George Gershwin

by Rodney Greenberg

Φ

to the memory of my parents

Phaidon Press Limited
Regent's Wharf
All Saints Street
London N1 9PA

First published 1998
© 1998 Phaidon Press Limited

ISBN 0 7148 3504 8

A CIP catalogue record for this book is
available from the British Library

Printed in Singapore

Frontispiece, Gershwin's
strong, slender hands
conjured up music by the
hour as he improvised at
the keyboard.

Contents

Preface

Gershwin's music was going to occupy a special place in my life from
the moment two kinds of home entertainment became linked in my
boyhood: home movies, and the 78rpm record. Two days before
Queen Elizabeth's coronation in 1953, my father unveiled a 9.5mm
movie projector he had bought, with a selection of silent films in
metal cans. Having teased the projector lens into focus, the clattering
of film through sprocket-wheels became integral to the entertainment.
I thought there had to be something else we could listen to while
Charlie Chaplin, Snub Pollard and a travelogue of New York flickered
their monochrome way across the beaded-glass screen. Searching
along the shelves of shellac records (long-playing vinyl was only just
coming in), I found a set of two HMV discs on which a certain
Leonard Bernstein, a name unknown to me, conducted Gershwin's *An
American in Paris.* (They were the only records whose labels had
'American' in the title, so they ought to fit the pictures.) Even now I
can never hear this piece without recalling where the sides ended, and
the way the hiss of shellac and the chatter of sprockets were submerged
as Laurel and Hardy cavorted to Gershwin's tunes. I was hooked.

When I took up music at Manchester University it did not seem
very respectable to talk too much about Gershwin. I remember
Rhapsody in Blue seeping one day through the supposedly sound-proof
walls of the practice cubicle next door, but generally Gershwin was far
down a syllabus ladder whose upper rung was our singing of
Palestrina's unaccompanied Stabat Mater and going home happy if the
tuning-fork revealed we had not slipped in pitch. Years later I was
amused to read how Gershwin liked to 'improve' on that purest
polyphony, and also discovered the main sources of an eclectic two-
piano *Divertissement* I had written as a student. Hearing the two-
piano version of *An American in Paris* for the first time, I realized with
a jolt that the two real composers jostling for prominence in my
student piece had been George Gershwin and the man he approached
for lessons in Paris, Maurice Ravel.

At the time I joined BBC Radio the 30th anniversary of Gershwin's death was coming up, so I offered to write a radio portrait. I had no idea that the finished tape had been sent to Ira Gershwin until his publisher, Chappell, forwarded a copy of his appreciative letter. I now wish I had caught the next plane to Hollywood to introduce myself. George would not have missed such a potential career opportunity.

Later I came under the wing of two BBC producers whose divergent opinions about Gershwin epitomize one of the central issues in this book. John Culshaw had come to head the Television Music Department from Decca Records, where his numerous achievements culminated in the first LP recording of the complete *Ring* cycle under Solti. In his book *A Century of Music*, Culshaw admitted his distaste for *Rhapsody in Blue*, 'in which are exploited all the less significant jazz idioms supported by every harmonic cliché of the previous two decades. ... his Piano Concerto in F reveals a complete misunderstanding of the purpose of musical form, though in a sense this is more forgivable (and less catastrophic) than his use of the jazz idiom which ... is hardly ever free from the metrical bounds of the bar line and achieves an intense monotony which is quite contrary to the nature of real jazz.'

The antidote to this came from an unlikely BBC Radio colleague, the musicologist and teacher Hans Keller. Unlikely because you would not think this rigorous, German-born scholar, possessor of a formidable musical intellect, could have much time for Gershwin. Yet the longer Keller lived the more vigorously he championed Gershwin's cause. Two months before Keller died in 1985, *The Listener* published his views on the same concerto: 'Ever since my mid-twenties, I have called Gershwin a major master of minor forms – like Chopin and unlike Webern, because to my mind, Gershwin is a greater composer than the fairly simple-minded Webern. Gershwin is a genius, in fact, whose style hides the wealth and complexity of his invention. There are indeed weak spots [in the concerto] but who cares about them where there is greatness?'

That two musicians I much admired could be at opposite poles in regard to Gershwin only reinforced my attraction to the music and the man behind it. Neither man is 'wrong' about Gershwin. Keller liked to quote a Talmudic fable about a rabbi who told a husband seeking a divorce that he was right about all the awful things his wife

did. When the wife's turn for interview came, the rabbi said she was right too. 'How can they both be right?' inquired a bemused scholar of his master. 'You know,' replied the rabbi, 'You are also right.' Gershwin is like that. You know that his best tunes have the stamp of immortality, but you would also be right saying that he could never have written the symphonies he talked about because they would not really have been symphonic. This Brooklyn boy who played truant and left school at fifteen wrote letters without a single spelling or grammatical error. But you could say that some of his statements on music are alarmingly uninformed and naïve, and you would be right. Gershwin certainly raised the profile of jazz music among a wider, more diversified audience than it ever had before. But you could say that he was operating within the terms of commercialized, white, big-band jazz rather than taking his impulses directly from its authentic, black roots – and you would be right.

I admire Gershwin because he would be the first to admit how much he didn't know about music, yet he carried on reaching people's hearts with it. The fact that he was able to overlay his insecurity with a sometimes breathtaking egocentricity makes him all the more endearing, because it was public concealment of private anxiety. Belief in oneself and one's talents are the necessary qualities for any artist, but in his case were essential to succeed in the viciously competitive world of popular music on Tin Pan Alley, let alone among the sceptics at Carnegie Hall. It is said he never learned to read music fluently, and that when he tried to play from the piano score of *La bohème* to impress a girl, he could not cope with all the sharps and flats. This seems extraordinary for someone who apparently zipped through thousands of pieces as a song-plugger, accompanied Todd Duncan at sight when he brought unfamiliar arias for his *Porgy* audition, and put countless notes down on paper. Who is right? More to the point, does it matter? His keyboard wizardry was a mixture of finger dexterity, memory, and a phenomenal capacity for instant invention – an alchemy which explains his admiration for a pianist such as Art Tatum.

He was envied for his facility and for his wealth, but popular success always breeds resentment. He was mocked for his invasion of the concert hall, but he would have chuckled to see himself at home in the 'UK Crossover Chart', invented in 1996 to accommodate new

records deemed impossible to categorize as either popular or classical. Gershwin was living through the 'crossover' controversy decades before the word was invented.

From the moment I was asked to write this book I wanted to diverge from the usual approach taken by Gershwin's biographers, working through his life chronologically. I felt he was one composer who could benefit from a different format, because he committed himself throughout his career to both theatre music and concert music with equal intensity. His life does not really divide into 'periods' as with other composers in this series. I have written about his Broadway musicals and his concert scores in separate chapters, to try and give the clearest focus to two parallel but distinct activities.

I am particularly happy that publication of this book coincides with Gershwin's 100th anniversary year. Amazingly, his entire professional career spanned just two decades. He is among that hapless group of famous composers – Mozart, Schubert, Bellini, Mendelssohn, Chopin – whose lives ended when young, at the height of their creative powers, and with incalculable riches still to come. Gershwin is rightly called a man of his time, but what a short time it was. If he had lived just over twenty years longer, he could have been at the New York première of *West Side Story* on his fifty-ninth birthday.

His brother Ira, who wrote the majority of his song lyrics, outlived him by forty-six years. Although this book is primarily about George's life and music, Ira is central to the story. I have tried to illuminate the unique creative partnership and the deep bond between them. Ira's widow, Leonore Strunsky, was a complicated woman who does not emerge from my narrative with the best of images, and the triangle of feelings which existed between her and the Gershwin brothers seems more complex the harder one looks at it. I can perhaps help redress the balance by giving her due credit for her generosity during her eight-year stewardship of Ira's estate, and for overseeing the start of an impressive project to have Gershwin's musicals accurately reconstructed and available on disc.

In his centenary year a new biography seems appropriate, because although his life has been well documented there are facets worthy of a fresh look. I have often found writings about the Jewish elements in Gershwin's music to be exaggerated or confused. His original scores have become more accessible, and the 'revisionists' are turning to

Gershwin with enthusiasm. His manuscripts have long needed sorting out, and sketches or short piano works neglected for years are now available on disc. His piano-rolls have also been transferred to disc using computer technology, enabling us to assess his pianism as never before. I felt that the essential classicism of Gershwin's song-structures, his instinctive response to words and the skilful harmonic schemes that underpin his famous tunes were features too often missed. The further we move from the Jazz Age of the 1920s, the more important it seems to place him properly within that era, and not be vague about what kind of 'jazz' Gershwin actually composed. I wanted to make specific comparisons between his concert music and works by other composers – something that biographers seem to avoid. The acceptance of his opera *Porgy and Bess* in the world's opera houses, after years of neglect and bowdlerized versions, merited a detailed look at its conception and its attitudes to black people. And there are glimpses of George that only came to light towards the end of Ira's life, as increasingly he recalled treasured memories.

To the many friends and colleagues who have assisted in my research and supplied Gershwin nuggets I might easily have missed, I express my warmest thanks. Caroline Underwood at Warner/Chappell Music guided my progress from the start. Mike Autton at HMV steered me through the massive range of available Gershwin recordings and helped me whittle them down to a list of recommendations, while Bill Holland at PolyGram commissioned a centenary CD album associated with the book. I am grateful to my editors at Phaidon Press, Ingalo Thomson and Daniel Cunningham, to designer Hans Dieter Reichert, and to picture researcher Michèle Faram. In particular, I am indebted to Michael Feinstein for telling me fascinating details about his years as archivist and friend to Ira, to Michael Tilson Thomas for his perceptive comments about a composer whose music he performs brilliantly, and to Larry Adler, who reminded me how George had accompanied him in an unrehearsed performance of *Rhapsody in Blue* at a party and remarked: 'The God-damned thing sounds as though I wrote it for you.' Larry must have told this story a thousand times. But – like a Gershwin tune – it always sounds as good as new.

Rodney Greenberg
London, 1998

I

A snapshot of George taken
in the Catskill Mountains
resort area, where he spent
a summer playing the piano
for hotel guests

George was a pretty wild boy. People used to say,
'Mrs. Gershwin has nice children, but that
son of hers, she's going to have trouble with that
son, George.'

Frances Gershwin Godowsky,
interviewed in 1990

Brooklyn to Tin Pan Alley

George Gershwin was the most charismatic of a handful of twentieth-century composers who liberated American music. His very beginnings can be traced back to two symbols of liberty – one noble, the other prosaic. First, the Statue of Liberty, dominating New York harbour. Second, a young man's hat, blown off by the stiff breeze as he stood at the deck-rail of a ship sailing past the statue. The vessel was crowded with immigrants, confused and excited as they caught their first glimpse of the majestic figure holding aloft her torch of freedom. It was the early 1890s, and the hat belonged to Morris Gershovitz. In later years, family legend would say that, as the hat blew away, it carried a scrap of paper stuffed inside. Scribbled upon it was the Brooklyn address of his uncle, Greenstein the tailor. Morris knew that Greenstein, having similarly left Russia for a new life in the United States, was the custodian of important information: the Lower East Side address of the girl for whom Morris had endured his arduous voyage – the girl he had fallen in love with in St Petersburg, and whom he was now pursuing to marry. It is not clear how he tracked her down, now that his uncle's whereabouts were bobbing in the waves. But such is the stuff of legend, and who would begrudge Morris indulging in a little picturesque invention? Morris's father, Yacov Gershovitz – though in reality a mechanic drafted into the Russian artillery – became romanticized into being an inventor. George Gershwin would later say that 'the only creative ancestry that I had seems to have been my father's father who, he tells me, was an inventor in Russia. His ingenuity had something to do with the Tsar's guns.'

Real or invented, the airborne slip of paper represented freedom for Morris Gershovitz because it symbolized a double escape: from tedious work in a St Petersburg shoe factory, and from the possibility of mandatory service in the Tsar's army. Like a character in a Broadway show, he duly turned up on the doorstep of his sweetheart Rose Bruskin and asked her to marry him. Rose and her family had

made the voyage from St Petersburg a year or two previously, her father having given up his business as a furrier. So there was much at stake for the couple as each of their respective boats passed Liberty Island. In Russia, Rose and Morris had not been confined to a ghetto, and their lifestyle had put them above Russia's 'huddled masses'. If anything, their living conditions in the overcrowded Lower East Side could not have been much of an improvement on those back home. But, like the forebears of Irving Berlin, Richard Rodgers, Aaron Copland, Leonard Bernstein and a host of others, they saw no future in a homeland where pogroms threatened their very lives. In setting sail, they were unwittingly ensuring that music in America would be immeasurably enriched. There is truth in the quip that the man who should take credit for founding the Broadway musical is not the Irish-born composer Victor Herbert, but Tsar Alexander III.

Rose Bruskin and Morris Gershovitz were married in 1895; she was nineteen, he twenty-four. They were living over a pawnshop when their first son was born on 6 December 1896. He grew up believing his name to be Isadore, and that it had been shortened to Ira; to his family and friends he was simply 'Izzy'. Not until 1928 did he discover that the name on his birth certificate was really Israel. For immigrant families, accuracy over names and dates in the face of officialdom had low priority. Often it was enough to have emerged from the

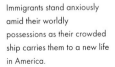

Immigrants stand anxiously amid their worldly possessions as their crowded ship carries them to a new life in America.

absorption centre at Ellis Island with some semblance of the name they had brought with them (Aaron Copland would have been known to us as Aaron Kaplan but for the slip of an immigration clerk's pen).

So clarity was not uppermost during the registration following the birth of a second son on 26 September 1898. Having progressed from being a foreman in a shoe factory, Morris had moved the family to the Williamsburg district of Brooklyn, and acquired a roomy two-storey house at 242 Snedicker Avenue. Here, across the street from a synagogue, his second son was born. In keeping with his enthusiastic self-Americanization, Morris had changed his surname to Gershvin, which a certain Dr Ratner misspelled as Gershwine on the birth certificate. The baby's first name was entered as Jacob, his paternal grandfather's name (normal Jewish custom was being followed in naming the child after a deceased relative), but he was never called anything other than George. When the child became a man, he simply dropped the final letter of 'Gershwine'. It has been suggested that the associated idea of being someone who would 'win' in the music business was not lost on the ambitious young composer. Nor was the attractive sound of 'Gershwin' lost on the family, who all adopted it from then on.

There were two further children: Arthur, born 14 March 1900, and Frances (known to all as 'Frankie'), born ten years to the day after Ira. Arthur became a stockbroker, at which he enjoyed greater success than his first love, songwriting – the family genes were to dictate only one

Not a rags-to-riches family: left to right, Arthur, the maid, George, Rose and Ira in Prospect Park, Brooklyn, 1901

Frances (Frankie) Gershwin photographed c. 1928; she said her brother George could be very conventional, and had once slapped her for using the fashionable word 'darn'.

genius in that direction. In people's recollections, Arthur is the least well-delineated of the four children. There is sadness in his remark: 'I am a leading composer of unpublished songs'. Frances, on the other hand, adjusted well to growing up with two other brothers as celebrities, and she herself was a capable enough singer to appear in various intimate Broadway revues. George liked to accompany her on the piano as she performed his songs at parties. (In 1930 she married Leopold Godowsky Jr, son of the virtuoso pianist. Just as Arthur was not granted his brother's musical prowess, Leopold Jnr did not inherit his father's wizardry on his own chosen instrument, the violin. Fate, however, did decree a measure of celebrity: he became co-inventor of the Kodachrome colour process.)

Ira's most vivid memory of his childhood was that 'we were always moving'. All four children were born in different houses. Between 1898 and 1916 the family lived in twenty-five apartments in Manhattan and three in Brooklyn. This was because once his father stopped being an employed person and went into business, he proved better at starting up a new enterprise than nurturing it. As composer and lyricist respectively, George and Ira would work relentlessly on a song until they could polish it no further. They did not inherit such powers of concentration from Morris; he became bored with each new venture. He liked to live within walking distance of his work, so every time he sold a business the family moved on. Cigar store, Turkish bath, pool parlour, bakery, restaurant – Morris went from one to another, in partnership with a relative. Financially, the low point was three disastrous weeks as a bookmaker at the Brighton Beach racecourse.

Where Morris was amiable, easy-going and artistically naïve (his oft-quoted remarks about his son's music were excused because they were unintentionally funny), Rose was a dominating force in the household. Somehow she harnessed the erratic income from her husband's exploits, to the extent that the Gershwins were never the archetypal immigrant family clawing their way upwards to escape the deprivations of the tenement. Their homes were well-furnished and they were always able to afford a maid. A stream of friends and neighbours would be entertained with lemon tea, cakes and perhaps a noisy game of poker. The children looked on, while actors in the Yiddish theatre or fellow-immigrants from Eastern Europe enthralled the household with outrageous songs and stories. George and Ira did

not have to wait for initiation into the delights of vaudeville and musical comedy. Though they could not have known it at the time, essential elements of their future Broadway successes were ever-present in the twenty-eight residences of their peripatetic childhood.

Rose was ambitious for her children. She became an unabashed social climber, and from her George must have inherited his driving ambition and a need to be respected and admired by the wealthy and famous – a desire he would gratify at countless parties where the social élite gathered round his piano and made him the centre of attention. In 1931 he said of his mother: 'She is what the mammy writers write about and what the mammy singers sing about. But they don't mean it; I do.' This squares oddly with aspects of his mother's behaviour. She was never one to dote on her children, not hesitating to criticize George for a musical flop or to suggest it was time he bought her a new fur coat. When he was undergoing surgery in California in a desperate attempt to save his life, she is said to have told Ira on the phone that it was useless for her to fly over from New York as there was nothing she could do.

It was probably due to Rose rather than her husband that the family spoke English from their earliest days in New York, rather than Russian or Yiddish. (Yiddish has been defined as 'Judeo-German', originating a thousand years ago among Jews settling in the Rhineland. Over the centuries it blossomed into an eclectic vernacular – mostly adapted from German, but absorbing Hebrew, Polish, Ukrainian, Russian, Romanian, Slavic and English elements. It is still a viable language, not to be confused with modern Hebrew.) Rose had grown up not in an obscure village – the kind of *shtetl* made familiar to worldwide audiences as the Anatekva of *Fiddler on the Roof* – but amid the sophistication of St Petersburg, the most western-influenced of Russian cities. Even before George's income made the family wealthy, Rose would spend money with abandon on poker games and betting on horses. She particularly loved diamonds, a passion matched by Ira's wife Leonore. In fact the relationship between Ira and his wife seems to have been a mirror-image of his parents, both men content to be the passive spouse steered by a dominating partner. Pianist and singer Michael Feinstein worked closely with Ira as assistant and archivist for the last six years of the lyricist's life. He attests to Leonore's volatile temper and the extraordinary fortitude with which her gentle,

'If you want to look good and you want to look rich, you wear furs': Rose proves her point in one of her favourite poses.

George's parents, Morris
Gershovitz and Rose Bruskin,
at about the time of their
wedding in 1895

submissive husband bore her tantrums. Feinstein believes their
troubled relationship stemmed from the blunt fact that Leonore would
have liked to have married George, but had to settle for Ira instead.

Only Ira – the first of Rose's three sons – was given a barmitzvah,
the traditional ceremony at which every Jewish boy is ceremonially
recognized as having attained manhood at the age of thirteen. This
religious milestone apparently meant little to Ira himself. The fact that
Rose and Morris never imposed it upon George and Arthur means
that, by the time they became teenagers, the family had left their East
European Jewish origins behind and were living a secularized existence
in New York's cosmopolitan melting pot. Attempts have been made to
prove strong Jewish influences on Gershwin's melodies, not least
because in 1929 he signed a contract with the Metropolitan Opera to
turn the Jewish folk-tale *The Dybbuk* into an opera (abandoned
because rights to the original Yiddish play, by Shlomo Ansky, were
already assigned). But apart from their awareness of Yiddish theatre
and its folk ingredients, George and Ira took a very wide cultural
canvas for their inspiration; the strong hand of their mother in
secularizing their education led to Jewish elements in their songs being
intertwined with many other layers of influence.

The two brothers roamed all over New York City in their youth,
absorbing the culture of Chinatown, Harlem and the West Side just as

much as Italian, Irish and Jewish sources. They were not imbued with Jewish ritual and practice in their boyhood, when it would have had most effect. Rose made sure the living-room curtains were drawn closed on the eve of sabbaths or festivals, so that her Jewish neighbours would be unaware she had not lit the ceremonial candles. Ira did seem to retain a fondness for one religious ceremony: the annual Passover *seder* meal, when families gather to sing traditional Hebrew melodies and recount the timeless story of the exodus from Egypt. The parallels with a musical play are obvious, and must have held an appeal for Ira. But we know from the harmonica virtuoso Larry Adler that, on the evening he was invited to Ira's house to celebrate the festival, Ira wore a silly top-hat like a vaudeville comedian, and had rewritten the ancient text for maximum comic effect. Adler, himself Jewish but not observant, was annoyed that a ritual full of historic resonances and deserving respect was being 'gagged up'.

The temperamental differences between Ira and George were apparent from earliest childhood, and in retrospect were fundamental to the creative partnership that was to develop. Ira was shy, introverted and gentle-natured like his father, never happier than when engrossed in lurid nickel-novels borrowed from a library behind a laundry for two cents a time. Later he progressed to hard-cover fare. His voracious appetite for books led him to try his hand at rudimentary poems and short stories. He was also good at sketching (a talent George would share and overtake), and loved going to as many nickelodeon theatres and movie-houses as his pocket-money would allow.

The operettas of Gilbert and Sullivan made an indelible impression, and Ira's later gift for word-play had its roots in the wittily-fashioned librettos of W. S. Gilbert. He became an ardent anglophile, and his well-stocked library included the major works of English literature. Apart from Gilbert, the English writer who influenced him most (and with whom he struck up a lasting friendship) was P. G. Wodehouse, creator of the 'Jeeves' books and a skilled lyricist, evident in the shows he wrote with Jerome Kern. Even if there had never been a brother with musical gifts, Ira would still have made his mark writing for the stage. We tend to think of the brothers' names as inseparable, but during George's lifetime Ira wrote lyrics for Vincent Youmans, Harold Arlen and Vernon Duke, among

others. After his brother's death his work with major figures including Kern, Kurt Weill, Arthur Schwartz, Johnny Green, Burton Lane and even Copland showed his talents to be largely undimmed – although none of these collaborations could match the halcyon days of working alongside George.

The key to George's boyhood temperament was his mother. From Rose he inherited not only his unswerving ambition. There was also an irrepressible urge to dominate, to assert, to be forever active. Unlike Ira, he was rarely seen reading a book. With fame this never changed; in his successive bachelor apartments, shelves of books provided chic decoration – mostly unread, apart from the occasional revelatory volume such as the novel *Porgy*, or reference books on music. His schooldays were characterized by bad reports, truancy and petty pilfering. His later-acquired eagerness to absorb everything he could learn about music was absent in the aggressive, street-wise trouble-maker whose exploits often meant that Ira had to placate George's teachers to bail him out. This, too, became embedded in their adult relationship: Ira, the devoted brother, would be intensely protective of George when he was beset by affairs of the heart, poor reviews, or pressures of meeting a producer's deadline.

Whichever street the family resided in, the youthful George would win out as its acknowledged champion roller-skater; he also threw his energies into competitive sports like punchball, hockey, handball and wrestling – and became resentful if he didn't win. He was at home in a rough-and-tumble street environment. In some of his photographs we see evidence of a broken nose, the legacy of either a sidewalk brawl or being kicked by a horse, depending on which story is believed. Although his father had moved the family from Snedicker Avenue when George was eight months old, it would be satisfying if, today, we could stand before a plaque commemorating his place of birth – in the way that Mozart's is honoured in Salzburg. But there was never a permanent plaque at 242 Snedicker because, although ASCAP (the American Society of Composers, Authors and Publishers) repeatedly put one up, so unruly did the neighbourhood become that each replacement was stolen. Eventually the entire area became the victim of failed urban renewal. Despite pleas from music-lovers, Gershwin's birthplace disappeared at the hands of a demolition squad.

Hester Street, Lower East Side, where Ira was born. George recalled spending 'most of my time with the boys on the street, skating and making a nuisance of myself'.

Happily, what George was not learning from books he learned in the streets of the Lower East Side. The depression of the 1890s was giving way to an optimism and an exuberance that overflowed on to the sidewalks from within the faceless tenements, drugstores and saloon bars. Amid the teeming alleyways and brownstone tenements, George's ears were assaulted by a never-ending tapestry of sounds that were storing themselves in his mind and which became part of his musical vocabulary: the arrogant honking of the newfangled 'automobiles'; the staccato clatter of the overhead railway; riveting machines on a construction site; the hurdy-gurdy man; the street-singer with his sentimental Yiddish songs and his swooning, out-of-tune fiddle; the repetitive, pungent cries of street-market vendors; marching bands blaring out John Philip Sousa's snappy military rhythms; ragtime pianists and sassy little jazz bands ushering in a succession of dance crazes; the voice of Caruso sailing out of a window from the magic horn of Edison's 'Patent Home Phonograph'. Down

on the crowded amusement park known as Coney Island, merry-go-round organs were oozing American folk-tunes or popular overtures by the Austrian operetta composer Franz von Suppé through punched paper rolls. And everywhere there was Negro music, tugging at the ears of a youngster who would devote almost the last days of his working life to creating the first all-black opera.

Recalling those childhood days, Gershwin used to claim that two key incidents consciously alerted him to music. The first, when he was six, was hearing Anton Rubinstein's *Melody in F* being played on a pianola as he stood barefoot outside a penny arcade. 'The peculiar jumps in the music held me rooted.' Considering his own hard-driven, unsentimental style of pianism, it is perhaps significant that the strict, rhythmic jangle of a pianola made such an impression. The other critical incident was at school at the age of ten, when one of his fellow pupils, an eight-year-old violin prodigy named Max Rosenzweig, was taking part in an afternoon concert. George had better things to do than to attend, but his ears were caught by the strains of Dvořák's *Humoresque* floating down the corridors from the assembly hall. 'It was a flashing revelation of beauty,' he recalled. He waited in vain outside in the pouring rain for the prodigy to appear, then turned up at the boy's home and begged to see him. They became close friends and 'Maxie' opened up the world of good music for his admirer. George was not about to take up Maxie's instrument, the violin. Instead, at the house of another friend who had a player-piano, he found his way around the keyboard and tried to make up some of his own tunes. Proudly, he played one to Maxie. The world of music may have lost George Gershwin if he had followed the eight-year-old's advice: 'You haven't it in you, Georgie. Take my word for it, I can tell!'

Two years later, Rose Gershwin unwittingly took a hand. Her sister, Kate Wolpin, had been giving Ira piano lessons. Rose, covetous as ever, decided a piano was the thing to have in the Gershwin household, so a second-hand upright was hoisted through a window. Ira watched glumly – clearly it was intended for him, but he had made little progress with Aunt Kate, and dime novels were still his real passion. Suddenly, George was at the keyboard. He rattled off some popular tunes of the day, which he had taught himself on his friend's piano. Ira later recalled that he was particularly impressed by his

brother's swinging, lightning-fast left hand, and various rhythmic effects. So the agility and invention on Gershwin's recordings were there from the start.

He had spent hours listening to 'ragtime piano' in cafés and bars. Inventive and technically skilled pianists such Eubie Blake, James P. Johnson, Zez Confrey and Luckey Roberts were influencing his untutored fingers. Ragtime – with its syncopation, adroit rhythmic surprises, and percussive piano tone – held him spellbound. Ragtime is said to have its roots in St Louis, Missouri, where its chief exponent was the black pianist and composer Scott Joplin. Joplin became particularly renowned for *Maple Leaf Rag*, and his 1902 'ragtime two-step' *The Entertainer* gained renewed fame in the 1970s because of its shrewd use as the theme in the film *The Sting*. When ragtime began to be heard in New York around 1896, introduced by a pianist called Ben Harney, it became all the rage. What particularly appealed to the youthful Gershwin was the constant feature of syncopation. The main, regular beat of the music was maintained by the pianist's agile left hand, but the right hand indulged in all manner of cross-rhythms that ran counter to the main beat, injecting the music with an ear-catching propulsion and an unpredictable, foot-tapping energy.

Syncopation, of course, was nothing new. Classical composers such as Haydn and Beethoven threw accents on to beats where they are least expected, and the mighty development section in the first movement of Beethoven's 'Eroica' Symphony includes gigantic, off-beat accents which syncopate the music to such an intensity that the original pulse is temporarily annihilated. Ragtime, in its far less elevated fashion, happily exploited two or more rhythms colliding with one another, and stabbing, independent accents between the two hands – literally, ragged time.

From the moment of George's surprise début on his mother's new piano, Rose released Ira from his sluggish progress through *Beyer's Piano Method* and accepted George instead as the son who would entertain her friends at the keyboard, and maybe bring some musical culture into the apartment. Even at that age, Gershwin showed a determination for seeking out whoever he felt could be most useful to his musical ambitions. His first teacher, a Miss Green, began leading him through Beyer's with such unawareness of his pent-up keyboard ambitions that George soon decided her lessons were not even worth

Above, James P. Johnson (1894–1955), whose 'stride' style of playing influenced Gershwin; right, Scott Joplin (1868–1917), named 'King of Ragtime'

the fifty cents she charged. He changed piano teachers three times, ending up with a Hungarian named Von Zerly who specialized in having his students flounder through flamboyant pot-pourris he had arranged from popular operas. Then he met Jack Miller, pianist with the local Beethoven Society Orchestra. George was now fourteen and had started attending concerts, particularly if a pianist was featured. He kept the programmes in scrapbooks, pasted alongside pictures of musicians he admired: Liszt, Busoni, Balakirev, Wagner, Sullivan. Miller offered to introduce him to his own teacher, Charles Hambitzer, and took him along for an audition. Anxious to make an immediate impression, George tore into the Overture from Rossini's *William Tell* in Von Zerly's transcription. When the histrionics ended, Hambitzer had one suggestion: 'Let's hunt out the guy who taught you to play this way and shoot him – and not with an apple on his head either!'

It was Gershwin's 'deadly seriousness' that, according to Hambitzer, made him offer the boy immediate lessons without payment. Hambitzer was a first-rate musician, one of the first pianists to perform Schoenberg in America. Reluctant to promote his own many compositions, he devoted himself to his teaching schedule with such

ferocious intensity that he was to die in 1918 aged only thirty-seven. Gershwin regarded him as the first great musical influence on his life, especially for introducing him not only to the music of such masters as Bach, Chopin and Liszt, but to Debussy – a true modernist in 1913.

The young George's enthusiasm for Hambitzer led him to drum up ten new pupils for his revered master. On his part, Hambitzer discerned exceptional gifts. 'He is a genius, without a doubt. He will make his mark in music if anybody will. He wants to go in for this modern stuff, jazz and what not. But I'll see he gets a firm foundation in the standard music first.' Two pointers to the future were evident. First, Gershwin's predilection for adventurous harmonies. Second, the tension between 'classical' concert music, and what his teacher dismissed as 'jazz and what not'.

Gershwin was already enamoured with songs he had heard by Jerome Kern and, in particular, with Irving Berlin's *Alexander's Ragtime Band*, a hugely popular hit written in 1911. His own first, uncompleted song, called *Since I Found You*, dates from about 1913. He had also composed a Berlin-inspired rag called *Ragging the Traumerei* (presumably based on Schumann's exquisite little piano piece), and a tango which he played at a college social. Then he decided to leave composition alone and concentrate on his piano technique, and on lessons in theory and harmony. For these, Hambitzer sent him to Edward Kilenyi (1884–1968), a Hungarian who had once studied under Mascagni, composer of the immensely popular opera *Cavalleria rusticana*. In Gershwin's estimation, his two most formative teachers were Hambitzer and Kilenyi. Unlike Hambitzer, Kilenyi was sympathetic to the young man's aspirations towards popular music. He predicted: 'You will face the same difficulty all Americans do trying to have their works performed. If you become a big success as a popular composer, conductors will come to you to ask for serious works.' Kilenyi spoke highly of Gershwin's 'extraordinary faculty to absorb everything, and to apply what he learned to his own music'. The boy's exercise books still exist, and prove him to be a fastidious student whose musical handwriting was neat and who liked to experiment with his own devices once he had learned the traditional rudiments.

All this was not enough to convince Rose Gershwin that her son was taking the right path. After his school graduation at the age of fourteen, she enrolled him in the High School of Commerce. It was as

though the archetypal Jewish mother was ensuring he entered a respectable, profitable profession. Only later did she realize the enormous earning potential her son had in the music business. In the event, his tutor books in accountancy did not keep George away from the keyboard. The year before, he had earned five dollars a week in a summer job, entertaining guests at the piano in a Catskills resort. Now he was on the lookout for a breakthrough that would put commercial studies behind him. Again, a friend was on hand. Ben Bloom, who worked in Tin Pan Alley, took George to meet Mose Gumble, manager of Jerome H. Remick and Co., one of New York's foremost publishers of popular music. Although Rose was now suggesting he try the fur business, George announced he was leaving college to take up a job at Remick's for fifteen dollars a week. His will prevailed. At the age of fifteen his formal education was at an end, and he became one of the youngest pianists ever to be employed as a song-plugger, or 'piano pounder'.

Tin Pan Alley is said to have taken its name from the jangling, tinny sound (likened to the clattering of kitchen pans) issuing from dozens of upright pianos being incessantly pounded in a small area of New York centred around 28th Street, from 6th Avenue to Broadway. This was the city's main entertainment district, crammed with vaudeville theatres and music halls. It was the ideal location for Remick's, a typical brownstone building crowded with song-pluggers and wily publishing executives for whom popular music was a frenzied, lucrative business. Hit songs had to be manufactured and distributed at breakneck pace, in stiff competition with dozens of other enterprising publishing houses. Everything depended on sales of sheet music, from which the public could sing and play their current favourites.

Now, for up to ten hours a day, Gershwin sat at an old piano in a tiny cubicle, pretentiously known as a 'professional parlour'. He had to be prepared to play any of Remick's songs at sight, in any key, for a constant stream of vocalists, theatre managers, bandleaders and vaudeville entertainers, using his charm and enthusiasm to sell as many as he could. Through the thin walls of his cubicle would come the racket of a dozen or more other pluggers doing the same. He had the energy and temperament to thrive in this bedlam. 'Coloured people would come in and get me to play *God Send You Back To Me* in seven keys,' he recalled. 'Some of the customers treated me like dirt.'

Fred and Adele Astaire in a
non-Gershwin 1922 musical
For Goodness Sake; already
a famous song-and-dance
team, in 1924 they would
become the stars of
Gershwin's *Lady, Be Good!.*

One who did not was Fred Astaire, who appeared in Gershwin's
cubicle one day to try out song-and-dance material for the touring
vaudeville act he performed with his sister, Adele. It was the start of a
friendship that ended only with the composer's death. Although
Gershwin made sure he kept up his studies of 'good' music outside
business hours, on some evenings the song-plugging had to go on into
the night, when he joined with vocalists or tap-dancers to promote
Remick songs at saloon bars or restaurants.

His gruelling years at Remick's were of incalculable professional
value. It was the ideal way for him to become a supremely practical,
'hands-on' composer, developing his keyboard facility to a
consummate degree. Later, on Broadway, it enabled him to write at
speed, chop and change his material at the whim of a stage producer,
or craftily rescue a song from a failed show and work it into another.

Many of the singers who visited his cubicle had a limited vocal range, so he became adept at switching from key to key as they got into difficulties, or transposing an entire song into another key on the spot. Hours of experimentation and improvisation meant that he never played a Remick song as printed, which in turn provided him with an arsenal of pianistic tricks to use in his own compositions. He also came face-to-face with the ruthless business side of the songwriting profession.

By 1915, his skill as a performer led him to be asked to record piano-rolls, which filled a ready market in an age when a close economic partnership had developed between music publishers and the player-piano manufacturers. Since 1900, player-pianos had been mass-marketed. Their appeal in the home or in bars and clubs was obvious. First-rate renditions of popular pieces, often 'orchestrated' by skilled editors who cut extra holes in the paper roll (so that more than ten fingers would be 'playing' a particular texture), were available at the turn of a switch. At home, even amateur pianists could manipulate various controls while the roll turned in the pianola, to add their personal 'interpretation' to what was being mechanically reproduced. Roughly between 1915 and 1926 (by which time he had long graduated from Remick's and was famous for *Rhapsody in Blue*), Gershwin recorded about 130 piano-rolls – sometimes under pseudonyms such as Fred Murtha, Bert Wynn or James Baker, so that customers believed they were getting a range of pianists for their money.

For him, it was principally a means of supplementing his income. He was paid thirty-five dollars to record six rolls, which he could polish off easily in one Saturday session. His crisp, dynamic piano style stemmed both from these piano-roll sessions and from various black pianists he observed in Harlem clubs. His later gramophone records, made on a normal grand piano, retain the unswerving, hard-driven touch of the pianola rolls. Several of the rolls contained pieces by composers other than himself, whose names have otherwise been forgotten. Modern techniques have enabled the fragile paper recordings to be played on an authentic player-piano, from which the music is digitally transferred to a computer and thence to compact disc. Such is the realism and clarity of these transfers that we can now enjoy the nearest equivalent to having Gershwin with us and playing in our own homes.

Inevitably, he was not satisfied with promoting Remick songs day after day. He could hardly wait to see his own in print. Remick's were adamant that he was being paid only to plug their own material, so his first published song was issued by the Harry von Tilzer Company, having been recommended by Sophie Tucker. Tucker was to become renowned as 'The Last of the Red Hot Mamas' (it is not clear who was the first), performing personal successes such as *My Yiddishe Mama* and *Life Begins at Forty* with irresistible conviction, clutching a handkerchief against the tears. At the time she became aware of Gershwin's music, young Miss Tucker billed herself as 'The Mary Garden of Ragtime' (Mary Garden being the opera singer who created the role of Debussy's Mélisande).

The song that had captured her fancy had been written by the eighteen-year-old Gershwin in collaboration with an aspiring young lyricist, Murray Roth, and it boasted the longest title in his output: *When You Want 'Em, You Can't Get 'Em (When You've Got 'Em, You Don't Want 'Em)* ('Em' referring, of course, to girls). The self-assured young composer waived an advance on his fee and chose to wait for royalties. When none were forthcoming, he settled for five dollars – his only payment for a song whose chief merit is that it was the first piece of sheet music to carry the name of George Gershwin.

He again collaborated with Roth to write *The Runaway Girl*, the first of his songs to appear in a musical. Performed at the Winter Garden, a theatre in the Shubert organization, the song led to Gershwin meeting Sigmund Romberg, who was Shubert's staff composer, best remembered today for his Viennese-style operettas *The Student Prince* and *The Desert Song*. Like everyone else, Romberg (yet another Hungarian-born figure in Gershwin's life) spotted his talents and encouraged him to submit further songs for the Winter Garden. From these, Romberg selected *The Making of a Girl*, which appeared among fourteen Romberg numbers in *The Passing Show* of 1916. Once more, Gershwin's efforts went unnoticed by the public – but this time his fee came to seven dollars. At last, in 1917, his hard-nosed employers, Remick's, published something by Gershwin. *Rialto Ripples* (written in collaboration with a Remick colleague, Will Donaldson) is a typical piano 'rag' of the period, complete with a 'trio' section in the middle. Although catchy in a repetitive way (Gershwin's piano-roll recording has just the right zest), it was hardly original. Joplin's piano

rags were clearly an influence, together with the music of Felix Arndt, an established ragtime composer (*Nola* was one of his hits) whom Gershwin often visited.

It was inevitable that the brilliant young piano-pounder, now increasingly getting his music performed and with a couple of published items under his belt, would finally react against Remick's constraints. He had served his time for nearly three years. 'The popular-song racket began to get definitely on my nerves,' he complained. 'Its tunes began somehow to offend me. Or perhaps my ears were becoming attuned to better harmonies. I wanted to be closer to production music – the kind Jerome Kern was writing.' At the wedding of his Aunt Kate back in 1914, Gershwin had been so struck by two pieces played by the band that he had rushed up to the conductor to find out who wrote them. The first turned out to be Kern's *You're Here and I'm Here*. The second was also by Kern: the now-classic *They Didn't Believe Me*. It is easy to see how the smooth,

Two smart dressers in a radio studio: Gershwin chats with his boyhood idol, Jerome Kern.

graceful contours of this melody, supported by subtle harmonies, made an impression. The first four notes can be regarded as coming from the pentatonic scale, heard when one plays just the five black keys of the piano in any octave. Gershwin developed an early 'crush' on the pentatonic scale, which became an unusually resourceful element in his melodies. (Why had he found Dvořák's *Humoreske* a 'flashing revelation of beauty'? Though he did not know it at the time, apart from one note the whole tune can be played on just the black keys!) In *They Didn't Believe Me* the first four notes of Kern's melody, speeded up, are identical to another pentatonic inspiration, *I Got Rhythm* – first rising, then falling.

Jerome Kern now became his role-model. 'Kern was the first composer who made me conscious that most popular music was of inferior quality, and that musical-comedy music was made of better material. I followed Kern's work and studied each song he composed. I paid him the tribute of frank imitation, and many things I wrote at this period sounded as though Kern had written them himself.' This did not diminish his admiration for Irving Berlin, whom he described many years later as 'America's Franz Schubert'. In 1918 Berlin actually offered him a job as arranger and musical secretary – then paid him the compliment of adding: 'But you're more than the skilled arranger I am looking for. This sort of job would cramp you. You are meant for big things.' Gershwin turned down the offer.

Early in 1917, Gershwin finally left Remick's. He found a job as pianist at Fox's City Theatre, accompanying vaudeville acts during the orchestra's supper break. The previous incumbent had been Chico Marx, the piano-playing member of the Marx Brothers comedy team. A humiliated Gershwin quit when one of the comedians ridiculed him for missing some cues in the manuscript he was sight-reading. The comedy routine continued in silence while he fled the theatre, not even bothering to collect his pay. The event left a scar on his memory. But this failure did lead directly to his meeting his idol, Kern, since he now secured a job as rehearsal pianist for *Miss 1917*, a musical in which Kern had collaborated with three of his favourite colleagues: the composer Victor Herbert, author-lyricist P. G. Wodehouse, and lyricist Guy Bolton. Though star-studded, the show failed; its rehearsal pianist is the only reason it is now remembered. But, by playing the piano for members of the cast who were singing at Century Theatre concerts, Gershwin was able to give two of his own

songs a public hearing. Among the audience there happened to be a Remick's representative, who was sufficiently impressed with one of the songs to get Remick's at last to publish a Gershwin tune, *You-oo Just You*. The words had been written by a motor-mechanic, Irving Caesar, whose ambition was to become a full-time lyricist. He had first met Gershwin during a visit to Remick's, where the young man's piano-playing had bowled him over. 'His harmonies were years ahead of his time; his rhythms had the impact of a sledge-hammer.' They wrote more songs together – hardly suspecting that not far ahead lay a collaborative effort that would change their lives.

Gershwin was by now completely familiar with a practice that is virtually non-existent in the modern musical theatre – the process of interpolation. An established composer such as Kern would provide nearly all the songs in a given production, but opportunities could be found for an unknown or up-and-coming composer (or more than one) to contribute a few more. This had benefits all round. New composers and lyricists could seize a chance to get their work heard. If their songs failed, they would either try again or quietly disappear. If the public sat up and took notice, it meant a promising new talent was suddenly on the scene. Either way, the principal composer's work remained untarnished, so his reputation was not under threat.

Gershwin, aware of the ruthless financial deals inherent in the songwriting profession through his drudgery years at Remick's, realized that normally only the writer of a complete musical score would earn a respectable fee on Broadway. He had to go beyond interpolating his efforts into other people's shows. The year 1918 was a good case in point, proving to be not a particularly fruitful one. He contributed five numbers to a revue called *Half-Past Eight*, which closed after a week's tryout. *Variety*, the showbiz journal, dubbed it 'not worth the war tax', which was a mere forty cents.

He then went on tour as accompanist to Nora Bayes, a celebrated vaudeville singer of the time. They did not get on, since his accompaniments proved too inventive for her. They were appearing in a revamped version of *Miss 1917*, now called *Ladies First*. The show is worth recall only because, among several interpolated Gershwin numbers, it included *Some Wonderful Sort of Someone* – the middle section of which foreshadows *Fascinating Rhythm* – and *The Real American Folk Song (Is a Rag)*, whose lyrics were by a certain Arthur Francis. This label disguised the fact that, for some time, Ira had been

writing lyrics for George. (Not wanting to capitalize on his brother's increasing success, he had modestly taken his other brother's name and adapted his sister's to contrive a pseudonym.) *The Real American Folk Song* was George and Ira's first song to be placed in a musical. When the show came to Pittsburgh it was seen by a twelve-year-old named Oscar Levant, who was destined to become closely bound up with Gershwin's life and music. Even then, Gershwin's piano-playing struck Levant as brisk, free and inventive.

One positive event that year was Gershwin's meeting with Max Dreyfus, head of the music publishers T. B. Harms (affiliated to the British firm Chappell). Gershwin's earnestness about his ambitions in popular music had its usual effect, and Dreyfus (who had 'discovered' Kern a decade earlier and would later promote Vincent Youmans, Cole Porter, Richard Rodgers and Kurt Weill) promptly decided he was someone worth gambling on. For a regular thirty-five dollars a week, Gershwin had only to continue offering his songs to Harms. It was an ideal arrangement, bringing Gershwin professional stability and Harms lucrative rewards, since the agreement lasted ten years and saw some of Gershwin's best output.

The following year, 1919, more than compensated for his frustrations. *I Was So Young, You Were So Beautiful*, one of the songs he had written with Irving Caesar, was interpolated in the musical *Good Morning Judge*, and it became the first to achieve real popularity beyond professional circles. Popular tunes were supposed to be thirty-two bars long, but here was Gershwin truncating the orthodox structure to twenty-two bars, with a charm and simplicity that announced a new voice to the theatre-going public.

But he had still not written a complete Broadway score. His chance came with a commission from 29-year-old Alex Aarons, who had given up the clothing business to produce musicals. *La La Lucille* was his first venture, and he chose the relatively inexperienced Gershwin to write the entire score. The musical director was Charles Previn, a cousin of André Previn's father. Although one song, *Nobody but You*, has remained a Gershwin favourite, the show, closed in August 1919 by an actors' strike, did not establish him as a major new talent. But he was only a few months away from creating the song hit that would carry the name of George Gershwin around the world.

2

A young man in a hurry:
studio portrait of Gershwin
in a stylish coat and bowler,
c. 1918

*Music must reflect the thoughts and aspirations
of the people and the time. My people are
American. My time is today.*

George Gershwin

Broadway to Aeolian Hall

At the end of World War I, Europe was left exhausted and largely
bankrupt. In America, things were different. The nation had emerged
with a vibrant economy and enormous self-confidence. As the 1920s
drew near, New York led the way in new fashions, new dance crazes,
new songs, new books and films, a proliferation of mass-circulation
magazines and lively radio-stations, the pulse of jazz, the competitive
architectural audacity of each new Manhattan skyscraper towering
above streets of well-stocked stores, their tills ringing praises to the
strength of the dollar. New York had escaped the ravages of Europe's
capital cities, and in the air was the excitement of a metropolis proud
of its position as the cultural and economic heart of the world's most
powerful country. Broadway was entering a boom-time, with new
theatres hardly able to keep pace with the supply of fresh productions.
Among the city's songwriting fraternity, commiserations over the
devastation the Great War had wreaked abroad were not on the
agenda. Songs of happiness, true love, nostalgia for Old America,
maybe with an exotic setting, and tunes irresistible for dancing were
their stock-in-trade. Rhythms were sharp, lyrics were 'peppy', and
America was the best place to be. For those songwriters most in touch
with the tide of popular taste, there were fortunes to be made.

    If ever a popular song achieved runaway success because its creators
unashamedly used an established hit-song as a blueprint, *Swanee* was
it. In 1919, one fact was inescapable to Gershwin and Irving Caesar:
the public were madly in love with a song by two now-forgotten
writers, Harold Weeks and Oliver G. Wallace. Their hit was called
Hindustan, a 'one-step' with a pseudo-oriental flavour. Could
Gershwin and Caesar manufacture an American version that would
cash-in on its popularity? Why not take Stephen Foster's *Swanee River*,
a universally-known piece of American folk-culture with Deep South
resonances, and marry its elements to the style of *Hindustan*? Lifting
the first word from Foster's title and using it as their own, their new
song was hurriedly sketched during dinner at Dinty Moore's

restaurant in Times Square, worked over on the bus home to the
Gershwin family residence on West 144th Street, and quickly
completed there – not without complaints from the regular gang of
poker-game players in the next room, disturbed by the noise of white-
hot creativity at the piano. Little did these family cronies realize they
were witnessing the birth of George Gershwin's best-selling song,
though they did break off from their game to give Papa Gershwin a
round of applause as he improvised a kazoo-like première on a comb
wrapped in tissue-paper.

Swanee was treated to exuberant staging in *Capitol Revue*, a live
presentation at the new Capitol Theatre movie-house to mark its
opening. Not even sixty chorus girls, dancing with electric lights
glowing on their shoes, could excite the audience to buy the sheet-
music in the lobby afterwards, nor later in the music-stores. But
Swanee was not destined for oblivion. Not long after the revue closed,
Gershwin and Irving Caesar attended a party hosted by Al Jolson.
With his customary panache, Gershwin extemporized a piano version
of the song while Irving Caesar – no professional singer – gave a lively
account of his lyrics.

Al Jolson was already billing himself as 'America's Greatest
Entertainer' (later he would inflate this to 'The World's Greatest
Entertainer'). Born in Lithuania into a devout Jewish family among
whom were several cantors, his real name was Asa Yoelson. His father
had emigrated to Washington DC, to be joined by the rest of the
family when Asa was about six. The possessor of dynamic energy and
a massive ego, Jolson developed a powerful stage presence and, made-
up in blackface, would sing his heart out in Negro-inspired tear-
jerkers such as *Mammy*. (In 1927 he starred in the first talking-picture,
The Jazz Singer.) By 1919 he was already a megastar. His parties were
thronged by celebrities, show-business magnates and starry-eyed gate-
crashers. That the young Gershwin sat at Jolson's piano enthralling the
gathering with his new song revealed much in common between the
two men: both were supremely confident in their musical talents and
greatly enjoyed displaying them. Common, too, were the familiar
leitmotifs of Russian-Jewish parentage and of revelling in their own
identification with all things American.

Jolson immediately realized the potential of *Swanee* and put it into
his own revue, *Sinbad*, at the Winter Garden. It brought the house

Swanee lyricist Irving
Caesar (1895–1996) once
said his songs had 'no
message at all – other than
I like people to sing my
work. Even better, I like
them to pay for it.'

down. Within twelve months, over two million copies of Jolson's recording had been bought. Sheet music sales topped a similar figure. At twenty-one, Gershwin was 'made', and Jolson found his own career boosted still further by a hit-song with which he would always be associated by his adoring public. Gershwin and Caesar were richer by about ten thousand dollars each in royalties, a fortune in those days.

A conventional song may have been its model, but *Swanee* does have innovative features. The verse, or opening section, is in F minor. Irving Caesar described Gershwin's piano-roll version of it as a traditional introduction typical of Yiddish musical theatre songs of the time. But when the chorus arrives ('Swanee, how I love you'), Gershwin switches to F major. *Swanee* and the songs of Schubert are from two different worlds. But minor/major switches are also an important means of expression and contrast in Schubert's songs, and Gershwin's ability to clothe words with apt key changes and harmonic surprises is, within his own terms, worthy of comparison with the greatest classical songwriters. Moreover, after the chorus (thirty-two bars, the normal Tin Pan Alley formula), Gershwin adds a sixteen-bar 'trio' ('Swanee, Swanee, I am coming back to Swanee'), allowing Irving

The sheet music cover of *Swanee*, 1919, Gershwin's runaway success, is dominated by superstar Al Jolson.

Caesar to cap his lyrics with a witty reference to the inspirational Stephen Foster ('I love the old folks at home'). For all this, *Swanee* remains a one-off in Gershwin's output. It was his one true 'pop' song, unconnected to and uninspired by any theatre plot-situation. It pre-dates the mature Gershwin style, standing on its own as a brilliantly fabricated commercial entity. Fellow songwriter Arthur Schwartz (composer of *Dancing in the Dark* and *You and the Night and the Music*) once remarked: 'It's ironic that George never again wrote a number equalling the sales of *Swanee*, which for all its infectiousness does not match in subtlety and individuality his later works.'

At the time it came from his pen in 1919, Gershwin was still studying music with Kilenyi. As one of his orchestration exercises he wrote a movement for string quartet, called *Lullaby*. Friends would form a quartet and perform the piece at parties, but he never attempted to publish or promote it. Larry Adler gave its first public performance, in an arrangement including harmonica, at the 1963 Edinburgh Festival. The original version, for strings only, was first performed in 1967 by the Juilliard Quartet, and finally published the following year. Another attempt at music outside the popular song genre also dates from 1919. Gershwin submitted a national anthem, *O Land of Mine, America* for a competition offering five thousand dollars to the winner. The judges included John Philip Sousa ('The March King') and Irving Berlin, and they awarded his entry the lowest prize of fifty dollars. His earnestness at not abandoning his interest in 'good' music was admirable, but he had yet to show signs of being capable of a breakthrough into the concert hall.

Meanwhile, the financial rewards he was reaping from *Swanee* gave him renewed confidence. He had tasted triumph on Tin Pan Alley and now his sights were set firmly on the Broadway musical, rather than on further single, commercial hits. His days as a lowly rehearsal pianist had allowed him to observe at first hand how a musical was put together, how songs needed to be planned according to their position within the score, the mechanics of a show's overall structure, the distinction between opening numbers, finales, dance-routines, filling-in material under dialogue, transitional music, reprises of earlier tunes as the story developed, and so on. The ideal vehicle for him to put some of these lessons to good use came his way in George White's *Scandals*. White, a multi-talented man of the theatre who had worked

with Gershwin in *Miss 1917,* was setting himself up to challenge the man in whose revues he had been a principal dancer – the master-showman himself, Florenz Ziegfeld.

Ziegfeld, born in Chicago, was the son of an austere martinet who ran one of the city's music colleges. As a boy he seems to have rebelled against the large doses of classical music his father tried to instill, and in later years he often alienated the excellent composers he hired for his shows, once they realized he operated with a shrewd business sense rather than a love of music in general. He was nevertheless genuinely obsessed with the theatre, and his annual *Ziegfeld Follies* had been delighting audiences since 1907 with stunning show-girls, lavish sets, dazzling costumes and extravagant dance routines. George White did not have the resources to compete on the same scale, but he was well on the way to becoming a major Broadway producer. His first edition of *Scandals* had opened in 1919, a week after Gershwin's *La La Lucille,* but White had not been happy with the quality of the score by Richard Whiting (who had been hired on the strength of his 1918 hit *Till We Meet Again,* which actually sold better than *Swanee*). So when Gershwin offered himself as the composer for the 1920 edition, White could hardly turn down the man whose *Swanee* had just swamped the musical scene.

Gershwin eventually wrote for five consecutive *Scandals,* ending in 1924 – over forty songs in all. White paid him comparatively little, but it meant that Gershwin's name was up in lights on Broadway every season for five years. But these shows cannot be said to have called upon Gershwin's deepest talents because they were really a string of sketches, dance routines and production numbers, devoid of anything resembling a plot. At their best, they were more topical and satirical than Ziegfeld's productions. They were also more sexually provocative; it was said that, while Ziegfeld glorified the American girl, George White undressed her. Gershwin was shrewd enough to realize that some fairly commonplace, utilitarian songwriting would suffice for much of the time, and many of the numbers were lifted from his sketchbooks or expeditiously crafted to suit a particular artist or even some scenic set-piece, such as the *South Sea Isles.* Two songs, however, are outstanding because of their quality of inspiration. In the 1922 *Scandals,* White provided a gleaming, white stairway on which fifty beautiful girls, dressed in a black leather material that reflected the

Opposite, song-cover from Scandals of 1920, the year Gershwin began writing for the series; the dapper peeping-tom eyeing the pretty girl epitomizes the titillating 'naughtiness' of George White's revues.

THE SCANDAL-WALK

SECOND ANNUAL EVENT

GEORGE WHITE'S SCANDALS OF 1920

WITH

ANN PENNINGTON

Book By ANDY RICE & GEORGE WHITE
Music By GEORGE GERSHWIN
Lyrics By ARTHUR JACKSON
Staged by GEORGE WHITE & WILLIE COLLIER
Scenery By LAW STUDIOS

ON MY MIND THE WHOLE NIGHT LONG 60
TUM ON AND TISS ME   -   60
MY LADY   -   -   60
QUEEN ISABELLA   -   60
THE SCANDAL-WALK   -   60
IDLE DREAMS   -   60
MY OLD LOVE IS MY NEW LOVE   60

T. B. HARMS
AND
FRANCIS, DAY & HUNTER
NEW YORK

spotlights, performed a true Gershwin show-stopper, *I'll Build a Stairway to Paradise*. The words were jointly by Ira (still under his pseudonym of Arthur Francis) and one of Broadway's foremost lyricists, Buddy De Sylva, who had written for *La La Lucille*. Ira had at one time written a lyric which he called 'New Step Every Day'. De Sylva latched on to one choice line, which he moved to the beginning and which became the title of the song for which George then provided the music – an example of fortuitous collaborative effort that typifies the best songwriting teams. Later, in the 1924 edition, Gershwin came up with one of his greatest successes since *Swanee*. His inborn melodic gift shines in *Somebody Loves Me*, a tune built almost entirely of simple scales and perfectly balanced little phrases – one of his favourite formulas.

Both of these songs exhibit a musical device known as the 'blue' note. Blue notes became such an integral part of Gershwin's melodic style that it is easy to assume he patented them. Not true. We find blue notes in an obscure *Barcarolle* for solo piano written in the 1870s by another Jewish composer, the eccentric French virtuoso pianist Charles Alkan – a rather haunting trifle which has been described by the British pianist Ronald Smith as 'the piece of Mendelssohn that Gershwin forgot to write'. One envious Broadway songwriter is said to have remarked: 'Sure, that guy Gershwin is a genius. I just wish he'd stop going around as though he'd invented the blue note.'

Essentially, blue notes have their origin in the African-American blues, wherein singers subtly 'bend' the pitches of certain notes to heighten the effect of melancholy or longing. With the singing voice, or on instruments which bend pitches easily, the bending of an ordinary note into a blue one is straightforward. But to capture on paper the flavour of the blues, there had to be a way of categorizing the most often-used blue notes and integrating them within the conventional western musical scale. Put in simple terms, composers 'flattened' the third and seventh notes of the scale, effectively turning them 'blue' to the ear. (In some tunes, the fifth note also gets 'flattened' and turns blue). The major scale becomes the 'blue-note' scale – the lifeblood, one might say, of the blues, the world of jazz, and the music of George Gershwin.

From childhood, Gershwin would also have responded to the potency of blue notes in the traditional cantorial melodies of Jewish

liturgical singing, and as a budding composer he was soon aware of the plaintiveness they could impart to his own vocal lines. In *I'll Build a Stairway*, the critical blue note falls on the first syllable of 'Paradise'; in *Somebody Loves Me* it colours the words at 'I wonder who' – twice, for added poignancy. Gershwin was taking these emotive inflections from religious, folk and jazz sources and exploiting them in his theatre songs (and later, in his concert music) to such a degree that his melodies convey a characteristic 'Gershwin sound' by means of this ingredient more than any other. Blue notes are also a component of the chords and harmonies he uses to support the tunes, making the mixture of 'white' and 'blue' notes a rich compound that beguiles the ear without the hearer realising how it is achieved, which is as it should be.

The word 'blue' was to gain immortality for Gershwin in 1924, through *Rhapsody in Blue*, but it was already to the fore in the *Scandals of 1922*. Buddy De Sylva had aroused in Gershwin the possibility of writing a sort of 'Negro opera', which they could try out in that season's revue. George White liked the sound of this experiment, and within five frenetic days Gershwin and De Sylva completed a twenty-five-minute miniature opera entitled *Blue Monday*. (The tension of working at this pace brought on constipation problems for Gershwin, who thereafter referred to his 'composer's stomach' – a lifelong nervous affliction which doctors were never able to alleviate.) The story was set in a basement cafe in Harlem, a Negro area of New York which conjured up a frisson of uninhibited sexual naughtiness and latent violence for the middle-class Times Square theatre-goers who were the basis of George White's audiences. After a prologue explaining that the piece is centred around 'a woman's intuition gone wrong', *Blue Monday* tells the over-sentimental tale of Joe and Tom, rivals for the love of Vi. Joe visits his devoted mother (shades of Don José in Bizet's *Carmen*), pretending to be on business. Tom suggests to Vi that Joe is really out of town to meet up with another woman. She shoots Joe in revenge, then learns the truth. So much, as they say, for the plot.

With such a feeble libretto, it was left to the still-inexperienced Gershwin to carry the action with his music. What he came up with was more a series of blues-inspired popular songs connected by jazz-like recitatives than an integrated piece of musical theatre. (The

Scandals staging was recreated in the 1945 film *Rhapsody in Blue*, an entertaining Hollywood 'biopic' based – at times very loosely – on Gershwin's life). Of the songs, *Blue Monday Blues* has a genuine Harlem atmosphere, and Vi's aria *Has Anyone Seen My Joe?* benefits by borrowing a languorous theme from Gershwin's *Lullaby* quartet movement. But for sheer mawkishness, Joe's closing 'mammy' song, *I'm Going to See My Mother*, takes some beating.

Several critics were merciless. 'Freeze-dried *Pagliacci*' and 'the most dismal, stupid, incredible blackface sketch that has probably ever been perpetrated' were among the press comments. The fact that the cast were actually white, but made-up in blackface (so that they could quickly wash away their Negroid appearance and be all set for the next production number), typified a degree of stereotypical racism among producers and writers of the time. Gershwin and De Sylva's artistic intentions, none the less, were honourable, and one anonymous critic did write more positively. 'Here at last is a genuinely human plot of American life ... there were crudities, but in it we see the first gleam of a new American musical art.' *Blue Monday* was the first intimation that Gershwin would never be content with supplying miscellaneous songs for Broadway revues. Something was driving him towards an integrated theatre piece, and in this case Negro music proved to be the mainspring. George White removed the ill-fated mini-opera from *Scandals* after only one performance because he was alarmed at how it depressed the virtually nonplussed audience. But in a sense *Porgy and Bess* was born – or still-born – on 28 August 1922, thirteen years before Gershwin's operatic masterpiece finally arrived on stage.

One musician who remained loyal to *Blue Monday* was the conductor on that night of disappointment for Gershwin. He was an up-and-coming, 32-year-old bandleader named Paul Whiteman, who had been hired by White as musical director, bringing his ensemble, the Palais Royal Orchestra, into the Globe Theatre pit. *Blue Monday*'s piano-score had been orchestrated by Will Vodery, a black arranger and long-time Gershwin supporter. Whiteman must have taken a liking to the piece because, more than three years later, he was to give two Carnegie Hall performances of a reorchestrated version under a different title, *135th Street*. This time the orchestration would be in the hands of Whiteman's close colleague, Ferde Grofé. Under its new name, the hybrid piece would fare little better with audiences and

Paul Whiteman (centre) discussing his two Carnegie Hall performances of *135th Street* with (left to right) critic Deems Taylor, composer/ arranger Ferde Grofé, singer Blossom Seeley and George Gershwin

critics than it had done at the Globe. But that would hardly matter, because by then the names Whiteman and Grofé would be synonymous with Gershwin's sensational breakthrough into the concert hall with *Rhapsody in Blue.*

Meanwhile, between 1920 and 1924, Gershwin kept up his unstoppable work-rate by contributing to diverse productions. His scores for the *Scandals* hardly counted as a full-time commitment and as usual he was eager to take on anything new. Two songs illustrate not only the stylish confidence he had achieved, but represent another brand of audience-pleaser now that ragtime and 'mammy' songs were beginning to wane: the titillating, mildly-naughty French song. One of its most enchanting practitioners was Irene Bordoni, who saucily introduced *Do It Again* in a risqué 1922 comedy called *The French Doll.* This number is a prime example of how effectively he could, by that time, set a given lyric using the simplest, most direct musical procedures. The words 'Oh, do it again' are sung to a little five-note

scale, falling and rising to suggest a tender insistence. They occur a second time over different harmonies. As ever, Gershwin's harmonies do not stand still; we are drawn into the song by some new harmonic surprise. Then the word 'no' is repeated five times, on the same note. These are very elementary devices, but in Gershwin's hands they are magic. The song perfectly expresses the allure of a pretty girl as she coyly, knowingly teases her loved one, but because of its classical poise it never descends into sentimentality. It remained one of Gershwin's own favourites.

The following year he came up with another song in capricious vein, once more sung by Bordoni, in a show called *Little Miss Bluebeard*. Its title was *I Won't Say I Will, But I Won't Say I Won't*. Again, there is the element of teasing, of playing hard-to-get. But Gershwin does not resort to a similar melodic idea just because the lyrics (again by Buddy De Sylva and the elusive Arthur Francis) express analogous sentiments. *Do It Again* used a smooth, seductive melody, yet now the element of tantalizing mischief is caught by little jumps in an angular tune – a felicitous match for the playful skittishness of the words.

Gershwin was moving ahead socially. Still in his early twenties, his fame was spreading as a brilliant pianist, a fluent composer with his finger on the pulse of popular taste, and a charismatic entertainer at parties. He was distancing himself ever further from his Brooklyn roots, mingling with influential people both inside the world of the theatre and beyond. Two friends, Herman Paley and Jules Glaenzer, became particularly helpful in promoting him.

Paley, nearly twenty years his senior, had been a Remick's staff composer and the company had published some of his songs. He had studied the piano with Hambitzer, Kilenyi, and the 'American Grieg', Edward MacDowell. His apartment was a lively meeting-place for people from a wide social circle, a place where Gershwin felt at home and where his piano-playing was the only activity guaranteed to stop the animated chatter about politics, literature and the arts – conversations valuable to the young composer, ever-conscious of his lack of formal education. It was at one of Paley's gatherings that Ira met his wife-to-be, Leonore. Even at that time the extrovert George dominated any gathering with his *joie de vivre* and his insatiable love of playing his music, while the more reserved Ira was content to

remain out of the limelight, talking quietly and smoking his pipe, beaming with pride at the effect his brother was having on all these cultured and witty people. As their fame grew, this endearing feature of their relationship never altered.

Jules Glaenzer was an executive of Cartier's, the jewellers. His fashionable parties were held at his East Side residence – a far cry from the Gershwin family apartment, now on West 110th Street. This is where the whole family would continue to live until 1925, entertaining boisterous relatives and friends who seemed to come and go at all hours as in some Marx Brothers comedy, playing poker and roaming noisily from room to room. In contrast, an evening at Glaenzer's might see Noël Coward and Lord and Lady Mountbatten rubbing shoulders with Charlie Chaplin, Jascha Heifetz and Maurice Chevalier. This had important consequences for Gershwin because up till this point he had not mingled with people of sophistication and his social graces were lacking. Even when introduced to a woman, he would forget to take the cigar out of his mouth. He began to attend to matters of etiquette and from now on would wear stylish and fashionable clothes. In his photographs – not just the studio portraits, but those taken at rehearsals, on a concert tour, relaxing with friends, or just writing a song at home with Ira – we see a man aware of his public image.

Tall, dark-eyed, with a muscular build, boundless vitality and good humour, Gershwin was already intensely attractive to women, and various (often exaggerated) stories about his sexual appetite recur among his biographers. Because of his work in the theatre he was surrounded by alluring and ambitious young women – showgirls, dancers, starlets – for whom George Gershwin was an obvious catch. Opportunities abounded – yet even at that age he enjoyed visiting brothels, and this need would become a lifelong addiction. His passion for work meant that these casual encounters with women were probably a necessary way of releasing his sexual energy so that he could get back to the 'real' business of life: his next batch of songs, his next theatre project.

Ira, aware of his brother's numerous affairs but always discreet, kept under lock and key a 'black book' listing the phone numbers of his women friends. Understandably, this area of George's life was not one upon which Ira or other family members wished to dwell. Underneath

his poise and charm, George was actually unsure of himself with women, and afraid of rejection. Of the hundreds of women he would meet and socialize with (possibly with an aim to marry), none came up to specification. A common excuse was that the woman, though available, was older and had children. Often he would fall in love with somebody already married, complicating the issue for himself from the start. Then there was the real fear of being socially outclassed if he chose the wrong partner, or – much worse – that she would not be musically intelligent enough for him. He decided against proposing to a girl brought up in the elegant area of Park Avenue because 'I'm a guy who will always have a touch of the tenement about me.' And as late as 1933, a chorus girl in his musical *Pardon My English* was discarded, despite George's initial enthusiasm, because she made the mistake of playing some Gershwin on the piano for him. He remarked that he 'couldn't live with that kind of piano playing' for the rest of his life.

Any chosen partner would have had to sustain his habit of talking endlessly and approvingly about himself and his work. Gershwin's egotism is unquestioned, but it was part of his inborn character and therefore unfair to regard it as deliberately hurtful. Sometimes it was plain funny. Thrown about in a taxi, he called to the driver: 'Careful man, you've got George Gershwin in the car!' At other times his insensitivity could border on offence, had not the recipient been aware of his innately benevolent nature. Once, having agreed to try receiving some baseball throws from the songwriter Harry Ruby, the balls were coming at Gershwin so fast that he pulled out of the game. He later explained that his hands were too valuable to risk injury. Ruby protested, 'What about my hands?' To which Gershwin replied, 'With you it doesn't matter.' Some time later Ruby reminded him of his remark. 'Well, it's true isn't it?' said Gershwin. Another songwriter, Johnny Green, remembers Gershwin sounding-off at length about his achievements to a woman after one of his concerts, eventually to stop and say: 'That's enough about me. Now what did you think about how I played?'

It was an attitude that was bound to permeate his relationships with women. He wrote a little waltz-song, which he would sing and play to his current dating-partner. It was, in effect, what his friend Kitty Carlisle (who later married playwright Moss Hart) described as

his 'mating call', because he left a blank space in the lyrics so that any name could be inserted – and of course varied according to which girl he was trying to impress. At one party he was getting along famously, cuddling an attractive companion on his lap, when someone asked him to play the piano. His electrifying dash to the keyboard meant that the astonished woman found herself dumped on the carpet.

With a boyish, joyful enthusiasm that made 'an evening with Gershwin a Gershwin evening' (a quote from Oscar Levant), he was unstoppable once at the piano. Even his mother advised him not to overdo it. 'The trouble is,' he protested, 'when I don't play at a party I don't have a good time.' Alongside this should be considered Gershwin's response to Harold Arlen, when Arlen asked him whether, since he always seemed so natural at the keyboard, he ever got nervous. 'Of course I do,' he replied. 'But I never let on.' The composer Burton Lane said that 'you could feel the electricity going through the room when he played. He could transpose into any key with the greatest of ease. He had total command of what he was doing. Musical surprises, unusual changes of keys. He was one of the few composers who had a real sense of humour.'

No two Gershwin performances were alike, and because he played only his own music, to the onlooker it seemed that everything was being newly-minted on the spot; his improvisations sounded like written-out, memorized pieces. Indeed, his astonishing ability to improvise at the piano was perhaps his greatest gift, because from his hours of improvising at parties would come an unending stream of ideas he could later recall, and work into his written-down music in the quietness of his apartment.

The brilliant Russian-born theatre director Rouben Mamoulian (among his achievements were the original productions of *Porgy and Bess*, *Oklahoma!* and *Carousel*) left us vivid recollections. 'George at the piano was George happy ... like a sorcerer celebrating his Sabbath. He would draw out a lovely melody like a golden thread, then juggle it, twist it and toss it around mischievously, weave it into unexpected intricate patterns, and hurl it into a cascade of ever-changing rhythms and counterpoints.' A view confirmed by the conductor Serge Koussevitsky (not one to be fooled by fake musicianship, and later the mentor of Copland and Bernstein and founder of the Tanglewood

Festival): 'As I watched him, I caught myself thinking, in a dream
state, that this was a delusion; the enchantment of this extraordinary
being was too great to be real.'

Oscar Levant (1906–72) met Gershwin in 1924, having moved to
New York from his native Pittsburgh. Levant's mordant wit and
lugubrious wisecracking are well-captured in several Hollywood films
(including *Rhapsody in Blue*), and he became a sharp observer of
Gershwin, who provided an effective foil to his neurotic personality.
Levant was a brilliant pianist and also wrote songs and concert music.
He had some lessons from Schoenberg, after the Austrian composer
(the first to abandon tonality) left Germany in 1933 and settled in Los
Angeles. As Gershwin also harboured ambitions to study with
Schoenberg it is worth noting that, compared with Gershwin's
audience-pleasing priorities, Levant's attempts to fuse jazz with atonal
disciplines have remained unperformed and virtually forgotten.
Michael Feinstein has tried to rescue his music from neglect and has
issued long-lost recordings on compact disc. Among them is Levant's
nervy, one-movement piano concerto, which is worth a hearing if only
to imagine what might have resulted had Alban Berg fallen in love
with jazz and blues. The impact of Gershwin's musical gifts meant
that Levant found himself creatively inhibited, and by 1942 he had
given up composing and was famous instead as a radio quiz-show
panellist – though he remained a devoted and dazzling performer of
his friend's works.

Levant's acidic sense of humour added a bitter-sweet tinge to his
recollections of Gershwin in full flow. 'Tell me George,' he remarked
during a pause in one of George's keyboard marathons, 'if you had to
do it all over again, would you still fall in love with yourself?' Levant
was bewitched by Gershwin's facility. 'He had so much fluency at the
piano and so steady a surge of ideas that any time he sat down just to
amuse himself something came out of it.'

The glittering round of parties that made Gershwin a society
celebrity were part of a social environment governed – none too
successfully – by the American law of Prohibition. Enforced
nationwide between 1920 and 1933, it forbade the manufacture or sale
of any drink containing more than 0.5% alcohol. It arose from the
passionate belief among mainly white Protestants that alcohol
consumption threatened law and order, especially among immigrants

Federal 'Dry Agents',
enforcing Prohibition,
dispose of twenty barrels of
illicit beer at Hackensack,
New Jersey, 23 July 1930.

in the industrial northern states. Most of these newcomers were
Catholic or Jewish and could see nothing wrong. Alcohol, surely, was
an essential part of their ancestral traditions. The Poles and Germans
loved their beer, the Irish drank beer or whiskey, and Jews from
numerous countries, Greeks and Italians had always enjoyed wine. But
Prohibitionists insisted that crime, violence and family degradation
were rampant through excess drinking. Their interdiction backfired,
however, and drinking became even more attractive because it was
illegal. Saloons re-opened as 'speakeasies' supplied by liquor from
underworld dealers in a national racket known as 'bootlegging';
during the 1920s there were around 30,000 speakeasies in New York
alone. Police were bribed and corrupted. Bootlegging grew into a vast
enterprise with connections to the Cosa Nostra (the American wing of
the Mafia), spawning gangsters among whom Al Capone was king.
The bootlegging industry may have played a vital part in the
establishment of jazz for a white clientele, because Prohibition
encouraged people to desert large theatres and seek their
entertainment in intimate venues enlivened by jazz music and cabaret.
Here they could defy the law unseen, and truly 'speak easy'. A
bootlegging trial in Chicago had to be abandoned when the jury were

found to have drunk all the evidence. Prohibition was repealed in 1933 because, finally, it was plain to all levels of society that it had failed.

One of New York's foremost critics and writers, Carl Van Vechten, observed that, despite Prohibition, one could drink one's way right through an evening simply by moving on from one party to another. So the glitterati who draped themselves around Gershwin's piano were part of a culture determined to flaunt authority and enjoy the added frisson of illegality in pursuance of their social pleasures. As soon as Prohibition had become the law of the land, Broadway revues started interpolating extra songs and sketches about it. Nora Bayes, who was touring in Gershwin's *Ladies First*, put in an extra number called *Prohibition Blues*. No one was more alert to the farcical aspects of an unenforceable law and its effects on American civil liberty than the Gershwin brothers.

George and Ira were honing their talents in a climate of limitless experiment and adventurousness in the theatre, art and literature. Eugene O'Neill was in search of what might be termed a purely American dramatic form for the stage. Clifford Odettes was writing sharp protest plays addressing social issues. George S. Kaufman was becoming a master of political satire, and his screenplays for the Marx Brothers comedies were among his prime weapons. The imported, sophisticated social observances of Noël Coward could be contrasted with the gritty realism of Elmer Rice, whose play *Street Scene* became the basis of Kurt Weill's operatic version. Maxwell Anderson was juxtaposing verse-dialogue and street-wise talk in his tragedies. The corrosive humour of W. C. Fields, the cowboy routines of Will Rogers, the perfectly-timed comedy of George Burns and Gracie Allen, Lucille Ball, Bob Hope and legions of vaudeville entertainers, the charm of Fred and Adele Astaire, the unbridled exuberance of larger-than-life Jewish performers including Jolson, Eddie Cantor and Fanny Brice, annual discoveries in Ziegfeld's scintillating *Follies*, among them Paulette Goddard (with whom Gershwin was to fall in love), Carole Lombard, Marilyn Miller, Ruby Keeler ... the two Gershwins were bound to flourish in this Broadway-centred hothouse of creativity and expertise, even though few guests at those supposedly-dry, liquor-free parties could have imagined what the genial, bookish Ira and his extrovert brother in masterly command of the grand piano would eventually achieve.

Early in 1923, George made his first trip abroad to write the music for a London revue, *The Rainbow*. The customs officer in Southampton glanced at his passport and remarked, 'George Gershwin, the composer of *Swanee*?' This gave him enormous delight. When a reporter then asked him for an interview, 'I felt I was Kern or somebody.' One of his collaborators was the playwright and author of mystery thrillers, Edgar Wallace. But the composer who would soon be as renowned in London's West End as he was on Broadway did not sail home as the toast of Piccadilly. *The Rainbow*, though not a flop, ran for only 113 performances. Gershwin admitted that, of all his theatre scores, this was his weakest. He had dashed off a dozen new songs in London and used some of them, plus a few 'spares' brought over in his suitcase, to patch the score together. None of the music has stood the test of time; for once, Gershwin's sheer facility was not enough.

Back in New York, November 1923 saw a more significant milestone, and another important indication that Gershwin's music was now too original to be confined just to the musical-comedy stage. The moving spirit was Eva Gauthier (1885–1958), a Canadian-born mezzo-soprano who could boast impeccable musical training in Europe. She appeared in the 1920 London première of Debussy's *Pelléas et Mélisande*, spent five years absorbing herself in the music of Malaya and Java, and returned to New York to embark on a distinguished career during which she presented unusual, provocative recital programmes and championed such modernists as Schoenberg, Bartók, Stravinsky, and any young contemporary American composers she considered worthy of promotion. Now she was planning a recital of 'Ancient and Modern Music for Voice' at the prestigious Aeolian Hall. Her programme would range from William Byrd to Schoenberg, and would include a group of modern American popular songs. Carl Van Vechten had no hesitation in suggesting to Miss Gauthier that Gershwin must be represented in what he mistakenly referred to as 'the jazz group'. Indeed, why not invite Gershwin himself to be her accompanist for these pieces?

Gauthier seized the chance to add extra distinction to her already innovative recital, and on 1 November 1923, the 25-year-old Gershwin strode on to the Aeolian Hall platform to make his first major public appearance as both composer and pianist. Gauthier had just

performed two songs by Hindemith. Now Gershwin would accompany her in an American selection: music by Kern, Berlin, Walter Donaldson, and himself. Schoenberg's *Song of the Wood Dove* (from *Gurrelieder*) would be heard immediately afterwards – for which her regular accompanist, Max Jaffe, would resume his seat at the piano. It was all very unusual and very newsworthy. The critic Deems Taylor described Gershwin's entrance: 'The singer reappeared, followed by a tall, black-haired young man who was far from possessing the icy aplomb of those to whom playing on the platform of Aeolian Hall is an old story. He bore under his arm a small bundle of sheet music with lurid black and yellow covers. The audience began to show signs of relaxation; this promised to be amusing.'

The next quarter-of-an-hour proved to be more than merely 'amusing'. Gauthier and Gershwin launched into Berlin's *Alexander's Ragtime Band* and followed it with Kern's *The Siren's Song*. After Walter Donaldson's *Carolina in the Morning* came three of Gershwin's own works. *Innocent Ingenue Baby*, the only outstanding number in a burleske which had run for a mere five weeks the previous winter, came between two songs guaranteed to set feet tapping in the staid Aeolian Hall: *I'll Build a Stairway to Paradise* and the inevitable *Swanee*.

Deems Taylor, an accomplished composer and the music critic for the *New York World*, happily reported the effect all this had on an audience which 'included a fair sprinkling of poseurs, highbrows and intensely class-conscious *cognoscenti*'. Gershwin's 'mysterious and fascinating rhythmic and contrapuntal stunts' (the sort of embellishments which had so upset Nora Bayes in their tour of 1918) were much appreciated. All his songs 'stood up amazingly well, not only as entertainment but as music'. Taylor praised their melodic interest and their 'almost classically severe form – the qualities that any sincere and interesting music possesses'. Such was the enthusiastic reception given to *Swanee* that singer and pianist returned to the platform to give, as an encore, *Do It Again* – which generated thunderous applause and had itself to be 'done again'. Gershwin had every reason to be well-pleased as he strode, smiling, off the platform to make way for the return of accompanist Max Jaffe and the very different world of Schoenberg. He could not have known that the next time he sat at the piano on the Aeolian Hall stage he would truly be making American musical history.

In general, the critics referred to this whole American section of Gauthier's recital as 'jazz songs' (following Van Vechten's mis-terminology), rather than 'Broadway songs' or 'show-tunes'. Before the abolition of slavery at the end of the Civil War in 1865, the music of the American Negro consisted mainly of work songs, blues, gospel songs and spirituals. None of this could reasonably be called 'jazz' because the word had not yet been coined. Negro music developed in the bigger cities and especially in New Orleans, which had a large population of 'creoles', descendants of early French and Spanish settlers who had inter-married with Negroes. Their natural tongue was French and much European tradition was in their musical character. One of the most prominent early jazz pianists was the creole 'Jelly Roll' Morton, who is credited with stating that he started using the word 'jazz' in 1902, to try and clarify the difference between what he felt should be termed 'jazz' and the existing ragtime. What ragtime did not exploit was the poetic, melancholic, vocal music of the Negro

Canal Street, the main thoroughfare through the Storyville district of New Orleans, the 'cradle' of jazz

Ragtime pianist and composer 'Jelly Roll' Morton (1885–1941) led the way in widening the scope of jazz while preserving its traditional spirit.

known as the 'blues', and it was this that Morton and like-minded composers developed into music to be played instrumentally, rather than sung.

Morton was among many jazzmen whose less blatant, mellower style succeeded in controlling and softening the more frenzied, purely Negro jazz around New Orleans. From about 1910, Negro musicians began to take their music to major cities like Chicago and New York, where white musicians (including Gershwin) were quick to respond to its appeal. Pure, 'classical' ragtime was practically out of fashion by 1917, the year of Scott Joplin's death and of the forced closure of the Storyville red-light district of New Orleans which drove most remaining jazz musicians north to the big cities. The newer music – jazz – offended many by its apparently chaotic and raucous din. Anti-Negro feeling was as prominent as ever among a significant proportion of the white population, so the Negro origins of jazz hardly facilitated its acceptance. Jazz was spreading too quickly for a clear understanding of its nature, and when white intellectuals such as Van Vechten termed show-tunes 'jazz songs', they were perpetuating – as late as 1923 – a widespread misunderstanding of black music in relation to the popular songs of the day.

The Gauthier recital was repeated in Boston two months later. It gained a warm review from critic H. T. Parker, who coined a resonating phrase to summarize his delight in Gershwin's achievement: 'He is the beginning of sophisticated jazz.' Writers such as Deems Taylor and H. T. Parker were certainly on to something. What they considered to be jazz was invading the concert hall; thanks to Gauthier, the show-tunes of Kern, Berlin and Gershwin were now fair game for recital audiences to experience in venues hallowed by the songs of Schubert, Schumann, Brahms and Hugo Wolf. And because of the rare quality of his tunes and the ear-catching inventiveness of his piano-playing, Gershwin was nominated their standard-bearer in making this crossover an exciting and culturally-acceptable process. Where they were misguided was that jazz had no need to wait for George Gershwin to appear in order for it to be acceptable as a distinctly American musical phenomenon – indeed, the one really original American contribution to the diversity of western musical culture, and moreover a music invented and promulgated by blacks. By the 1920s jazz was a widespread, multi-faceted, vibrant form of

musical expression and public entertainment, spreading from its earthy New Orleans origins to every part of the globe. But it was also falling victim to the gleeful appropriation of its musical elements and financial potentialities by mainly middle-class white performers and entrepreneurs.

From the early 1920s jazz was under constant attack. For many, it was a symbol of crime, drug addiction, alcoholism and prostitution. Jazz and ragtime had begun sweeping the country at the same time as the Prohibition lobby were gaining force. An article in the journal *New York American* in 1922 (the year before Gauthier's recitals) warned that 'moral disaster is coming to hundreds of young American girls through the pathological, nerve-irritating, sex-exciting music of jazz orchestras. The degrading music is common not only to disorderly places, but often to high-school affairs, to expensive hotels, and so-called society circles.'

Fortunately for the vitality and distinctiveness of American popular music, ragtime and jazz penetrated into its very bloodstream, despite such press sentiments. Tin Pan Alley songs became enlivened, and steadily progressed from their origins in black minstrel shows or vaudeville ballads. But jazz remained inextricably linked with anti-black discrimination. When the black pianist-composer Duke Ellington installed his band at the Cotton Club in New York in 1927, its staff and performers were all black too, in common with most other speakeasies. The customers, however, were white. The ten dancing-girls in its gaudy floor-shows were chosen with a white audience in mind. It was essential they were comparatively light-skinned, and in white company they could virtually pass for Caucasians.

Throughout this whole period of black exploitation (in America's wider culture and not just in music and show business), Gershwin and the best of his creative colleagues were setting themselves a higher purpose than sequestering black music and transmuting it for their own ends. Their love and respect for its vigorous, youthful traditions were genuine, and their excitement in grasping the possibilities it offered was inevitable at a time of insatiable public demand for novelty, especially in a period rich in musical experimentation and cross-fertilization.

The entrance to New York's Cotton Club, whose floor-shows were backed by Duke Ellington's uninhibited jazz, to the delight of the all-white clientele

Leonard Bernstein was fascinated by the influence of black musicians on American art music. In 1939 he made it the subject of his Bachelor's thesis, writing: 'American music owes one of its greatest debts to the Negroes, not only for the popularly acknowledged gift of jazz, but for the impetus which jazz has given to America's art music. This incentive has come in two ways – melodically and rhythmically – with further support from tone colour and contrapuntal feeling. Both the scale patterns and the rhythm patterns, as first manifested in jazz itself, were used freely in symphonic composition by men like Gershwin.'

Among the audience at Gauthier's New York recital was Paul Whiteman – one of the key personalities in the process of making jazz 'respectable' which, rightly, offended large numbers of true jazz executants and listeners. He had conducted Gershwin's *Blue Monday* and been impressed by its trail-blazing intentions. Now Gershwin was enthralling a recital hall audience with popular show-tunes and jazz-

inflected pianistic fireworks. Wheels that had been turning in Whiteman's mind must have accelerated their motion. He had long nurtured an ambition to lift jazz from 'out of the kitchen' and make it acceptable in the concert hall. All was in place. Gershwin and Whiteman were made for each other.

3

Gershwin poses proudly
beside the original sheet
music of *Rhapsody in Blue*.

The Rhapsody in Blue *represents what I have
been striving for since my earliest composition.
I wanted to show that jazz is an idiom not
to be limited to a mere song and chorus that
consumed three minutes in presentation.
I succeeded in showing that jazz is not merely a
dance, it comprises bigger themes and purposes.*

George Gershwin
in *Theatre Magazine,* June 1926

Rhapsody in Blue

Paul Whiteman (1890–1967), born in Denver, Colorado, was an orchestral viola player before joining the US Navy and rising to become conductor of a forty-piece Navy band, towards the end of World War I. After the war, he was among the first to put together a dance band which specialized in 'orchestrated jazz'. Such music had enormous appeal for dancing, but because the music was tightly-organized, written-out by ingenious arrangers, and carefully rehearsed, there remained little allowance for individual jazzmen to ad-lib their solos. So the improvisatory spontaneity and invention of real jazz was largely absent. The distinction is immediately clear when one compares, say, a Louis Armstrong recording of the 1920s (with his Hot Five or Hot Seven ensembles) with one by Whiteman, who began making records in 1920 (*Whispering* was one of his best-sellers). At a time when all the finest jazz musicians were black, Whiteman hired only white personnel, and everybody concerned made a great deal of money by entertaining the public with skilful, often brash and elephantine dance-numbers and popular song arrangements in which they joyfully exploited all the styles and tricks of the less famous, black jazz pioneers. Whiteman had an efficient publicity machine, and because of the various bands he led around the hotel circuit on the west coast, an extensive European tour in 1923, and, from 1920, his band's residency at New York's Palais Royal, he was soon riding the crest of a wave and being lauded as the 'King of Jazz'.

This is not to say that Whiteman was not an excellent musician. But his music could never be taken seriously by jazz lovers or jazz critics, for whom a better designation might have been 'King of His Kind of Jazz'. His mission to spread his music to an ever-wider public was expressed in his 1926 book, *Jazz*, in which he suggested that America's 'common people' were avid for as much jazz music as they could get, but that they lacked 'the courage to admit they took it seriously'. Two years earlier this belief lit the touch-paper for Whiteman to present big-band arrangements in a prestigious concert

location. That way, he reasoned, everyone would see that jazz had come to stay, and that it deserved recognition as 'a new movement in the world's art of music'. He resolved that the Paul Whiteman Palais Royal Orchestra would present 'An Experiment in Modern Music' at one of New York's prime centres for classical music, and Gershwin would be one of his star turns. His first choice of auditorium was nothing less than Carnegie Hall, with its nearly 3,000 seats. But it was already booked on his chosen day, 12 February 1924, which was Abraham Lincoln's birthday. (Whiteman would not have been unaware of the appropriateness of proclaiming the 'emancipation' of jazz on this date.) So the venue would have to be the scene of Gershwin's recent triumph, the 1,300-seat Aeolian Hall.

He put out a somewhat grandiose summary of his intentions: 'To sketch, musically, from the beginning of American history, the development of our emotional resources which have led us to the characteristic American music of today.' Leaving aside this lofty talk, Whiteman was aiming for a highly-publicized event that could only boost his band's popularity, and even the choice of New York was cynically rationalized. 'Novelty, not luck or ability, is what gets by there. New York doesn't care about merit so much as it does about something new to tickle its eyes, its palate or its ears.'

Strictly speaking, his project was not actually novel. A jazz musician named James Reese Europe had performed jazz numbers with his Clef Club Symphony Orchestra at Carnegie Hall as far back as 1912 (and again in 1914). New York newspapers had sent along their music correspondents, who had been 'astounded by the sound of syncopated music'; the concert had brought 'a very storm of tumultuous applause'. Whiteman, in a brilliant piece of showmanship, added an extra twist: a distinguished committee would attend his concert, and afterwards hand down judgement on the central question, 'What Is American Music?' A news item in the *New York Tribune* of 4 January 1924 explained that this committee would comprise 'the leading musical critics of the United States'. It included some illustrious names: Sergey Rachmaninov, Jascha Heifetz, Efrem Zimbalist and Alma Gluck. An odd selection to pass opinion on American jazz, to be sure. Unlike Stravinsky (who attended Whiteman's concert, and whose *Ragtime for Eleven Instruments*, a movement entitled *Ragtime* in *L'Histoire du soldat*, and *Piano Rag*

Following page, Paul Whiteman and his orchestra. Ferde Grofé is at one of the two pianos, back row, second from right. Whiteman's Rhapsody score listed twenty-three players, but double bassist Albert Armer seems to have missed this photo-call; his instrument is propped against Grofé's piano.

Music had all appeared between 1917 and 1919), Rachmaninov neither played nor composed anything in the jazz idiom. Rachmaninov was, of course, Russian-born. So were the two violinists, Heifetz and Zimbalist. The soprano Alma Gluck, though educated in America, came from Romania; her place on the panel was presumably due to being the wife of Zimbalist. How these particular luminaries were expected to come up with expert definitions of American music is hard to say. None the less, Whiteman had undoubtedly pulled off a coup in getting such star names to be associated with his venture. His publicity agent further fuelled the excitement by ensuring that, on the day, major figures in the world of serious music would be among the diverse audience of song pluggers, vaudeville artists, Tin Pan Alley entrepreneurs, jazz fans and general curiosity-seekers. In addition to Stravinsky could be seen Walter Damrosch, Fritz Kreisler, Ernest Bloch, John Philip Sousa, Leopold Godowsky, Moriz Rosenthal, Mischa Elman, John McCormack, Amelita Galli-Curci and Leopold Stokowski. They rubbed shoulders with yet more personalities from the worlds of theatre, literature and commerce.

Whiteman had talked to Gershwin about his notion for a 'jazz concert' some time before February 1924, even to the extent of asking him to contribute a concerto-like piece in which he would be the solo pianist. Gershwin sketched a few ideas, but felt under no pressure to start serious work on such an unusual commission when he was so busy with his Broadway commitments. His surprise can be imagined when, late on the evening of 3 January at a billiard parlour, where he was relaxing with Ira and Buddy De Sylva, Ira brought to his attention a *Tribune* news item in an early edition of the following morning's paper. The final paragraph was startlingly specific: 'George Gershwin is at work on a jazz concerto, Irving Berlin is writing a syncopated tone-poem and Victor Herbert is working on an American suite.'

Gershwin rang Whiteman the following morning to register his amazement that a work he had not even begun was being publicized as being in production for a high-profile première only five weeks ahead. His latest musical, *Sweet Little Devil*, was going through final rehearsals ready for its New York opening on 21 January, and he was polishing up with Eva Gauthier the songs they would be performing in Boston on the 29th. This was not a good time to be diverting his energies. Whiteman replied that Vincent Lopez, a rival bandleader,

was planning to steal the idea of his experimental concert and there was no time to lose. Knowing that Gershwin was flattered to be involved, and aware of his capacity for strenuous work in order to meet deadlines, Whiteman was able to persuade him to get started. He was less successful with Irving Berlin, who failed to produce his 'syncopated tone-poem' and probably never could have done. His genius was for song hits, not extended pieces. Victor Herbert, always a prolific professional, did deliver his *Suite of Serenades* – which proved to be his last composition.

Most of the 'jazz concerto' was composed on an old upright piano in the back room of the Gershwin family apartment at West 110th Street. The manuscript was in the form of a two-piano sketch, a time-honoured method used by composers for a work intended to be orchestrated later. The first piano part showed what Gershwin would be playing as soloist, while underneath ran a second piano part outlining the music for the accompanying jazz band. We know the starting-date was 7 January, since Gershwin wrote it under his signature at the top of the first page. But there is nothing to show when he finished it. At one time he said he took ten days, at another that he took 'three weeks, on and off' – which is more likely. Whichever the case, he worked amazingly quickly. Since Whiteman had allocated five days of rehearsals, the whole piece, including orchestration, needed to be finished within a month. Its original title was *American Rhapsody*. But, so the story goes, Ira happened to have been to a gallery exhibition of Whistler paintings bearing such descriptive titles as *Nocturne in Black and Gold*, and from then on, a piece which has blue notes at its very heart became *Rhapsody in Blue*, for Jazz Band and Piano – interestingly, not the other way round. Gershwin would similarly title his *Second Rhapsody* as being 'for orchestra with piano'. (In both rhapsodies the solo piano is, nevertheless, as much centre-stage as in the *Concerto in F* and the *Variations on 'I Got Rhythm'*.)

In 1931 Gershwin gave his first biographer, Isaac Goldberg, recollections of the rhapsody's genesis. He recalled that he was on a train to Boston for the out-of-town previews of *Sweet Little Devil*. 'I had already done some work on the rhapsody. It was on the train, with its steely rhythms ... I frequently hear music in the very heart of noise. And there I suddenly heard – and even saw on paper – the

complete construction of the rhapsody from beginning to end. I heard it as a sort of musical kaleidoscope of America – of our vast melting pot, of our incomparable national pep, of our blues, our metropolitan madness.' Gershwin's words were probably tidied-up by Goldberg, but in essence there could be no clearer summary of the rhapsody's content and spirit. He also gave Goldberg a sort of manifesto-after-the-event, which shows how closely his thinking had matched Whiteman's. 'There had been so much chatter about the limitations of jazz. Jazz, they said, had to be in strict time. It had to cling to dance rhythms. I resolved, if possible, to kill that misconception with one sturdy blow.'

In the light of these remarks, his choice of a free, rhapsodic form (instead of an 'extended blues for orchestra', his first intention) makes sense. He would not be a slave to conventional forms of either popular or classical music. The piece would have a shape, but a shape resembling, say, one of Liszt's *Hungarian Rhapsodies* (music with which he was certainly familiar), where his tunes would not need scholarly development and where he could work at speed, linking together the various bits of thematic material already in his head (and, to some extent, in his sketchbooks) to create something episodic, yet coherent.

Much speculation has abounded as to whether Gershwin would have been technically capable of orchestrating the rhapsody himself. As each page of the piano manuscript was finished, it was handed to Whiteman's orchestrator, Ferde Grofé, who confirmed in 1938 that Gershwin did not have sufficient knowledge of orchestration in 1924. (Only eighteen months after the rhapsody, Gershwin accomplished his own orchestration for his piano concerto, and thereafter for all his concert works.) But in view of the tight deadline it would have been foolish for him even to have tried. In any case, Gershwin himself was the first to agree that Grofé was the key figure in enabling the piece to be spectacularly successful under Whiteman's baton.

Like Whiteman, Ferde Grofé (born in 1892) had been a violist, playing for over ten years in the Los Angeles Symphony Orchestra. He joined Whiteman in 1920 as pianist and arranger, and his skills were so wide-ranging that he could play nearly every instrument in the band. It was his talent that gave them their distinctive sound, with well-timed contrasts between solos and ensembles, and a multitude of novel effects and timbres gleaned from his intimate knowledge of the

Grofé, Gershwin, S. L. Rothafel ('Roxy') and Whiteman at the Roxy Theatre, New York, where the film *The King of Jazz* had its première

various instruments. His success under Whiteman was immediate: the year he joined, their recording of *Whispering* sold a million-and-a-half records. From then until 1924, every Whiteman number came via Grofé's pen, including all the arrangements featured in the Aeolian Hall 'experiment'. (After leaving Whiteman he would occupy himself with conducting and composition; his *Grand Canyon Suite* was performed and recorded by Arturo Toscanini, the legendary Italian conductor of the NBC Symphony Orchestra, and remains a popular item in the American repertoire.)

Grofé practically moved in with the Gershwins during this hectic period. 'I learned to value the atmosphere of George's home,' he recalled, 'and the sweet hospitality of his mother and father. Mrs

Gershwin watched our labours with loving interest, and taught me to appreciate Russian tea, which she brewed for us when we rested.'

Gershwin annotated some tentative instrumental indications in his sketch for the jazz band. Understandably, he had clear ideas about which instruments should be featured in certain passages. But he was to a considerable extent in awe of Grofé who, speedily and meticulously, noted specific instrumentations in his orchestral version, allocating Gershwin's themes to given individuals with all the expertise acquired in the four years he had grown to know every aspect of Whiteman's line-up. For instance, 'Ross' meant the versatile Ross Gorman, who would play several kinds of clarinet and 'double' on oboe and saxophone. Even though Whiteman had enlarged his normal nine-piece Palais Royal orchestra to twenty-three for this special event, Grofé skilfully contrived that several other bandsmen besides Gorman would alternate between a variety of instruments, giving the piece a rich palette of jazzy coloration. Grofé would be playing one of the two orchestral pianos, and a second pianist would double on celeste (one of the characteristic sounds of Whiteman's band was the inclusion of one or two pianos). These were the professional skills Grofé brought to his adaptation of Gershwin's manuscript during the ten days he orchestrated the two-piano version. The 25-year-old composer could not have matched them, with or without the crushing time-schedule.

For all his clarity of thought regarding the shape of the rhapsody, Gershwin was receptive to improvements suggested by colleagues. (He had already changed the title, thanks to Ira.) But it might be assumed that the choice of thematic material, at least, was his personal domain, and legend has it that the famous central slow theme, marked Andantino Moderato, came to him while playing the piano at a party, and that Ira urged him to use it in the rhapsody. But there is no reason to disbelieve Grofé when, in a radio interview, he revealed a different source. Apparently, when Gershwin started to compose this heart-tugging section, Grofé had misgivings. It is worth quoting the Grofé interview at some length, because it shows how one of the most famous tunes in the world found its way into the rhapsody despite the composer's original intentions.

I'd take so many pages, go home and work at it, and everything was going along fine. When we got up to the part where the immortal strain

in E major begins, George had something in the pastoral – something, if I recall it correctly, in six-eight time. Up to that point I thought he did a splendid job, but there, all of a sudden, he had a different mood. It didn't seem to fit in there. I said, 'Why don't you write something more melodic?' Well he thought about it. He said, 'Did I ever play you this theme Ferde?' He had it in E flat. I said, 'What is that? Gee, I think it's beautiful. Now that would really fit in there.' He said, 'I wrote that about four or five years ago at Remick's. That's tripe. Sentimental.' I said, 'I don't care what you call it, I think it's a very lovely strain. Please give me a lead-sheet of that, and I'll take it home. I want to play it because I think it's beautiful.' And the thing haunted me all night long – I just couldn't sleep. So I got back the next day to see if he'd gone ahead with ... you know, the pastoral thing. And he'd written a few more bars, I think he'd almost completed it. I said, 'Why don't you use this?' He said, 'I don't like it. It's just too cheap.' I laughed. Just then Ira walked in; we called him Izzy in those days. I said, 'Ira, I wish you'd settle this argument. George has a lovely strain here, I think it really belongs in the rhapsody.' He said, 'Well let's hear it.' George played the theme, and Ira said, 'Yeah, I remember that. You wrote that some years ago.' Well between Izzy and I we finally convinced George that he should use it. I went home, came back the next day, and sure enough he had put it up a half-tone, E major. And that's the story, the real story, of the immortal E major melody.

At the end of Grofé's manuscript score, he scribbled the date on which he finished the orchestration: 4 February, only eight days before the première. Gershwin's solo part was written at the bottom of each page, possibly to make last-minute alterations easier. Just before what Grofé called 'the immortal E major melody' there is a completely blank page of manuscript paper giving room for a continuation of the big, virtuoso piano cadenza that leads into it. Gershwin had originally intended to improvise this long solo.

Had he done so he would have been reviving eighteenth-century practice. Cadenzas, originally, were improvised embellishments inserted into opera arias by the vocalist. At the time of Handel's operas and the *bel canto* aria they became wanton opportunities for singers to show off. Later, composers adopted them for instrumental concertos, allowing the soloist to parade invention and skill on the spot, and Gershwin would have been treading this path. In Grofé's manuscript,

Victor Herbert, Gershwin's
mentor at the rehearsals of
Rhapsody, had achieved
fame as a conductor and
as the composer of over
forty operettas.

Opposite, the first page of
Gershwin's two-piano
manuscript as given to
Grofé for orchestrating; the
starting date is shown, but
the famous clarinet
glissando was only invented
during rehearsals.

most of the cadenza is shown as we hear it today, but Gershwin kept his options open as to when Whiteman would bring in the orchestra – Grofé has scrawled, 'Wait for nod.' An unusual reminder in concert music, but not unique. Beethoven opened his Fantasy for Piano, Chorus and Orchestra with a long, pyrotechnical solo that he improvised at the first performance. In the conductor's score was the German equivalent of 'Wait for nod.'

Ultimately, only a few extra bars were ever added to Gershwin's sketched cadenza before the score was published – but even these apparently caused him some trouble. In their original form they prompted Victor Herbert, who was of course present at rehearsals, to suggest to Gershwin – thirty-nine years his junior – that the musical progression he had been playing sounded too plain. So the rising sequence and final, spread chord we now hear at the end of the cadenza, and which never appeared in Grofé's score, can be attributed to Gershwin's respect for Victor Herbert.

Another rehearsal improvement proved more momentous. In Gershwin's piano sketch, the rhapsody begins with a clarinet trill followed by a rising scale into the first theme. There are seventeen notes in the scale, and Gershwin intended them all to be sounded, because the figure 17 is written over them. In Grofé's original orchestration this indication was faithfully followed in the clarinet part, and at the rehearsals Ross Gorman initially played the scale exactly as written. At some point, just to enliven the session, the virtuoso clarinettist turned the last half of the scale into a glissando – a jazzy, sliding 'wail' which so captivated everyone present that Gershwin insisted it be incorporated into the performance. It has been played thus ever since, and is printed that way in the published score. Gorman's experimental little joke led to what is arguably the most famous opening bar in the whole of American music.

Simon Rattle has defined the rising scale as being 'stolen from one of Bessie Smith's trademark wails, but after it what you hear is pure Jewish cantor music'. A more accurate definition would be 'Jewish klezmer music', echoing as it does the style of abandoned, improvised clarinet figuration essential to the vagrant 'klezmer bands' which originated generations ago in the Jewish communities of Eastern Europe and which joyously entertained the guests at festive occasions ('klezmer' is Hebrew for 'vessel of song'). Other than through the

efforts of Giora Feidman, former principal clarinet in the Israel Philharmonic Orchestra, klezmer music received a significant boost when the violinist Itzhak Perlman visited Poland in 1995 to trace his Jewish roots. He embraced the music with characteristic zeal, his subsequent concerts and recordings spreading the genre worldwide, reminding us that the fiddle, rather than the clarinet, was once its quintessential instrument. We shall meet a sudden appearance of klezmer fiddling in *Concerto in F* and in *An American in Paris*. Simon Rattle's underlying point is that only in America could such disparate elements – the yearning voice of blues-singer Bessie Smith and the Yiddish folk-tunes of Gershwin's forebears in Old Russia – collide to define the sound of New York, as instantly as a Strauss waltz conjures up Old Vienna.

By the day of the concert, Gershwin was quietly confident that his hastily-written piece would not go down badly. But Whiteman, suddenly realizing the enormity of what he had taken on, and with so much ballyhoo, worked himself into a state. 'I slipped around to the entrance of Aeolian Hall. It was snowing, but men and women were fighting to get in the door. I went backstage again, more scared than ever. Black fear simply possessed me. I paced the floor, gnawed my thumbs and vowed I'd give 5,000 dollars if I could stop right then and there.'

Reading their programmes, the audience recognized that they were in for a long afternoon. Whiteman had divided the music into sections with headings such as 'True Form of Jazz', 'Legitimate Scoring versus Jazzing' and 'Semi-Symphonic Arrangements of Popular Melodies'. There would be twenty-six separate musical movements in all, with Gershwin's piece next to the last. Incongruously, Whiteman would end the concert with the first of Elgar's *Pomp and Circumstance* marches, under the heading 'In the Field of the Classics'. Maybe he had become fond of it during his US Navy band days – certainly it was worlds away from anything else on the programme.

Some people were heading for the exits by the time Gershwin made his entrance to take his place at the piano. Despite the important-looking category headings in the printed programme, many of the numbers had started to sound alike, and boredom was in the air. The ventilation system had broken down, and even on a cold

The ubiquitous *Rhapsody in Blue* is propped on the piano for this picture taken just before a concert in Seattle, 1936.

February day the crowded hall had become unpleasantly humid. But from the moment Gorman's clarinet wail rose into the air, everything changed. Gershwin's virtuosity at the keyboard eclipsed anything heard earlier from Zez Confrey. By the end of Gershwin's rhapsody, it was clear that the originality of its invention, its unconventional yet convincing structure, its brilliantly effective piano part, its attractive tunes coloured by Grofé's masterful instrumentation, and its sheer verve had all combined to save the day. The applause was almost frenzied. 'At half-past five on the afternoon of February 12, 1924,' Whiteman exulted afterwards, 'we took our fifth curtain call.'

Unsurprisingly, no clear answer to the question 'What Is American Music?' ever emerged from Whiteman's extravaganza. Instead, the significance of that wintry February afternoon at Aeolian Hall lay with the fact that it had launched the *Rhapsody in Blue*. This was the one item in the over-long programme that occupied music critics and journalists in the days that followed – and their reactions ran from enthusiasm to revulsion. Henry O. Osgood, critic for the *New York Courier*, went over the top in calling the piece 'greater than Stravinsky's *Rite of Spring*'. Deems Taylor, in the *World*, was more

insightful: 'His rhapsody has all the faults one might expect from an experimental work, but it also revealed a genuine melodic gift and a piquant and individual harmonic sense to lend significance to its rhythmic ingenuity. Mr. Gershwin will bear watching; he may yet bring jazz out of the kitchen.' In the *New York Times*, Olin Downes was especially perceptive about Gershwin's struggle to project musical ideas that were not always within his technical means. He described the rhapsody as showing 'extraordinary talent, just as it also shows a young composer with aims that go far beyond those of his ilk, struggling with a form of which he is far from being a master. Often Mr. Gershwin's purpose is defeated by technical immaturity, but in spite of that he has expressed himself in a significant and on the whole highly original manner.' Lawrence Gilman, chief music reviewer for the *Tribune*, decided to praise the work's rhythm, and Grofé's orchestration, while denouncing its other aspects: 'How trite and feeble and conventional the tunes are, how sentimental and vapid the harmonic treatment, under its guise of fussy and futile counterpoint. Weep over the lifelessness of its melody and harmony, so derivative, so static, so inexpressive. And then recall, for contrast, the rich inventiveness of the rhythm, the saliency and vividness of the orchestra colour.' It seems odd that Gilman was able to isolate Gershwin's rhythmic invention from the actual tunes it propelled, praising one but damning the other.

Undeniably, Gershwin glued his segments together with a fair amount of 'padding' – the main reason why it is possible to make all sorts of cuts in performance. The critic Pitts Sanborn put his finger on this when he wrote that the music 'runs off into empty passage-work and meaningless repetition'. One of the most cogent appraisals of the rhapsody had to wait until 1955, and an article in *Atlantic Monthly* by Leonard Bernstein. (Bernstein made two recordings of *Rhapsody in Blue*, playing the piano part himself and directing the orchestra from the keyboard. The finer of the two, made in 1959, is with the 'Columbia Symphony Orchestra', an alias which CBS had to use, due to contractual requirements, for what was actually the New York Philharmonic. His 'live' 1983 recording with the Los Angeles Philharmonic does not have quite the same 'pizzazz'.)

Bernstein wrote: 'The Rhapsody is not a composition at all. It's a string of separate paragraphs stuck together. The themes are terrific –

inspired, God-given. I don't think there has been such an inspired melodist on this earth since Tchaikovsky. But if you want to speak of a composer, that's another matter. Your *Rhapsody in Blue* is not a real composition in the sense that whatever happens in it must seem inevitable. You can cut parts of it without affecting the whole. You can remove any of these stuck-together sections and the piece still goes on as bravely as before. It can be a five-minute piece or a twelve-minute piece. And in fact all these things are being done to it every day. And it's still the *Rhapsody in Blue*.'

Bernstein's observation is borne out by numerous recordings in abridged versions. In the days of 78rpm records it would need four 12-inch sides to contain the whole piece, which runs to about sixteen minutes. But Gershwin's own recordings with Whiteman's orchestra, made by Victor in 1924 and 1927, delivered all the essential material on only two sides. And, from countless arrangements and transcriptions, one can cite a 1944 78rpm Decca recording by the Phil Green Orchestra on two 10-inch sides which needed only six-and-a-half minutes to get through all the main features. Bernstein was right – it's still the *Rhapsody in Blue*.

Whiteman was not slow to capitalize on his 'experiment'. He gave a repeat concert at Aeolian Hall and two more at Carnegie Hall, and took the rhapsody on tour, initially with Gershwin as soloist. By the summer of 1924 public interest was so acute that, on 10 June, the Victor company assembled Whiteman's band, with Gershwin at the piano, in their studio in Camden, New Jersey, to make the very first recording of the rhapsody – a classic 78rpm disc which sold a million copies and is now available on compact disc. The music was condensed to nine minutes.

Though recorded acoustically, this record proved superior, in terms of the spontaneous excitement in its performance, to an electrical recording Victor made in April 1927, by which time the band's personnel had changed. In any case, by 1927 Gershwin had become irritated at the way Whiteman was performing the rhapsody. The previous year he had heard Whiteman's orchestra (with a different pianist) give its London première at the Royal Albert Hall, and he was not pleased by Whiteman's exaggerated tempo changes and general 'jazzing up' of the orchestral passages. Rehearsing for their 1927 recording session, Gershwin realized that things had not changed. The

two argued, and Whiteman left the studio. So although the record label would credit Whiteman as conductor, the man who stepped in to save the day and wield the baton was actually Nathaniel Shilkret, one of Hambitzer's piano pupils, who was, by that time, music director for Victor Records. Despite the argument Gershwin turned in a fine performance, and the record was issued in England by HMV.

Grofé made new orchestrations in 1926 and 1942, each time for a larger orchestra. The 1942 version is the one commonly heard in concert, being effectively laid out for full symphony orchestra. But nearly all the 1920s flavour of the original is lost. Simon Rattle and Michael Tilson Thomas are among those who have preferred to perform and record Grofé's authentically pungent scoring of 1924. Tilson Thomas has even recorded a version in which he conducts a jazz band based on Whiteman's layout, cleverly synchronized to accompany Gershwin's own solo performance on a piano-roll.

It was estimated that, in the ten years following its première, the rhapsody earned a quarter of a million dollars for Gershwin. The Gershwin brothers were actually surprised to learn that Max Dreyfus was publishing the sheet music. They believed the piano part was so difficult that only a few pianists would want to buy it. Even George never claimed it to be an unflawed masterwork, though he could not resist proudly displaying the score in an illuminated case in his penthouse apartment. There are awkward transitions, repetitions of little motifs just for the sake of moving to another key with some easily-generated excitement (known in the trade as 'sequences'), and naïve moments where a real sense of harmonic purpose is lacking. The Gershwin biographer Joan Peyser is among writers who heap too much praise on its construction, saying that, after the E major central section, 'the composer skilfully brings the listener back to B flat major, where he began.' In fact there is nothing particularly skilful about the way Gershwin gets back to his home key. He only returns to it for the last six bars, a triumphant peroration of the opening clarinet theme, and it comes without effective preparation – just three loud chords on the orchestra, jerking the music into B flat. He could have inserted almost any three chords and finished the work in another key alto-gether. Musically speaking, he simply helps himself to one of the stock-in-trade devices any Tin Pan Alley arranger would have employed when knocking-up a popular medley.

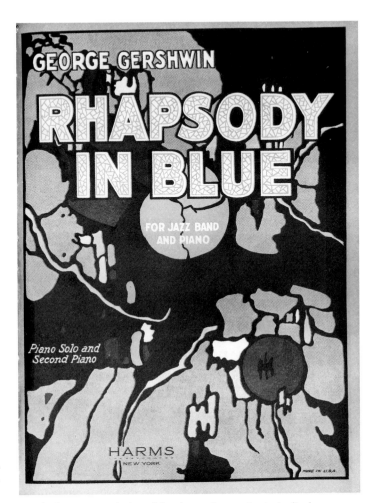

The art deco cover of the original sheet music, a bestseller in its arrangement for piano solo or two pianos

The lasting popularity of the rhapsody remains in its lively rhythms, its strong and memorable tunes, and the entertaining element of interplay between virtuoso piano soloist and orchestra – the essential ingredients of the typical, Romantic piano concerto. Indeed, its nearest classical models are probably the flamboyant concertos of Liszt, not only in a similar looseness of form, but in the constant working of tiny elements of themes into the texture at different speeds and in varied rhythms, giving a certain unity.

Gershwin's piano writing encompasses all the tricks and effects he had perfected while practising at home or during his slavish hours in

Remick's cubicle: ragtime rhythms; syncopated, 'stride' leaps in the bass; Rachmaninov-style writing with soaring, chordal melody in the right hand over sonorous arpeggios in the left; dazzling Lisztian cadenzas; bullet-like repeated notes with crossed hands (to be further exploited in the last movement of *Concerto in F*); pile-driving double-octaves straight out of Tchaikovsky's First Piano Concerto; sultry saloon-bar broodings in the left hand; chirpy, oriental-sounding crushed notes and pentatonic motifs evoking New York's Chinatown.

Despite the technical shortcomings, Gershwin achieved his objective: the rhapsody is a scintillating musical encapsulation of urban America in the 1920s, with all its exuberant madness, energy, restlessness and optimism. At the razzmatazz opening ceremony of the 1984 Olympic Games in Los Angeles, the solo part was played by eighty-four pianists on eighty-four white pianos. Worldwide, the message was clear: the Games had come to America. The rhapsody is not jazz, but it does show Gershwin achieving something at which he became ever more accomplished: seizing certain features in American popular music which he loosely referred to as 'jazz', and incorporating them into pieces based, as regards their formal shape, on nineteenth-century European models. He would never be really close to the folk roots of jazz.

The role which blacks had played in the origins of jazz was still being largely ignored, and confusion over what the word actually encompassed still reigned. Whiteman's own manager, Hugh C. Ernst, made only a condescending nod towards the real roots of jazz in his brochure for the Aeolian Hall concert. 'The experiment is purely educational. Mr. Whiteman intends to point out the tremendous strides which have been made in popular music from the day of the discordant jazz, which sprang into existence about ten years ago from nowhere in particular, to the really melodious music of today, which – for no good reason – is still being called jazz.' Words which seem to endorse the views printed in the *New York American* two years previously, and to sanction that journal's concern for young American girls falling victim to 'the weird, insidious, neurotic music that accompanies modern dancing'.

The rhapsody is the first major opus in a line of compositions in which Gershwin was not out to write jazz, but creatively to use jazz traits in the music he wanted to compose. Many Europeans had

Opposite, a scene from the 1930 film The King of Jazz. Gershwin's Rhapsody was given lavish Hollywood treatment, with Whiteman's orchestra perched on a giant piano seating five 'pianists'.

already flirted with pseudo-jazz in their concert or ballet works: Milhaud in *La Création du monde* and *Le Boeuf sur le toit*, Satie in *Parade*, the Stravinsky pieces mentioned earlier, and even Debussy's little piano prelude, *Golliwog's Cakewalk*. It is unlikely that Gershwin, in 1924, was familiar with any of these except perhaps the Debussy (from his lessons with Hambitzer). What sets him apart is that his assimilation of jazz attributes is genuinely American, since he learned his craft in Tin Pan Alley and on Broadway. Unlike the Europeans, the 'feel' of jazz was in his bones from the start. With *Rhapsody in Blue* he had made a journey that 'crossed the tracks' between serious and popular music, and the repercussions would be with him until the end of his career, leading to misunderstandings, suspicion and hostility from both camps. None the less, the rhapsody was crucial in helping to establish twentieth-century American concert music as a bona fide art-form, and in paving the way for later American-born composers.

When, in his 1979 film *Manhattan* (a cinematic exploration of the neuroses and complexities of twentieth-century living in New York City) the director Woody Allen reached for musical extracts that could most aptly underscore the images of his beloved metropolis, it was to Gershwin that he instinctively turned. What could best accompany the evocative, opening panorama of street scenes, bustling New Yorkers, the garish lights of Broadway, proud skyscrapers, fireworks cascading over Central Park at night? Fifty-five years earlier, George Gershwin had portrayed in music everything Woody Allen was now trying to express through the camera – and had named it *Rhapsody in Blue*.

4

George and Ira photo-
graphed c. 1924, the year of
their first joint success, *Lady,
Be Good!*

*I liked to do the songs just the way they were
written. There's a tendency for a good many
singers to take and mutilate a melody the
minute it's given to them. But you don't want to
change a Gershwin song around. It's too good.*

Fred Astaire

Master of the Broadway Musical

When George Gershwin began writing for the musical theatre, initially with interpolated songs and then with his first full-scale musical *La La Lucille* in 1919, he was entering an American entertainment tradition going back more than a century. 'Negro theatre' had flourished before 1800, and by the early nineteenth century a playhouse had been established in New York catering exclusively for blacks. Interest in the Negro as entertainer, with his native songs, dances and amusing patter, began to grow among white people. In 1843 a group of white performers calling themselves the 'Virginia Minstrels' transformed themselves into 'blackface' (using what became the standard method of applying burnt cork to blacken their skin) and, for the first time, an evening at the theatre was built round the concept of the minstrel show. This team soon disbanded, but imitators proliferated – to the extent that within a year a similar troupe was welcomed to the White House to give a command performance.

New York became the centre for the main development of the minstrel show, America's first significant indigenous entertainment. Blackface minstrelsy, a not-too-distant relative of Gershwin's *Blue Monday*, gave white performers free rein to sing Negro songs, dance Negro dances, impersonate slaves, and fire off jokes based on plantation life in an exaggerated Negro dialect. By later Broadway standards these productions were enthusiastic but artistically crude; there was no real script, no plot, no complete musical score. A set formula developed: ballads and jokes, followed by a variety bill, and ending with funny travesties of stage plays, or stories about life among the blacks, especially Harriet Beecher Stowe's anti-slavery novel, *Uncle Tom's Cabin*. Blackface minstrel troupes were in general a white man's theatricalization of a black man's art, presaging Whiteman's position vis-à-vis Negro jazz. The heyday of the minstrel show ended with the Civil War, but it remained a popular format.

From the 1870s onwards, American theatre enjoyed a veritable invasion of Gilbert and Sullivan. Beginning with *HMS Pinafore*, their

operettas were taken to American hearts, so much so that *The Pirates of Penzance* had to have its première on Fifth Avenue by a British contingent from the D'Oyly Carte Company to prevent an American production getting in first and pirating the show. *The Mikado* was a particular triumph. Two entertainment forms clashed amicably when a blackface minstrel troupe turned it into a spoof version called *The Black Mikado*, which must have lacked the respect Oscar Hammerstein brought to his reworking of Bizet's *Carmen* into the all-black musical *Carmen Jones*, nearly a century later.

Two further imported traditions – operettas from Central Europe, and Yiddish theatre – were paramount in setting the scene for Gershwin's innovations. European operetta composers (Johann Strauss, Jacques Offenbach, Rudolf Friml, Sigmund Romberg, Franz Lehár) were dominating the American musical theatre to such an extent by the early 1900s that, faced with the popular rage for tuneful favourites such as *Die Fledermaus, Orpheus in the Underworld, The Desert Song* and *The Merry Widow*, native-born composers naturally felt intimidated. Even the operetta composer most celebrated by Americans as the founder of the musical, and the one who had direct contact with Gershwin, was actually Dublin-born: Victor Herbert (1859–1924) became a household name through his 1898 Broadway production *The Fortune Teller*, with its hit number *The Gypsy Love Song*.

From the Yiddish theatre, already familiar to the Gershwin brothers since their youth, would come George's fascination with minor-key tunes and unusual melodic intervals, and Ira's deft command of manipulating the English language. Only immigrants, such as those who cultivated the Yiddish theatre in New York and for whom English was neither their native language nor the language of their shows, could unintentionally invent new ways of enhancing it – often with a kind of hilariously fractured grammar. Ira's *circa* 1921 lyric for his brother's 'Party Song' (that is, not written for a show) entitled *Mischa, Jascha, Toscha, Sascha* is a homely tribute to Yiddish theatre, celebrating four eminent Jewish violinists (Elman, Heifetz, Seidel, Jacobsen), with the humour and irreverence typical of those productions. Other, more subtle Yiddish theatre influences were at work throughout the brothers' collaboration, especially in their ability to delineate sentiment without a song becoming banal, or to deal with larger-than-life stage characters and frankly silly plots in an engaging way.

Operettas from abroad were written by one composer and his librettist; they tended to feature exotic locations, opulent settings and costumes, and aria-style songs in which the music was more memorable than the words. In contrast, home-grown Broadway revues (of which an outstanding practitioner was George M. Cohan, writer of the song *Give My Regards to Broadway*) specialized in rapid-paced songs and comedy routines, lively dance numbers, and topical jokes and political references. And a revue – unlike an operetta – was often cooked up by many chefs. By the time George and Ira were ready to embark on their series of mature musicals, they had assimilated all these historical references and were eager to present theatre-goers with the most modern versions of them.

After *Rhapsody in Blue*, George had the pleasure of redeeming his London flop *The Rainbow* by crossing the Atlantic again in 1924 for his only musical written specifically for the West End (it never transferred to Broadway), a deliberately English-style musical called *Primrose*. It was the last musical he would write before Ira became his regular lyricist, the words being shared by Ira and an English writer, Desmond Carter. The score was closely-integrated (not just a stop-start succession of numbers) and the influence of Gilbert and Sullivan was present (witness one of the song titles, *Isn't It Terrible What They Did to Mary Queen of Scots*). The musical aptness that Gershwin brought to his score, especially the song *Berkeley Square and Kew*, pleased London audiences and showed that, having just turned twenty-six, he could master any style. He even included a tongue-in-cheek ballet sequence. When the original manuscripts for the pit band were discovered in about 1986, three of the songs were found to be orchestrated in Gershwin's own hand. (To this day, it is highly unusual for a Broadway composer to write his own orchestrations, or even to have the necessary scoring ability.) They are the earliest known examples of Gershwin's orchestration. Coming seven months after he had *not* orchestrated the rhapsody, and a year before he would orchestrate his piano concerto, they suggest that Gershwin welcomed the chance to advance his skills during his London trip and prepare himself technically for bigger things.

Gershwin, ever the workaholic, was thoroughly enjoying the hectic pace he had set himself. Within three months of returning to New York from the successful *Primrose* première, his first major musical-

comedy success opened on Broadway. He had tasted failures prior to *The Rainbow*: his earlier *Dangerous Maid* and *Our Nell* had survived only five weeks during their out-of-town try-outs in 1921 and 1922. These disappointments were put behind him as effusive press notices greeted what became a turning-point both for himself and Ira: *Lady, Be Good!*

By the time this show opened in December 1924, the revue as a Broadway format was in decline. Unrelated musical numbers, loose plots (or none at all), miscellaneous skits and the casual process of interpolation were all proving unsatisfactory for a theatre-going public that had begun to stay away. Even shows by Ziegfeld, Kern and Berlin were losing money. Gershwin's new musical, though not as closely-knit as later ones, at least attempted a story-line, and its song and dance numbers mostly fitted the action and advanced the plot. A sister-and-brother dance team has fallen on hard times, but they find fortune through plot devices such as disguise and mistaken identity that would not be out of place in an *opera buffa* by Rossini or Mozart. The two dancers were played by Fred and Adele Astaire, who had just returned from a successful run in London and were overjoyed to be collaborating with the composer of the West End hit *Primrose*. For George, it was the fulfilment of a long-held ambition. Amid the racket penetrating his cubicle at Remick's, he had once said to Astaire: 'Wouldn't it be wonderful if some day I could write a show, and you and Adele would star in it?' Years later he commented, 'We just laughed then. But it came true.'

Lady, Be Good! also brought to an end Ira's reluctance to reveal himself as George's lyric-writer. Not only had he worked with many other composers by this time, who all knew the real identity of Arthur Francis, but he had discovered that in England there was actually a professional musician by the name of Arthur Francis. Ira's own name now appeared on every song he wrote. In any case the secret was out, if at times garbled. George had told him how funny it was to read, in a London press review of *Primrose*, that some of the lyrics were the work of 'his sister Ira'.

The show inaugurated a sequence of seven musicals the Gershwin brothers were to write for the producing team of Aarons and Freedley. George's friend Alex Aarons, who had given him his first break with *La La Lucille*, had teamed up with a former actor, Vinton Freedley. A

Opposite, the Astaires grace the cover of the title number from Lady, Be Good!, a musical comedy that set new standards on Broadway.

mark of the loyalty the Gershwins felt towards them is that the sequence spanned nine years up till 1933, and included some of their finest work. Five would be among the best musicals of their period: *Lady, Be Good!*, *Tip-Toes*, *Oh, Kay!*, *Funny Face* and *Girl Crazy*. (The two flops were *Treasure Girl* and *Pardon My English*.)

Apart from the title-song, the score of *Lady, Be Good!* included three more outstanding numbers: the wistful *So Am I*; a self-suffering, satirical comment on thwarted romance called *The Half of It, Dearie, Blues* (audiences in 1924 knew this was aimed at Bert Savoy, who impersonated a grotesque harlot in Ziegfeld's *Follies* with the catch-phrase 'You don't know the half of it, dearie') – Gershwin's recording of it in 1926 with Astaire includes unrehearsed banter between them as Astaire, in the confines of the recording studio, goes into a tap-dance around Gershwin's pentatonic tune; and the immortal *Fascinating Rhythm* – not 'Fascinatin', which many of today's vocalists or designers of Gershwin promotional material appear to think is an improvement on Ira's adjective. George had written the first eight bars of this tune while in London, and later reflected: 'It's rather strange I should have written, in a foreign city, what I consider to be one of the most typically American rhythmic themes I've ever done.' An early sketch of the song was called *Syncopated City*. The restless, nervous energy of

Gershwin on board ship returning to New York with producer Alex Aarons, after successfully launching the London production of Lady, Be Good! in 1926

New York in the 'roaring Twenties', with one dance craze succeeding another, is the phenomenon Ira's words pretend to rail against, although the singer protests too much and is actually enjoying being infected by the rhythm bug:

Each morning I get up with the sun,
Start a-hopping, never stopping
To find at night, no work has been done.
I know that once it didn't matter
But now you're doing wrong;
When you start to patter, I'm so unhappy.
Won't you take a day off? Decide to run along
Somewhere far away off, and make it snappy!

Even on the page this lyric looks breathless. What gives the song its captivating momentum is the ingenious syncopation George had put into his tune even before the words were added. The words 'Fascinating Rhythm' have six syllables and are given six notes. But this melodic cell is repeated three times, and each repetition starts on a different beat of the steady chord rhythm that supports it. So the tune, like the feverish effect of the rhythm bug, pulls against the intrinsic beat of the music, and the ear is bewitched by its unexpected accents.

Arthur Schwartz singled out Ira's words for this song as 'a truly phenomenal feat, when one considers he was required to be brilliant within the most confining rhythms and accents'. The intricate tune indeed posed great problems for Ira. Now that he was his brother's exclusive lyricist, he had to get used to George's strong views about how best to fit words to his notes; by nature he would have the final say if there was an argument. A tune or rhythmic idea that flowed effortlessly from George's fingers as he amused himself at the piano might mean days of work for Ira, who admitted he felt like taking a year off whenever they had just finished writing a show. George would be buzzing off to a round of parties and diving into his next assignment. Schwartz said he often wondered how Ira's leisurely temperament ever managed to keep pace with George's supersonic velocity. Ira was known as a hard man to get out of an easy chair. 'I have a whole day's work ahead of me,' he once announced. 'I'm going to change the ribbon on my typewriter.' (Ira much later confessed that

Ira, having memorized George's latest tune, would make numerous drafts to fit the right lyrics.

without George he would have been contented as a book-keeper.) The ultimate in self-effacement was written by Ira as a postscript to the introduction in his book, *Lyrics on Several Occasions*, a fascinating account of his life as a lyricist. 'Since most of the lyrics in this lodgment were arrived at by fitting words mosaically to music already composed, any resemblance to poetry, living or dead, is highly improbable.'

When asked the inevitable question, 'Which comes first, the words or the music?', Ira liked to reply: 'The contract.' George once offered some casual clues as to how they crafted their songs. 'Usually the music comes first. I hit on a new tune, play it for Ira, and he hums it all over the place for a while until he gets an idea for the lyric. Then we work the thing out together.' Typically, the studious Ira did not describe the process as being so simple. 'I would learn it very quickly, memorize the tune. Then I'd work and work on it, starting at midnight, sometimes at two in the morning, and work till six or seven in the morning.' He habitually worked at night because of the quietness outside. So, independently, did George. They must have slept through as many New York mornings as a night-shift worker on the subway. Then would come their joint sessions at the piano. Ira would set up a bridge table at the top end of the keyboard, lay out his

pencils, paper, Roget's *Thesaurus* and some dictionaries (apparently used only rarely) and, note by note and line by line, another Gershwin song would painfully emerge.

There was undoubtedly an alchemy at work that enabled each to sense what the other had in mind. But an enormous amount of discussion, trial and retrial went into every detail. Ira had already earned the nickname 'The Jeweller' from other songwriters, thanks to his endless polishing of every line until he was satisfied. Sometimes he would ask George for a few extra notes at a given place in the melody, so that some spare words that meant everything to his lyric could be accommodated. George would oblige – unless he felt otherwise. In the case of the lines 'I'm all a-quiver' and 'Just like a flivver' in *Fascinating Rhythm*, they argued on and off for days, George finally getting his way by insisting both lines must end with a two-syllable word because the rhythmic sense of his tune demanded

Stage two of the collaborative process: the brothers at the piano, here shown at work on *A Damsel in Distress* in Hollywood, 1937

it. It was just as well that Papa Gershwin was not party to these
sessions; with the thick, Russian-Jewish accent that he never lost, he
proudly referred to his son as 'George Goishwin, composer of
Fashion on der River.'

This collaborative method – graphically described by Ira as 'fitting
words mosaically to music already composed' – was quite the reverse
of some other famous teams. As their partnership developed, Richard
Rodgers came to wait until Oscar Hammerstein supplied a virtually
finished lyric before reading it over and letting it inspire the music.
Rodgers's previous collaboration had been with Lorenz Hart, who
fitted his lyrics to music Rodgers had already provided, as in the
Gershwin partnership. The melodies which Rodgers provided for
Hart's complex lyrics were as a result more adventurous, more
chromatic than those for the less cerebral Hammerstein, whose lyrics
for *The King and I* or *The Sound of Music* brought forth a high
proportion of 'white note' tunes. With his many co-writers, Jerome
Kern was also happy to fit his music to existing lyrics. Irving Berlin
was a genius in both disciplines, though it has been ruefully observed
that he decided to write his own words as soon as he realized a
composer doubled his royalties that way. Cole Porter also wrote his
own lyrics, which revel in dazzling word-play and are more advanced
in sheer technique than is his music, which rarely strays into
chromatic harmonies or novel rhythmic tricks so beloved of
Gershwin. If Gershwin knew his own worth, Porter could adopt a wry
haughtiness when it came to matters of collaboration. Asked to name
the authors of a tune that happened to be on the radio, he correctly
answered 'Rodgers and Hammerstein' ... then added: 'If you can
imagine it taking two men to write one song.'

Gershwin admired these superlative songwriters; in their turn they
recognized they could never compete with his facility at the piano.
Playing of such invention and virtuosity marked him out as a real
concert soloist, something to which neither they, nor hordes of Tin Pan
Alley composers and song-pluggers, could aspire. Irving Berlin could
only play in one key – F sharp, mainly on the black keys of the piano.
He had designed for him upright pianos with levers which shifted the
hammer mechanism along the strings to change key within or between
songs – the sort of thing the teenaged Gershwin had accomplished
through brain and hands for his clients in Remick's cubicle.

The original score of *Lady, Be Good!* included a unique example of a Gershwin song of exceptional quality which none the less would never find a permanent place in a production. When the show was tried out in Philadelphia, one of Adele Astaire's numbers was *The Man I Love*. After one week, it was taken out; the show was over-running, and the song's sweetness had not won much applause. But it was published, and a copy reached Lady Mountbatten in New York. She asked Gershwin to autograph it, and back in London her favourite band (the Berkeley Square Orchestra) started playing a special arrangement. Other dance bands took it up, and it spread to Paris. In 1927 Gershwin put the song into the original production of *Strike Up the Band*. This never reached Broadway – again the song was without a home. Later that year came a third attempt: Ira rewrote it for the Ziegfeld show *Rosalie*, but afterwards he could not remember the star, Marilyn Miller, even rehearsing it. Finally Gershwin's publisher, Dreyfus, issued *The Man I Love* as an independent, popular song. Whereas *Swanee* had been designed for that very purpose, *The Man I Love*, in its rootless state, became not merely a popular song by default, but the one Gershwin composition

Adele Astaire introduced *The Man I Love* in *Lady, Be Good!*, but the song had a chequered history before achieving fame on its own.

that comes to everyone's lips (along with *Rhapsody in Blue*) at the mention of his name.

Why was its route to fame so difficult? Looking back with detachment, Gershwin explained that the song could not function as a production number. 'It allows little or no action while being sung.' This is a rather strange comment, considering so many of his love-songs bring the stage action to a halt, and are spoiled if too much 'business' goes on around them. But his further points show a composer who knew his public. 'It lacks a soothing, seducing rhythm; instead, it has a certain slow lilt that subtly disturbs the audience instead of lulling it into acceptance. Then, too, there is the melody, which is not easy to catch; it presents too many chromatic pitfalls. Hardly anybody whistles or hums it correctly without the support of a piano or other instrument.'

In other words, the song was ahead of its time, standing as a perfect example of what Deems Taylor had said after the first Gauthier recital: a popular song in a classically severe form. Like any masterpiece, not a note can be altered without diminishing its beauty. Apart from the naturalness of its melody and the perfect proportion of its phrases, Gershwin's harmonic subtlety is working at full stretch. The first bar is in the major, the second in the minor. Yet the melody notes are the same – the second phrase a fragmented echo of the first. The tune is static, hypnotic – but Gershwin's harmony is already on the move. This is being 'harmony conscious' at a high level, and it goes on throughout the whole song. In the year of *Lady, Be Good!*, he told an interviewer: 'I think of melody as a line, a single thread – as the body of the music, and the harmony as the clothes you put on it. I can take a melody and harmonize it a thousand different ways.'

Show-tunes are routinely performed in whichever key the vocalist or musical director prefers. But, for the purpose of illustration here, Gershwin's original key for *The Man I Love* was E flat. At the middle section ('Maybe I shall meet him Sunday/Maybe Monday – maybe not'), Gershwin drops down from E flat into C minor, emphasizing the increasing feeling of uncertainty. (So far there has been a quiet confidence that 'he'll come along'.) In technical terms this is known as 'going into the relative minor key'. To revert to the 'Eroica' Symphony for a moment, three of its movements are in E flat, the

energetic, confident, 'home' key of the symphony. But between the first and third movements, Beethoven places a troubled funeral march in C minor, the 'relative minor'. In a microcosmic parallel, Gershwin uses the same keys for the outer sections of his song and the contrasting middle section. In terms of key relationships, this is about as classical as a composer can get. After Ira's lyric passes its point of greatest doubt, the music eases back into the 'home' key of E flat for 'He'll build a little home' and the optimistic ending. These harmonic subtleties, where an effortless switch in tonality tugs at the heartstrings, are common to all of Gershwin's finest love-songs, and they do not come from Negro blues or minstrel songs or Yiddish tunes. They come from a popular composer with an extraordinary sense of classical harmony and classical proportion. Furthermore, his songs are what we call 'memorable' because the tunes are created from the simplest arrangement of notes, sparingly used and built into perfectly proportioned phrases within the overall structure.

Gershwin would always have problems with large-scale structure, because his real genius lay in perfecting a 32-bar song. He was an absolute master of the small-scale form – and the same can be said of Chopin, Schumann or Grieg. Schoenberg said that, whereas a talent learns from others, a genius learns from himself. Gershwin learned from himself the compression of substantial emotions and musical procedures into a tiny frame, which makes songs such as *The Man I Love* miniature masterpieces and helps to explain why this one in particular went over the heads of its first musical-comedy audiences in the 1920s.

Gershwin's mature songs are peerless as a basis for improvisation by jazz soloists. This is because of the richness of their melodic scheme, and the sheer number of chord changes he is capable of achieving in thirty-two bars. Numerous recordings are available that testify to the effectiveness of Gershwin's songs as purely instrumental numbers in the hands of legendary jazz performers such as Louis Armstrong, Gerry Mulligan, Coleman Hawkins, Oscar Peterson, Art Tatum, Dizzy Gillespie, Sidney Bechet, Benny Goodman, Stephane Grappelli and a host of others – all spinning their personal flights of fancy around the bedrock of Gershwin's enduring melodies. The most idiomatic interpretations of his songs on record are not by a Broadway

'Composing at the piano ...
has become a habit'; the
cigar-smoking songwriter is
captured in a cartoon by
John Minnion.

star, but by a consummate jazz artist: Ella Fitzgerald, in her definitive
1959 *George and Ira Gershwin Songbook* recordings. For a while, *Oh,
Lady, Be Good!* was her 'theme tune'.

Gershwin's days at Remick's reinforced his instinct that there was no
need to tamper with the conventional popular-song structure he
inherited. After a few instrumental bars (in his published songs
Gershwin keeps these very short, but in the theatre they could be
extended to suit the action), the vocalist enters with an introductory
section, the verse, which sets the scene by giving an idea of the song's
mood and tempo, and whose lyrics help focus on the sort of situation –
love affair, loneliness, happiness or whatever – is about to be narrated.
Verses varied in length; the norms were sixteen bars (*Oh, Lady, Be
Good!, Do It Again, The Man I Love, Fascinating Rhythm*) or twenty-
four (*I'll Build a Stairway to Paradise, Someone To Watch Over Me, 'S
Wonderful, But Not for Me*). *Swanee* is so unusual that its verse extends
to thirty-two bars, and there are variants like the verses of *I Was So
Young* (twelve bars), *That Certain Feeling* (fifteen) and *Liza* (eighteen).

Ella Fitzgerald made landmark recordings of over fifty Gershwin songs, arranged and conducted by Nelson Riddle.

Following the verse is the main body of the song, known as the refrain or chorus (the part we generally recognize, even if the verse has not been familiar); it is thirty-two bars long and comprises four sections of eight bars each. Usually an AABA structure prevails, since the first eight-bar melodic idea A is repeated, the second time giving way to a contrasting section B (often in a different key), and the song ends with a final version of A. These thirty-two bars might be sung through twice or more with different words, depending on how much of a story the lyricist has to tell. The melodic structure of this refrain can lend itself to endless possibilities depending on how the composer treats each eight-bar section, and on how he inserts the B section (known as the 'release' or 'bridge'). The minor-key section of *The Man I Love* is an especially inspired example of a release. Bernstein used to do a party trick playing miscellaneous show-tunes and pretending to forget how the release music went. To keep going he would drop into the one from *The Man I Love*, and it always seemed to fit. Leaving aside this musical prank, a composer of Gershwin's stature worked hard to make this simple song template appear natural and inevitable, with the B section somehow sounding 'right' for whatever A material it was bridging.

It is significant that even so acclaimed an artist as Ella Fitzgerald was required to go back to the original published songs and learn the verses of her *Songbook* collection for her sessions with recording producer Norman Granz, because she had never performed them regularly before. She recorded eight *Songbooks*, featuring different composers and lyricists, between 1956 and 1963, by which time verses had come to be neglected by the majority of vocalists. So what was part of a singer's 'bread-and-butter' in Gershwin's day – an opening section into which George would distil many an enticing melody that was quite different from the refrain, and lyrics into which Ira poured as much effort as the rest of the song – was in danger of becoming lost. Admittedly, many Tin Pan Alley composers took very little trouble over their verses.

With *Rhapsody in Blue* at its beginning and *Lady, Be Good!* at its end, the year 1924 had proved a high point in the progress of both Gershwin brothers. George was famous and financially secure, and Ira was earning more money than ever before through his *Lady, Be Good!* royalties. Thanks to these earnings, the close-knit family moved, in 1925, to a handsome greystone house at West 103rd Street, in the elegant neighbourhood around Riverside Drive. Now they could all enjoy living in a style expected of their celebrity and social position. The house, on five floors, included a billiard room, plenty of space for the Gershwin clan to entertain their relatives and play poker, and a top floor fitted-out as living-quarters and workroom for George. (When Ira married Leonore the following year, they took over the fourth floor.)

This new-found, spacious elegance did not mean that life in the Gershwin ménage was any less feverish than it had been at 110th Street. The billiard room especially became a mecca for friends or complete strangers, who would drop in, help themselves to a game, and review the gossip. Visiting one evening, the playwright S. N. Behrman found that neither Arthur nor Ira could identify any of the people happily crowding the billiard table and strolling about the house. Behrman impatiently asked Ira where George could be found. 'He's taken his old room in the hotel round the corner,' sighed Ira. 'He says he's got to have a little privacy.'

This must have been an extreme case, because Arthur Schwartz did catch Gershwin at work among the mêlée and he gives us a revealing picture of George's single-mindedness. 'The thing that struck me

about his genius in its composing phases was that he had a power of
concentration greater than anybody I've ever seen. I was at the
Gershwin house when five or six different things would be going on –
people yelling, people playing ping-pong and card games, people
eating ... and George would be sitting there at the piano writing. Or
without the piano, just with paper. I couldn't work that way, and it
was one of the things I envied. I envy his talent, in any case. But I
envied that power of concentration.'

Schwartz's observation that Gershwin worked with or without the
piano raises an interesting point, because George himself said: 'Often
I have written my tunes with people in the same room or playing
cards in the next. When I find myself in the desired mood I can hold
it until I finish the song. Composing at the piano is not good practice,
but I started that way and it has become a habit.' Away from the
piano, he was almost certainly revising existing material or making a
fair copy. To a composer whose inspiration literally poured out of the
keys as his hands ran over them, working at the piano was an essential
part of the creative act. Gershwin liked to be photographed with pipe
or cigar in mouth and pencil in hand, his manuscript on the piano-
rest. A rare view of him working away from the keyboard is a snapshot
taken outdoors in brilliant sunshine; tanned and in shorts, he is at a
small table orchestrating – rather than composing – *Porgy and Bess*.

Morris Gershwin was fascinated by the elevator which connected
all five floors at 103rd Street. He loved to dress up in the uniform of an
elevator attendant as worn in smart hotels, and escort guests up and
down on party nights. His daughter Frances called him 'a darling
person, a real shnook' (Yiddish for a likeable, unassertive character).
Frances admitted that, when young, she was sensitive and somewhat
ashamed about her father's accent when she introduced him to her
friends. 'I used to admire George; he had such confidence in himself
that this didn't matter. He would take my father to places with him.
He had no false sense of social values, no false pride about things
like that.'

Speaking proudly about George's new tone poem *An American in
Paris* in 1928, Morris would say: 'It's a very important piece. It takes
twenty minutes to play.' He once stood nervously outside George's
workroom and heard his son obviously hit a blank spot in composing,
since the keyboard explorations had petered out. Morris timidly

opened the door and hummed his own little suggestion. 'How about that George – is that any help?' George enjoyed spreading his father's unconscious humour among his friends. One of his favourites was of the time he and Ira had been discussing Einstein and his theory of relativity. 'Imagine working for twenty years on an idea,' marvelled George, 'then being able to write it down on three pages.' Morris was silent for a moment, then shrugged: 'It was probably very small print.' While Rose Gershwin always seemed to take a cool, objective view of George's achievements, her husband's pride knew no bounds. Combined with his acquired American accent, it even rescued him from a brush with the law. When a New York traffic cop stopped Morris for speeding, the officer declined to issue a ticket when his victim pleaded: 'Don't you know who I am? I'm the father of Judge [George] Goishwin.' His son's celebrity status was acknowledged by *Time* magazine in July 1925, when Gershwin became the first American-born musician to appear on the cover.

George with his mother in a snapshot from the family album; she survived him by eleven years.

Three months earlier, *Tell Me More!* had opened on Broadway. Gershwin had teamed up again with producer Alex Aarons (for once, without Freedley) to write a romantic musical with a typical plot-line: heroine pretends to be a shop-girl to put her lover's affection to the test. At first it had a disappointing run compared to *Lady, Be Good!*, but later it was more successful both in New York and in London, though none of its music is now remembered. If the show had retained its original title, as used on its try-out tour, the history of the American musical would have been slightly different. *Tell Me More!* was initially called *My Fair Lady*. Ira, the committed anglophile, had lifted these words from the English folk-song *London Bridge Is Falling Down*. They survived as the title of one of the songs, but – happily for Lerner and Loewe – not the show itself.

Gershwin helped supervise the London production, enjoying as always the round of parties in Mayfair, the adulation of his British admirers, and the ordering of fashionable new suits in Savile Row. He also found time to collaborate again with the indefatigable Eva Gauthier, who timed her London commitments to coincide with his trip and who now repeated the recital they had given in New York's Aeolian Hall at the London venue bearing the same name. This time the publicity-conscious mezzo called the event 'From Java to Jazz'. Once again, some critics were disgruntled and confused by the 'American Popular Song' segment of the programme; as in New York two years previously they confused 'jazz songs' with Broadway numbers, and reviewed these pieces as being 'jazzed by George Gershwin'. Gershwin, again, only accompanied the American selection. Playing the piano for the remaining songs – or, as reported, 'accompanying with insight the non-ragged numbers' – was one of the most distinguished accompanists of his day, the British pianist Ivor Newton.

Gershwin's work-rate continued to amaze. That year, 1925, ended with three new Gershwin products being given their premières within days of each other. Apart from *Concerto in F* at Carnegie Hall, December brought the musical *Tip-Toes* and also *Song of the Flame*, described by its producers as 'a romantic opera'. His name was also prominent at Carnegie Hall a second time, when – for just two performances – Paul Whiteman loyally but unsuccessfully revived the

miniature opera *Blue Monday* in a semi-staged version under its new title, *135th Street*.

Song of the Flame was an uncharacteristic attempt by Gershwin to step into the world of operetta. It proved he was no Rudolf Friml or Sigmund Romberg. The scoring and some of the songs were the work of Herbert Stothart, an excellent musician who later found his *métier* in Hollywood films, and the experienced lyricists were Oscar Hammerstein and Otto Harbach. None of this talent could make a real success out of an elaborate and colourful production centred on a peasant revolt in Tsarist Russia. There was a large orchestra, ballet scenes and chorus numbers. 'Mobs, riots, balls and carnivals,' reported one reviewer. 'Yet the play lacked what used to be known as "that something".'

Gershwin left this flirting with pseudo-Slavic tunes behind him and instead produced the true successor to *Lady, Be Good!* in *Tip-Toes*, a sophisticated comedy about two brothers in a penniless vaudeville trio trying to pass off their sister 'Tip-Toes', the vivacious dancer in the team, as a wealthy marriage prospect. Some of its numbers remain Gershwin classics: *Sweet and Low-Down*, *Looking for a Boy*, and especially *That Certain Feeling*, in which Gershwin seems to delight in showing just how much melodic mileage he can get out of repeating the same note. Ira was flattered to receive a letter complimenting him on his lyrics from the esteemed Lorenz Hart. 'It is a great pleasure to live at a time when light amusement in this country is at last losing its brutally cretin aspect. Such delicacies as your jingles prove that songs can be both popular and intelligent.'

It is not surprising that the Gershwins slowed down somewhat in 1926, especially since George took time out to enjoy himself in London while supervising the West End productions of *Lady, Be Good!* and *Tip-Toes*. Almost as a throwaway, they contributed a clever production number to a Broadway revue called *Americana*. The song, *That Lost Barber Shop Chord*, showed them harking back to Sir Arthur Sullivan's popular Victorian ballad *The Lost Chord* and linking its idea with *Play that Barber Shop Chord*, a ragtime hit from about 1910. It was the kind of eclectic novelty that, with his knowledge of musical styles down the years, George could turn out with ease, and which gave his brother an opportunity for clever word-play. As so often in

the musical theatre, it gained the accolade 'the high mark of the revue' only to become a forgotten trifle once the show closed.

Their main efforts went into their only new production that year, *Oh, Kay!*. Prohibition had now been in force for nearly six years, and plots based on bootlegging were no longer novel. But this production brought together the gifts of the Gershwin brothers and those of writers Guy Bolton and P. G. Wodehouse, and its star was the magnetic Gertrude Lawrence, making her début in an American musical but long fêted for her stage roles, especially in collaboration with Noël Coward. Her presence as Kay, the sister of an English duke who turns up at Long Island on his yacht full of illicit rum, ensured the production was a major success. Four of its numbers have found their place in the canon of Gershwin unforgettables: *Maybe, Clap Yo' Hands, Do, Do, Do* and *Someone To Watch Over Me*. This last song is one of Gershwin's very finest, with its characteristic pentatonic opening (the first nine notes can all be played on the black keys) and the plaintive leaps at the end. The tune's wistful sense of longing, however, was not the original concept. Gershwin's constant experimentation at the piano, and his ability to seize on a fruitful idea as soon as it flew from the keys, were on full alert as he played for Ira a

George, Guy Bolton and Ira in Beverly Hills, 1930

fast-paced dance he had written. It had a peculiar rhythmic 'kick', cutting off a series of four-note phrases. As George played, the brothers talked, and unintentionally the dance got slower. Suddenly there came a point when both realized this was not an up-tempo tune after all; in its languid state it would make a wonderfully arching love-song. Ira set to work unremittingly on his lyrics, and came up with a lover likened to a lost lamb seeking its shepherd. In the release of the song we find two lines which typify the way he could combine wit, elegance and tenderness within a mere handful of notes and across the rhythm of the music, weaving in a masterly 'internal rhyme': 'Although he may not be the man some / Girls think of as handsome.' Ira confessed to Michael Feinstein that there was an autobiographical slant to these lines. Plump, bespectacled bookworm that he was, the glamorous Leonore had nevertheless entered his life to watch over him.

Ira's mastery is evident, too, in the ensemble number *Bride and Groom*, which celebrates Kay's wedding. It starts with a fleeting chorus that is over in barely a minute. But we can only marvel at the cleverness of Ira's puns that marry two ubiquitous wedding marches – Mendelssohn's from *The Midsummer Night's Dream* and Wagner's from *Lohengrin*. Like all his lyrics, they are a delight to see on the page. Meanwhile George, though not going so far as to quote Wagner, did make Mendelssohn's melody the basis of his part in the pastiche.

It's never too late to Mendelssohn;
It doesn't matter how long you have tarried.
Two hearts are at Journey's Endelssohn –
And we're invited here to see them married.
Two fond hearts will always blendelssohn –
At least we're all expecting them to swear it.
A gay honeymoon they'll spendelssohn;
We hope they Lohengrin and bear it.

After one particularly trying day of rehearsals for *Oh, Kay!*, Gershwin reached for some bedtime reading and chose a book given him by his close friends Lou Paley (brother of Herman) and his wife Emily. It was a short, recently-published novel by DuBose Heyward, a native of Charleston. Edwin DuBose Heyward (1885–1940) had grown up among the labourers, fishermen and stevedores of South Carolina,

and his novel was a vivid portrayal of the influence modern America had upon a small, tightly-knit black community in Charleston, and of their songs and dances, loves and sorrows. The book was named *Porgy* after its hero, a crippled beggar who got about on a wooden cart drawn by a goat. Gershwin said later that he became so absorbed by the story, he read it straight through into the night. He was convinced it had everything he was looking for as the basis of a serious musical play, or maybe a 'folk opera'. At four in the morning he wrote to Heyward and suggested they meet.

Not long afterwards Heyward and his wife Dorothy were in Atlantic City, New Jersey for a vacation. Gershwin came down from New York to meet them, and learned that Dorothy was already using her husband's novel as the source for a play, due to be staged in 1927. The two men took a brisk walk to discuss the proposal Gershwin had made in his letter. Heyward recalled that his first impression of Gershwin was 'singularly vivid. A young man of enormous physical and emotional vitality, who possessed the faculty of seeing himself quite impersonally and realistically, and who knew exactly what he wanted and where he was going.' Gershwin always seemed this way to anyone meeting him for the first time. He could talk about his music with such a degree of objectivity that he appeared almost to be speaking about someone else, and would allude to himself in the third person. Kay Swift, the woman with whom he would enjoy the closest relationship, observed that she didn't think he was 'out of focus at any time'.

Heyward continued: 'We discussed *Porgy*. He said that it would not matter about the dramatic production as it would be a couple of years before he would be prepared technically to compose an opera. It was extraordinary, I thought, in view of a success that might have dazzled any man, that he could appraise his talent with such complete detachment.' There the matter would rest until 1932.

Porgy opened on Broadway in September 1927, a couple of weeks after the Gershwin brothers began pre-Broadway try-outs of an ambitious new satirical show, *Strike Up the Band*. While the Heywards' play would run for 367 performances, the Gershwins' efforts were soon running into trouble. After two weeks in Philadelphia their musical closed without reaching Broadway. George

S. Kaufman, one of the leading satirists of the time, had written the book for the show. But an affluent and optimistic theatre-going public refused to warm to his cynical portrayal of how easily one country can declare war on another, a plot made deliberately ridiculous in that tiny Switzerland, a neutral country, has war declared on her by mighty America – all on account of the price of cheese. Kaufman, spotting two elderly gentlemen in the theatre foyer before a performance of the failing musical, quipped to the Gershwins: 'Here come Gilbert and Sullivan to fix the show.'

The lightness of touch in Gershwin's score, its patter-style songs and lively choruses, all combined with Ira's word-spinning lyrics, had indeed shown more than a flavour of Gilbert and Sullivan, updated to the late 1920s. But Kaufman's earnest message was not something for which a public yet to live through the stock market crash of 1929, and the subsequent posturing of politicians, preferred to spend an evening in the theatre. Just as *The Man I Love* was ahead of its time, so was the show itself. A Philadelphia critic wrote: 'Satirical musical shows have never been a success in America. Nor do Americans like to be laughed at on stage.' To which Kaufman added the immortal definition: 'Satire is what closes on Saturday night.'

It seemed as though the Gershwins were heading for another critical disaster when *Funny Face* began the obligatory out-of-town trials shortly afterwards. (The speed with which Gershwin turned out these 1920s musicals is astonishing. *Strike Up the Band* folded in mid September, yet the Broadway opening of *Funny Face* was already in his diary for 22 November.) All concerned in the production of *Funny Face* (originally called *Smarty*) found themselves embroiled in seemingly endless revisions to re-shape it for Broadway. It was at times like these, with about half his songs being dropped and replacements being contrived at breakneck speed, that George's galley years at Remick's and work as a rehearsal pianist stood him in good stead. Ira stayed up all night to keep pace writing new lyrics. 'Of rejoicing there was none,' he said. Even *How Long Has This Been Going On?* was thrown out. It reappeared the following year in *Rosalie*, true to Gershwin's 'never waste a good tune' policy. He seemed to have more ideas for tunes than he could ever use, and he kept sketchbooks into which he could dip at random. In his early

days he used to label the most promising ones 'G.T.' to identify them as a 'Good Tune'.

Arriving back in New York following the try-outs of *Funny Face*, he realized he had left in his hotel two sketchbooks, containing about forty song ideas. When they couldn't be found, he shrugged it off. 'There are plenty more where those came from.' He once said he liked to write six tunes a day, so he could get the bad ones out of his system.

The grinding toil to recast the show was rewarded. As was the norm during the revues of the 1920s, the book of the show provided the Gershwins with the slimmest of plots. Opportunities to integrate song and story to higher dramatic purpose would come with later projects, but for the moment producers hired them to write tuneful, ear-catching songs with smart lyrics that would provide happy vehicles for star performers and sell plenty of records and sheet music. In this case, the stars were again the Astaires, singing and dancing their merry way through a plot revolving around hidden jewels and incompetent crooks. Fred Astaire was given the chance to anticipate his trade-mark film appearances in black silk top hat, white tie and tails. His song-and-dance number *High Hat* exploited a Gilbert and Sullivan patter-song structure, Ira's lyrics being tossed about between Astaire and a male chorus. *My One And Only* served as his first important solo love-song, and Gershwin knew exactly where to place the all-important blue note – on the first syllable of 'crazy':

My one and only,
What am I gonna do if you turn me down,
When I'm so crazy over you?

Isaac Goldberg saw in this melody an encapsulation of Gershwin's melodic inspiration: 'It begins Yiddish and ends up black.'

Two further songs show Gershwin's mastery of economy in taking simple intervals, such as a third, and linking them to create a flowing, compact melody. Tunes built this way have two prime qualities: they are easy to sing, and easy to remember. The title-song *Funny Face* has the interval of a rising third as the basis for its opening, while the greatest hit in the score, *'S Wonderful*, has a falling third six times in its first sixteen bars. Rhythmically these songs are not intricate, but as usual there are shifting harmonies at almost every turn.

Fred Astaire's dance routines in white tie and tails are part of film legend, but they originated in the chorus number *High Hat*, from *Funny Face*.

'S Wonderful also saw Ira perfect a new device, that of contraction between the word 'it's' and the next one. The 's' was split off, and attached to the following word. This slurring effect produced the casual, colloquial ''S wonderful' and ''S marvellous'. And in the verse of the song we find him knocking the ends off words: 'passion' and 'emotion' become 'pash' and 'emosh'. One can imagine the brothers sweating over these apparently simple devices at the piano until they had come up with something seemingly so effortless and natural.

As always, Gershwin was spending hours at parties, improvising variations on these latest hits. Often he played his newly-composed songs forgetting that the public had not yet had the chance to hear them, which drew from George S. Kaufman the acerbic comment: 'George's music gets around so much that the first-night audience thinks it's a revival.' A lyric in *Jubilee*, a musical which Cole Porter co-wrote with Moss Hart, has a character based on the renowned society hostess Elsa Maxwell saying of her next party: ''Twill be different in every way ... Gershwin's promised not to play.'

Although the level of Gershwin's invention in the three musicals written between 1928 and 1929 was never higher, resulting in a few well-remembered songs, the shows themselves were soon to be eclipsed by the successful new version of *Strike Up the Band*. The first of the three, a Ziegfeld production named *Rosalie*, was a joint score by Gershwin and Sigmund Romberg. Most of George's contribution was salvaged from previous shows, including *How Long Has This Been*

Going On?. This deceptively languid tune does not begin safely in the home key but spends the first sixteen bars drifting downwards, only to reach it on the very last note. There is a perfectly-placed blue note on 'going', immediately made 'non-blue' at the next word, 'on'. Gershwin slides in and out of blue shading in the space of just the song's title.

The Gershwins ended 1928 with their fifth Aarons and Freedley production, *Treasure Girl*. This proved an ultimate example of how even a score containing some fine Gershwin numbers (*Oh So Nice, I Don't Think I'll Fall in Love Today, Where's the Boy?, Feeling I'm Falling, I've Got a Crush on You*) and the star attraction of Gertrude Lawrence could not prevail over a silly play about buried treasure. It closed after sixty-eight performances, a humiliation for all. Gershwin returned to the Ziegfeld fold the following summer but fared little better with his next revue, *Show Girl*, that seemed to have everything going for it, including comedian Jimmy Durante, the Duke Ellington band in the pit and Al Jolson's wife Ruby Keeler as its singing star.

Al Jolson had spotted Ruby Keeler when she had been a teenaged dancer in a speakeasy. Their meeting exemplified the lyrics of a song she would sing in her 1933 film *42nd Street*: 'Forty-Second Street, where the underworld can meet the élite.' The élite Jolson was indeed summoned by the underworld, in the person of gangster Johnny Costello, Ruby's boyfriend. 'She loves you, so you'd better marry her,' warned Costello, 'else there won't be a certain singer on Broadway no more – get me?'

Although none of Gershwin's close friends seem to have verged on criminal activities, interaction between show business and organized crime was inevitable in the racy atmosphere of New York, fuelled by Prohibition since 1920. There was many a thin line between funding a Broadway revue, or promoting some other kind of popular entertainment, and making illegal earnings from bootlegging. One of the finest chroniclers of the American social scene in the 1920s, F. Scott Fitzgerald, made his most famous character, Gatsby, a racketeer and gangster who throws glittering parties in his Long Island mansion and wants to be considered 'respectable'. In real life, at innumerable speakeasies and cabaret clubs, showbusiness people would mingle with shady characters from the criminal fraternity while illicit liquor appeared wantonly at their tables.

Jolson took Johnny Costello's advice and married Ruby Keeler shortly before Gershwin's new musical, *Show Girl*. But on the opening night in Boston not even Jolson's bizarre compulsion to jump out of his seat, run up and down the aisle and join his wife in belting out *Liza* – a stunt deliberately repeated when *Show Girl* moved to Broadway – could help draw subsequent audiences. Ziegfeld accused the Gershwins of contributing to the show's failure, and refused to pay them royalties. They sued (the only time they ever resorted to litigation) but received nothing. Ziegfeld maintained he was broke. Fortunately the charming *Do What You Do* survived the show's demise, as did *Liza*, which has become a favourite basis for jazz improvisation. Its first seven notes show Gershwin's pentatonic fingerprint, and Art Tatum used to play endless coruscating variations over its potent chord structure, much to George's delight.

Three months after the opening of *Treasure Girl*, on 25 October 1929, the Wall Street stock market crashed. Since 1918 America had been a rich nation in a poor world, Europe having virtually bankrupted itself through the economic strain imposed by World War I. In the late 1920s speculators were madly buying and selling for instant capital gain, but their luck ran out when a serious decline in stock prices caused panic on the floor of the Stock Exchange. On the day of the crash, shares worth 30,000 million dollars were rendered

Confusion spreads among the crowds outside the Wall Street Stock Exchange as shares plummet in 1929.

worthless. The savings of millions of Americans were wiped out, and the effect on the community at large was disastrous: riots, protest marches, suicides and widespread unemployment put an end to the heady, flippant Twenties, ushering in a more sober decade and all the social miseries of the Great Depression.

No single cause lay behind the Depression, but the nation was quick to blame its most recent three Presidents – Harding, Coolidge and Hoover – for not dealing with the economic problems left unsolved after the war, and turned its scorn on the perceived incompetence of bankers, brokers, industrialists and politicians. It was a climate ripe for a revival of the anti-war, anti-tycoon satire *Strike Up the Band*, and the Gershwins seized their opportunity. Morrie Ryskind, a gifted humorist who would later write for the Marx Brothers, was brought in to help adapt Kaufman's savage book and 'sweeten' it for theatregoers – literally replacing cheese with chocolate as the bone of contention, and transforming the former American–Swiss conflict into a dream fantasy in the mind of an industrialist and militarist, Horace J. Fletcher, a man with a grievance against the government in Washington for not raising the tariff on Swiss chocolates.

In his revised score Gershwin replaced about half the original numbers, though certainly there was no need to drop the rousing title-

Collaborators in musical satire: the Gershwin brothers with George S. Kaufman (left) and Morrie Ryskind

march. He had rewritten this five times in 1927 before he was satisfied
with it; according to Ira, he had slaved over four versions at the piano,
before the final one came to him while lying in bed. No single song
has become an often-heard Gershwin 'standard' (the one obvious
contender, *The Man I Love*, could hardly have been retrieved from the
1927 production, having by this time achieved fame on its own), but
this in itself bears testimony to the degree of integration between
music and action. Gershwin showed unprecedented skill in pointing-
up details of characterization and incisively underlining the acidic
nuances in Ira's lyrics. Opening in January 1930, the new version of
Strike Up the Band was hailed as a resounding success, running for
191 performances.

Gershwin added a new aspect to his career on opening night, by
conducting one of his musicals for the first time. He had made two
appearances the previous year conducting *An American in Paris*, for
which he had gone back to his old teacher Kilenyi for some guidance
in podium technique. Reports on his conducting are mixed, but some
musicians may have found that what he lacked in technique he more
than made up for in enthusiasm. Isaac Goldberg described him as
conducting not just with a baton, but 'with his cigar, his shoulders, his
hips, his eyes and whatnot. Nothing but a sense of propriety keeps
him from leaping over the footlights and getting right into the show
himself.' Had Gershwin lived longer, it seems unlikely that he would
have developed into a composer-pianist capable of directing orchestras
in his own music at the level of Bernstein or Copland. But he must
have acquitted himself well; he soon increased his conducting
commitments, including the premières of *Girl Crazy* and *Of Thee I
Sing*, and the hardened professionals in his pit orchestras would not
have tolerated a charlatan in the conductor's spotlight.

The second Gershwin musical of 1930 boasted an incredible line-
up below the footlights: Benny Goodman (at this time playing not
clarinet but saxophone), trombonists Glenn Miller and Jack
Teagarden, Jimmy Dorsey on alto sax, and Gene Krupa on drums.
The cornetist Red Nichols, already well-known through running his
own dance-band, had brought these as yet unrecognized talents
together and he joined them in the orchestra pit. The show was *Girl
Crazy*, which abandoned the topicality of the year's earlier success in
favour of a light-hearted story about a New York playboy banished by

his father to Arizona because he is 'girl crazy'. On arrival he opens a 'dude' ranch staffed by Broadway chorus girls, and falls in love with the local postgirl – played by the nineteen-year-old Ginger Rogers. Another future megastar was making her Broadway debut: Ethel Merman, a performer of impeccable diction and shattering power who brought the house down by holding a high C for sixteen bars in *I Got Rhythm* while the band continued with the melody.

Gershwin had finally broken free of the family ménage in 1928 and was now living at 33 Riverside Drive in a luxury penthouse, superbly appointed in 1920s art deco style complete with gymnasium, and with an adjoining apartment for Ira and Leonore. Here he auditioned Merman for the three songs he had planned for her. She recalled being astonished that he offered to change anything she did not like. This, however, confirms the general view that, although he would not tolerate having his work pulled about, he was always ready to be flexible with singers if they wanted to discuss changes in the run-up to

Ethel Merman (she shortened her name from Zimmerman) in *Girl Crazy*, the show that made her a Broadway star

a production. He also advised Merman: 'Don't ever go near a teacher. He'll only ruin you.' Larry Adler was given the identical warning.

There was a curious schizophrenia in Gershwin's attitude to tuition. All his life he pursued professional guidance from esteemed teachers and composers, but underneath there was an uneasy feeling that formal lessons might compromise his creative spontaneity. Impressed by the arresting talent of a young Merman or Adler, he felt compelled to issue a note of caution. In 1930 he wrote: 'Many people say that too much study kills spontaneity in music, but although study may kill a small talent, it must develop a big one. In other words, if study kills a musical endowment, that endowment deserves to be killed.' It was probably because of this ambivalence that he never settled down to study with anyone for very long, no matter how much he thirsted for knowledge nor how much his tutors enthused about his gifts.

Thanks to its Wild West setting, and the energy level generated by the budding jazz luminaries in the pit, *Girl Crazy* was remembered as being 'merry and very loud'. The Gershwins were happy to return to the style of their 1920s successes, providing love-songs, comedy numbers and production routines that would show off the principals. They had rescued *Embraceable You* from an unfinished score for a Ziegfeld extravaganza called *East Is West*, after he had suddenly cancelled it – the beginning of strained relations with the mercurial impresario. Now it became one of two Gershwin classics performed by Ginger Rogers, the other being *But Not for Me*. Both songs show Gershwin's love of 'conjunct' melodies – that is, tunes formed by notes which lie next to each other, and which therefore maintain a particular smoothness. The recurring motif in *Embraceable You* is the rising three notes at the beginning. *But Not for Me* is one of his most inspired tunes, beginning with gentle oscillations of only three conjunct notes. They form a phrase which – surprise, surprise – is immediately repeated over different harmonies, then give way to yearning upward phrases and a resigned, falling cadence that matches the unrequited love expressed in Ira's lyrics – one of their rare songs on this subject. Sometimes the charm of a Gershwin song lies in the way Ira's words actually diverge from the mood of George's tune, one undercutting the other. Here the melody is a simple, heartfelt love-song, but Ira's lyric is deliberately cliché-ridden, almost bored with its own self-pity:

I was a fool to fall
And get that way;
Heigh ho! Alas!
And also, Lackaday!

Ira was always proud if he could work the title of the song into his last line, but 'with a twist'. Here he came up with:

When ev'ry happy plot
Ends with the marriage knot,
And there's no knot for me.

A song like this could easily sound banal, but the craftsmanship both brothers lavished on its construction raises it beyond mere sentimentality. As for Merman's massive hit, *I Got Rhythm*, the salient aspect is how much less rhythmic complexity it manifests compared with its highly-syncopated predecessor, *Fascinating Rhythm*. Gershwin is being pentatonic again – four notes of the five-note pentatonic scale ever rising and falling (in the entire song no two consecutive phrases go in the same direction). The rhythmic interest is in the way the tune keeps pulling away from the main pulse, with three 'I got ...' phrases beginning a beat later than we would have expected (that is, at the beginning of the bar) then a fourth tumbling in to end 'on time' with 'Who could ask for anything more?'. Gershwin loved this fusion of pentatonic fragments and syncopated rhythm so much that he returned to the tune in 1934, as the basis for an entertaining set of concert variations for piano and orchestra.

Whereas *Strike Up the Band* had taken war and bungling international diplomacy for its themes, the subject of Gershwin's only 1931 musical – which proved to be his greatest and last Broadway triumph – was closer to home: an American presidential campaign. George and Ira once again teamed up with Ryskind and Kaufman in a show full of laughter and mockery, *Of Thee I Sing*. The principal characters are Wintergreen, a man who wants to be President, and his running-mate for the Vice Presidency, Throttlebottom. Their campaign issue is 'Love'. If love is the most important issue in life, then it must be the best thing to run an election about.

The dining room at 33 Riverside Drive; in the living room beyond, Gershwin's Steinway piano

The Senate, the White House, the Supreme Court, the devious machinations of ambitious politicians – nothing was off-limits throughout a fast-paced evening of satire. At last the Gershwins were devoting their talents to a production which jettisoned time-honoured, tired Broadway formulas, one in which the plot was highly worked-out and not subservient to a miscellaneous succession of songs and production numbers. And yet, this unprecedently integrated approach did not inhibit Gershwin from writing tunes that lived in the memory long after leaving the theatre.

Ira juxtaposed the patriotic line 'Of Thee I Sing' (from *My Country! 'Tis of Thee*, a veritable American national anthem which shares the same tune as *God Save the King*) with the slangy word 'Baby', creating the show's rousing title-song and setting its irreverent tone in one blow. When he performed it with George early in the production stages, 'there were one or two objectors who thought it was going a bit too far. Our response was that we'd replace it with something else if the paying audience didn't take to it. Weeks later, one could hear a continuous 'Of Thee I Sing, Baby' when friends

greeted one another in the lobby at intermission time.' Ira was also at
pains to point out that the show had no verse-and-chorus songs.
George's music complemented the dialogue and the action to a greater
degree than ever before, so that even the few songs that can stand
alone – *Who Cares?*, *Love Is Sweeping the Country*, *Wintergreen for
President* – are, in performance, integral to the overall dramatic
structure.

The production enjoyed the longest run of any Gershwin musical –
441 performances. George had cast a wide stylistic net to underscore
the plot's kaleidoscopic twists and turns, dipping artfully into the
sounds of a Salvation Army band, or of a Viennese waltz, or quasi-
operatic recitatives. Moment by moment, he matched the barbed wit
of Ryskind and Kaufman and showed himself to be an accomplished
musical satirist. The *New York Daily News* reported that 'there are
almost as many gags in Gershwin's music as there are in Kaufman and
Ryskind's book.'

It was unquestionably the brothers' finest achievement on
Broadway, recognized the following year when it became the first
musical-comedy to win the Pulitzer Prize. The circumstances of the
award led to what Ira described as 'the only time George ever got
angry at me'. The wording of the Pulitzer's brief could not
accommodate the man who wrote the score. The award was for
Drama, and its recipients were therefore Kaufman and Ryskind for
their book, and Ira for his lyrics. When Ira told George he would not
accept unless his brother was included, George insisted the rules be
obeyed. Ira hung the certificate in his bathroom, and took years to get
over what he considered an injustice. In 1943 the Pulitzer committee
changed their policy, allowing eligibility for composers and giving
Richard Rodgers a special award for *Oklahoma!*.

Just as the escapist Hollywood movies of the 1930s – Fred Astaire
and Ginger Rogers dancing their way through sumptuous sets, acting
out fragile plots in over-sized rooms shining with lots of white paint –
took people's minds off their problems, so did *Of Thee I Sing*. But,
unlike such film fare, it was not merely an escapist piece of
entertainment: a new genre had been achieved. Writing to Kurt Weill
in 1942, Ira observed how audiences a decade earlier had craved not
just escapism, but the experience of a finely-crafted musical play with
wit and intelligence. 'We were in the midst of the worst Depression

the country had ever known, and at the same time George and I had the biggest hit we ever had – *Of Thee I Sing*. I felt then that it was a tough period for any new show unless it was so extraordinary that it could overcome the prevailing tone of gloom.'

Nowhere are the fluctuating creative fortunes experienced by the most accomplished theatre people more apparent than in the events of 1933, when the Gershwins tried to repeat their stunning achievement only to be rewarded with two resounding flops. *Pardon My English* was, in Ira's words, 'a headache from start to finish'. They embarked on it principally out of loyalty to their long-time producers Aarons and Freedley. But this, the seventh collaboration, proved so disastrous that the production team split for good, Aarons moving to Hollywood and Freedley fleeing to Panama to escape his creditors. The feeble plot was centred in Dresden and featured an English nobleman with a split personality, his behaviour alternating between that of a dapper aristocrat and an underworld thug. The famous English musical-comedy star Jack Buchanan was meant to be the big draw in this role, but though the song-and-dance persona was perfect for him, the gigolo one was decidedly not. Buchanan bought himself out of his contract during the try-outs and from then on almost everyone else involved felt like deserting the rapidly-sinking ship. Numerous rewrites failed to save its Broadway run, and after forty-six performances – the shortest of any Gershwin production – it was mercifully laid to rest. But the score shows Gershwin as inventive and resourceful as ever, the schizophrenic story-line and the Dresden setting allowing him to mix lilting Viennese waltz-rhythms with those of the American dance-craze, the foxtrot.

Later in the year came *Let 'Em Eat Cake*, the last in the trilogy of Kaufman–Ryskind satires. It was a positive attempt to achieve a sequel to *Of Thee I Sing*, bringing back the characters of Wintergreen and Throttlebottom, now defeated in the presidential election. In revenge, Wintergreen embarks on a left-wing revolution to overthrow the new administration. In the theatre, all of this proved a miscalculation. New York audiences gave the thumbs-down to images of a dictatorship and a blue-shirt army (a spoof on Hitler's brown-shirts) running their country. The show's fate was sealed by reviews such as Brooks Atkinson's, who felt that '[the Gershwins'] hatreds have triumphed over their sense of humour.' The one Gershwin number to have

outlived this failure is *Mine*, an unusual attempt by him to write an extended song with two melodies in counterpoint; in it the ensemble chorus comes downstage and sings, directly to the audience, a counter-melody whose words comment on the sentimental refrain 'Mine, love is mine' being simultaneously sung by Wintergreen and his wife.

Let 'Em Eat Cake closed after only ninety performances, an ignominious end to the Broadway career Gershwin had launched fourteen years earlier with *La La Lucille*. Had he lived longer, he would undoubtedly have returned to Broadway after writing *Porgy and Bess* and songs for Hollywood films. Part of the tragedy of his early death is that we shall never know how he would have continued to develop the American musical if he had lived through World War II and seen the changed face of a world recovering from the effects of Fascism and political chaos, which his farewell to Broadway tried to lampoon. Gershwin's legacy runs through the neglected political satires of Marc Blitzstein, to the sharp-edged Kurt Weill, the popular successes of Rodgers, Porter and Loewe, down to Bernstein and Stephen Sondheim, to the stunningly-staged historical melodramas of Alain Boublil and Claude-Michel Schönberg, and to the dominant composer of musicals since the 1970s, Andrew Lloyd Webber. None would deny Gershwin's influence.

Intertwined with all his work in the theatre, Gershwin was writing music for the concert stage. If that activity, the subject of the following chapter, has always been more controversial than his Broadway scores, it only serves to show how unquestionably the world has taken his songs to its heart. In the hands of many composers producing the concert music of today, melody has regained something of a foothold after the rampant atonalism of the post-war years. It is refreshing to turn to a man who straddled both camps and whose melodic gifts were among the greatest of any composer. With his usual brand of disarming immodesty, Gershwin himself defined the key to his mastery of the Broadway musical: 'I have more tunes in my head than I could put down on paper in a hundred years.'

Gershwin the concert pianist, captured in an atmospheric portrait by Edward Steichen, 1927

George Gershwin is the only songwriter I know who became a composer.

Irving Berlin, c. 1961

Concert Music

When Irving Berlin described Gershwin as the only songwriter he knew who became a composer, he was appraising the extra dimension that took Gershwin beyond not only Berlin's own achievements, but beyond those of all his associates in Tin Pan Alley. Gershwin's fellow song-pluggers at Remick's who became songwriters were satisfied to have their material used on Broadway and if possible to write hit numbers that would make them rich and famous. What they did not possess was the aspiration to write extended works for the concert hall, with titles like 'Rhapsody' or 'Concerto' or 'Overture', based to a considerable extent upon European classical forms and unconnected with any theatre-piece.

Broadway material heard in concert tended to be in the form of orchestrated suites, usually put together by professional orchestrators rather than the composer. These expert musicians would string together the best-loved tunes and dances from a given show or maybe from a composer's entire output, a practice that has continued at American venues like the Boston Pops or the Hollywood Bowl and at concerts of 'light classical' music all over the world. In Gershwin's day, as in ours, skilled orchestrators were also responsible for taking a composer's piano draft of his new musical and arranging it for the musicians in the orchestra pit; in addition, they constructed a short, rousing overture using themes from the score in the tradition of a Verdi opera or Strauss operetta.

Even if Irving Berlin had written something for Whiteman's concert in 1924, it is safe to assume it would not have been structured any more ambitiously than a medley resembling a musical-comedy overture. The man who did fulfil Whiteman's commission, Victor Herbert, was a thoroughly-trained cellist and composer whose concert works included two cello concertos and large-scale pieces for orchestra and chorus. But he was writing these in the nineteenth-century Romantic tradition, without incorporating anything so stylistically foreign as jazz or ragtime. Even Gershwin's first idol, Jerome Kern,

steered clear of large forms, except for *Scenario*, a suite based on tunes from his vastly successful musical *Show Boat*, and a meandering *Portrait for Orchestra* inspired by the life of Mark Twain. In structural terms they show none of Gershwin's originality and it is doubtful that Kern was solely responsible for compiling and orchestrating them.

So where did Gershwin get his compulsion to 'cross the tracks' and invade the concert hall? Certainly it was within him by the time he took up song-plugging at Remick's. His colleagues were bemused by his eagerness to explore music completely foreign to the song-fodder clattering away in their cubicles. 'Sometimes when George spoke of the artistic mission of popular music,' said Harry Ruby (the songwriter with the powerful baseball throw, and composer of *Three Little Words* and *Who's Sorry Now*), 'we thought he was going highfalutin. The height of artistic achievement to us was a "pop" song that sold lots of copies, and we just didn't understand what he was talking about.' There is a story of a fellow piano-pounder hearing Gershwin practising a Prelude and Fugue from Bach's *Well-Tempered Clavier* and asking: 'Are you studying to be a great concert pianist, George?' 'No,' came the reply, 'I'm studying to be a great popular-song composer.' He was already steadfast about how the two worlds of music could feed off each other, and that it would be natural for him to engage in both with equal commitment. In 1926 he tangled with a critic, A. Walter Kramer, who wrote to a monthly journal stating that jazz did not belong in classical music, rubbing salt into the wound by suggesting the orchestration of Gershwin's recent piano concerto had been done by 'someone else'. In the next issue Gershwin fended off that insinuation and replied to Kramer that '… word-trouble surrounds the colloquial use of the phrase "classical music". It means as many things as there are people to say it. A man writes a piece of music which he considers serious, but which is pretty awful; he labels his work "classic" and an unsuspecting public accepts the label. From any sound critical standpoint, labels mean nothing at all. Good music is good music, even if you call it "oysters".'

Dvořák, who spent three years in America from 1895, is forever linked with the country through his 'New World' Symphony, which was superficially inspired by what he took to be American Negro music. He was clear-sighted enough to advise that American concert music would never thrive as an indigenous entity if it kept on

imitating European models. A musician who had died nearly three decades before Dvořák's sojourn, Louis Moreau Gottschalk (1829–69), is regarded as the first authentically American 'classical' composer. Born in New Orleans, he became the first American composer to achieve recognition abroad, having studied in France and received high praise from Chopin, who predicted a future as 'the king of pianists'. His fame rested on hundreds of small piano pieces which successfully integrated the folk music and dance rhythms of his native region with Chopin's own pianistic language. Gershwin seems never to have referred to Gottschalk but it is possible he knew about him; he would certainly have been attracted by the elements of jazz and ragtime which made Gottschalk something of a prophet. He would also have admired the virtuoso challenge of the more elaborate pieces, the invigorating way Gottschalk used syncopation and South American rhythms, and the way he exploited pianola-like textures or the strumming of a banjo.

Just as Vienna had its First and Second 'Schools' of composers, America had two of its own – the First and Second 'New England Schools'. They were basically unexceptional imitators of seventeenth- and eighteenth-century European masters, but from their number emerged someone whose music did not fall entirely into their mould. Edward MacDowell (1861–1908) had a distinctive personality and he specialized in two areas dear to Gershwin's heart: expressive songs, and short pieces for piano.

Like Gottschalk, MacDowell studied in Europe. He so impressed Liszt that he arranged for his own publishers to print MacDowell's two suites for piano. Today he is remembered mainly for his two piano concertos and the gently lilting *To A Wild Rose*, the first movement of a piano suite called *Woodland Sketches*. Gershwin would have been introduced to his music by Hambitzer, and the heavy influence of Grieg would not have been lost on him. MacDowell's first concerto shares its key, A minor, with Grieg's own, and the descending, dramatic octaves with which Grieg's soloist makes his opening flourish are echoed in *Rhapsody in Blue* just before the four 'Victor Herbert' bars Gershwin added at rehearsal.

MacDowell was an unassuming, Frankfurt-trained American who returned to his native country and produced music closely shadowing his Romantic idols – Schumann, Chopin, Liszt, Wagner, Grieg. These

were also the composers the young Gershwin was hearing at his earliest concerts, and whose pictures he was pasting into his scrapbooks. Because of the rarity of performances, he did not come under the influence of the most adventurous American pioneer of all, Charles Ives (1874–1954), nor the unfairly-neglected Charles Griffes (1884–1920), whose music was promoted by Eva Gauthier with her usual gusto. Rather than the church music and scenes of American life central to Ives, Griffes turned for inspiration to Debussy, Skryabin, Japanese folk-music, and other non-Western sources.

Gershwin would have known almost nothing about these American 'classical' composers at the time of *Rhapsody in Blue*. By 1924 none of them had, in the wider public sense, achieved the liberation of American music from European domination, nor the integration of American elements within formal structures that would prove satisfying to concert audiences and carry their composer's name around the world. Griffes's music only gained some temporary acclaim just before his premature death at thirty-six. Until 1924, performances of Ives's music were mostly at church recitals; he gave up composing two years later and spent the rest of his years revising his works and seeing them at last gain international respect. He was the only one of this group who had some real impact in America and beyond through his innovations.

At the time he wrote the rhapsody Gershwin could also have had little knowledge of the principal figures who were to be recognized as the next generation of American composers. His process of liberation began earlier than theirs because his breakthrough happened in his early twenties and his musical style was immediately accessible to concert-goers. Virgil Thomson, Howard Hanson, Roger Sessions, Roy Harris, Henry Cowell and Walter Piston all made prime contributions to American music – yet all were very close to Gershwin in age. More renowned than any of these was 'The Dean of American Music' – Aaron Copland, two years younger than Gershwin and sharing a Brooklyn upbringing and Russian-Jewish parentage.

Gershwin, one of the most non-intellectual and instinctive of composers, was capable of disingenuous pontificating about classical music as his fame grew and he was courted for interviews in the musical press. It is almost absurd to read the simplistic analysis he once put forward about the process of musical creation (even allowing

Aaron Copland (1900–90);
Gershwin craved recogni-
tion for his concert works,
but it was Copland who
came to be regarded by
the musical establishment as
the father of modern
American music.

for the greater understanding of Berlioz in our own day): 'To my
mind all artists are a combination of two elements – heart and brain.
Tchaikovsky – although he was a good musician – was apt to stress
the heart too much; Berlioz was all mind. Now Bach was that glorious
example of the unity of the two.'

When it came to placing himself within his own objectives he
made more sense, and his remarks in a 1933 article called 'The
Relation of Jazz to American Music' express the fundamental creed
behind his concert works. 'Jazz I regard as an American folk music; not
the only one, but a very powerful one which is probably in the blood
and feeling of the American people more than any other style of folk-
music. I believe that it can be made the basis of serious symphonic
works of lasting value, in the hands of a composer with talent for both
jazz and symphonic music.' We need not look far to identify the man
with these dual talents. Clearly he is the former Brooklyn teenager who
practised Bach in Remick's 'professional parlour'.

It is a sobering thought that all controversy associated with
Gershwin's invasion of the concert hall rests on a mere six
compositions that only need a total of an hour and forty minutes to
play. They are *Rhapsody in Blue* (1924), *Concerto in F* (1925), *An*

American in Paris (1928), *Second Rhapsody* (1931), *Cuban Overture* (1932) and *Variations on 'I Got Rhythm'* (1934).

Gershwin's concert pieces therefore span exactly the most productive and successful years of his Broadway career, being evenly distributed between *Lady, Be Good!* and *Let 'Em Eat Cake*, ending when he began devoting himself to composing his opera. It was as though he needed a 'fix' of 'serious symphonic' composition every so often during that decade, no matter how frenzied the pace of his Broadway commitments.

There were smaller-scale works too. For solo piano, he published Three Preludes (he wrote several more, and once performed six of them in concert), and a collection of eighteen song transcriptions issued in 1932 as *George Gershwin's Song Book*. There are a few other small piano pieces, some of them merely sketches, and his last instrumental composition, *Promenade*. Written in 1936 for the Astaire–Rogers film *Shall We Dance*, this tiny gem was originally a light-hearted interlude whose title in the film score had been *Walking the Dog*.

Gershwin's 'national anthem', *O Land of Mine, America*, which was awarded the lowest prize in the *New York American* competition he had entered in 1919, has mercifully vanished, despite being published anonymously in that journal on 2 March 1919. But his other piece of instrumental juvenelia, the quartet movement *Lullaby* dating from about the same period, is a charming piece that deserves to be heard occasionally at concerts in its transcription for string orchestra. In this guise it makes soothing listening and shows a completely different aspect of the young Gershwin, his head otherwise full of ragtime and jazzy rhythms. The music appears seamless and lies well on the instruments, the melody line being the province of the first violins rather than the harmonica, as in Larry Adler's special arrangement.

There is no mistaking Gershwin's mature fingerprints, even in this student exercise written for his teacher Kilenyi. It has a 'blue' feel to its harmonies, and the melody does not sit rigidly on the barline – as with *I Got Rhythm* a decade later, the tune already pulls away from the beat with little syncopated shifts. The melody itself has the mature Gershwin ring: four conjunct notes moving gently up and down over changing harmonies, its singability proved by his re-use of it for *Has Anyone Seen My Joe?* in *Blue Monday*. The piece has a proper shape, an ABA structure, the first A dwindling to almost nothing before a new

idea – reasonably contrasted – enters with echoes not only of Grieg but of Delius, a composer Gershwin could hardly have known at that stage. The main theme, A, returns, marked to be played louder and therefore has a greater urgency. The glistening, high 'harmonics' in the introduction, recurring delicately at the end, and the way the movement fades away with a pizzicato farewell, show a keen ear for string coloration.

Did Gershwin really possess all this finesse so early? The student manuscript must have been doctored somewhat by his quartet-playing friends before reaching the Julliard Quartet and its later transcription for full strings. This does not detract from the quality and potential of the first 'serious' piece from a young man otherwise busy with *La La Lucille.*

A few months after the *Rhapsody* première, Walter Damrosch recommended to the New York Symphony Orchestra, of which he was conductor, that they commission a work for piano and orchestra from Gershwin. A contract to have the piece ready in eight months, and for Gershwin to play the solo part in seven of their concerts (an irresistible commission for Gershwin, and a courageous hunch by Damrosch), was quickly arranged.

Damrosch (1861–1950) was an unsnobbish maestro who gave new music a chance without ever being really comfortable in the contemporary repertoire. Born in Breslau, he had established himself as an amiable and popular conductor, especially for his long-running music-appreciation broadcasts on NBC radio which spread awareness of classical music to listeners throughout the US and Canada. He gave the American premières of several Wagner operas, Tchaikovksy's fourth and sixth symphonies, and the last two by Brahms. Obviously he deemed Gershwin capable of writing an extended piece, but had to endure some press criticism suggesting it was all a publicity stunt, since Gershwin had neither orchestrated his recent rhapsody nor proved himself with anything for piano and symphony orchestra. His judgement would be vindicated. Gershwin decided to write a piano concerto, and the result was a work that continues to eclipse all other American concertos in popularity. For Gershwin, the pattern would become all too familiar – critics from the 'serious music' camp jealously hostile to this rich, fast-track songwriter encroaching on their territory without even the proper training.

Walter Damrosch, who conducted the first performance of Concerto in F. In 1938 he wrote that he had tried to wean Gershwin from Broadway, but 'the lure of the lighter forms in which he had become such a master proved too strong.'

Stories – apochryphal or otherwise – sprang up almost every time Gershwin set about something new. Often he would instigate them himself; at other times his friends would talk freely about his current work and his latest ambition, inevitably embroidering here and there. In the case of the concerto, Gershwin himself told the *New York Tribune*: 'I started to write the concerto in London, after buying four or five books on musical structure to find out what the concerto form actually was! And, believe me, I had to come through – because I had already signed a contract.' He also bought the then standard treatise on writing for instruments, Cecil Forsyth's 1914 textbook *Orchestration*. Gershwin was determined to orchestrate the piece himself.

His remarks to the *Tribune* make good copy, but it would be silly to imagine Gershwin had no idea about concerto structure. He had been listening to concertos at concerts since his teens, and presumably exploring some of them with Hambitzer and Kilenyi. Now, reading his reference books, he would have been struck by the variety of concertos written after the time of Haydn and Mozart, which none the less paid homage to a Classical design. He could not truly have been ignorant of 'sonata form' – the structure established and nurtured by those Austrian masters which formed the basis for the opening movements (and sometimes subsequent ones) in Classical and Romantic sonatas, symphonies, concertos, and chamber music such as string quartets.

Sonata form organizes a movement in such a way that we are taken through two main 'subjects', or themes, in contrasted keys. After this 'exposition', which has led us to a different key from the one we started in, the material is adventurously worked-over in a 'development' section. Lastly, a 'recapitulation' of the opening material presents subtle modifications to the themes and also to the key relationships to enable the movement to end in the 'home' key. There may be a 'coda' to round off the design and say some final things about the melodic material. Not only would Gershwin have grasped at least the gist of this by 1924, but it would not have escaped him that every great concerto writer had taken this structure and modified it freely according to his wishes, often straying far from the original rules.

About the only aspect of his concerto, however, that tallied with established practice was that it would be in three movements. His original title was *New York Concerto*; as with the rhapsody, it was the

vibrance and energy of the metropolis that were to be the mainspring of the outer movements, though the middle one was planned as a contrast. This is plain from a 'work sheet' he prepared before writing the music, with its pithy outline:

1. Rhythm
2. Melody (Blues)
3. More Rhythm

It is also interesting to see him summarizing how he would set out the first movement's material: 'Charleston; First (dotted) theme; Percussion effect; Effects for piano; Effects for brass; Double Charleston.' No matter that this scheme does not closely resemble the finished music. This is not a composer thinking in 'sonata form' terms at all. Instead, the important factors seem to be rhythm and colour. There is nothing to suggest how these separate 'effects' will join up to make a convincing shape, which should not surprise us. His priorities and talents would never lie with complex musical development on a substantial scale. It is what Gershwin does instead that should engage our interest.

As with the rhapsody, he did not stick with his original title. He started the concerto in July 1925 and the manuscript sketch refers to 'New York', but by the time it was finished and orchestrated it had become the more traditional-sounding *Concerto in F*. For a newcomer to large-scale orchestration, he must have torn into his work with customary zeal. The concerto existed as a two-piano sketch by September, and the job of orchestrating it was finished by 10 November, as noted on the manuscript. He then hired an orchestra of sixty, conducted by his friend William Daly, to try out the piece (a luxury afforded by few 'serious' composers). Gershwin later described his 'greatest musical thrill' as being 'the time I first heard my *Concerto in F* played by an orchestra. That was an experience I guess I'll never forget.'

William Daly had first met Gershwin at Remick's. He was a shy, academic man who had been a brilliant pianist even as a boy, and who later turned to orchestrating theatre music and conducting pit orchestras. Gershwin once described him as 'the best friend I have' (quite a statement from a man whose friends were numbered in hundreds) and Daly became his favourite conductor, orchestrator and

musical adviser. Damrosch attended this rehearsal, and Gershwin readily accepted advice from both him and Daly as regards improvements to the scoring.

The question of how much help Gershwin had with his orchestrations will never be fully resolved. He willingly submitted his concerto sketches to Daly, but his opera and all his concert works exist in neatly-written manuscripts in his own hand, and to suggest that his scores were extensively worked-over by masters of orchestration who have somehow been happy to remain unacknowledged is only to enter the arena of mischief typified by one Allan Langley, a freelance viola-player and not very successful composer. In an article provocatively entitled 'The Gershwin Myth' in 1932, Langley implied that Gershwin was covering-up the help he had from others, and that Daly was one of his principal 'ghost writers'. Langley had played the viola in *An American in Paris* under Gershwin's baton and had decided, after watching both Gershwin and Daly during rehearsal, that Daly knew more about the score. The implication was that this must also have been the case with Gershwin's concerto, rehearsed with Daly three years previously.

George photographed in his penthouse with William Daly, preparing for the first all-Gershwin concert at New York's Lewisohn Stadium, August 1932

In a withering rebuttal, Daly wrote: 'I would be only too happy to be known as the composer of *An American in Paris*, or of any of Gershwin's works, or as the orchestrator of them. It is true that I orchestrate many Gershwin numbers for the theatre, but so does Robert Russell Bennett. The fact is that I have never written one note of any of his compositions, or so much as orchestrated one whole bar of any of his symphonic works. I suppose I should really resent the fact that Langley attributes Gershwin's work to me, since Langley finds all of it so bad. But fortunately for my *amour propre*, I have heard some of Langley's compositions. He really should stay away from ink and stick to his viola.'

The controversy seemed to be resolved but the orchestration problem refused to go away. It still occupied Ira years after his brother's death, when he gradually discovered that almost all of George's concert scores had been tampered with or 'improved' on their way to the printing press in modern editions. Ira was convinced that George's 'mistakes' in instrumentation really were the sounds he intended. The culprit was Frank Campbell-Watson, the music editor for Gershwin's publisher, New World Music, who claimed that his revisions had been done with Gershwin's approval. This is inconceivable, since at the time of his death Gershwin was satisfied with his existing concert scores, having heard them performed numerous times. Only *Rhapsody in Blue* and *Cuban Overture* escaped Campbell-Watson's 'improvements'. He assigned the revision of *Second Rhapsody* to Robert McBride and the *I Got Rhythm* variations to another arranger, William Schoenfeld. This upset Ira and he appealed to the publishers. The process of reprinting Gershwin's scores according to the original manuscripts in the Library of Congress has still not been completed. (Michael Tilson Thomas sought out the original manuscript of *Second Rhapsody* in the library as an authentic basis for his 1985 recording and for his subsequent performances.)

Gershwin cast the first movement of the concerto in a very free version of 'sonata form' enlivened by the rhythm of the 1920s dance craze, the Charleston. Sledgehammer blows on the timpani, cymbal clashes and rolls on the side-drum make an arresting opening. The Charleston motif that follows becomes a dominating force that drives the music along, apart from when Gershwin – who has an abundance of tunes up his sleeve, compensating for development and transition –

relaxes into more sustained and reflective passages. He described the Charleston as 'quick and pulsating, representing the young, enthusiastic spirit of American life. American life is nervous, hurried, syncopated, ever accelerando, and slightly vulgar. I should use the word 'vulgar' without intent of offence. There is a vulgarity that is newness. It is essential. The Charleston is vulgar, but it has a strength, an earthiness, that is an essential part of symphonic sound.' Gershwin is being almost completely intelligible; only the term 'symphonic sound' seems ill-chosen.

Other striking features about the movement include the originality of the piano's first entrance, on a low note which gives way to an upward glissando (a cousin to the clarinet wail of *Rhapsody in Blue*?), and the fact that this leads not to any of the motifs the orchestra has excitedly introduced, but to a languid blues theme for the soloist in a different mood and tempo. Within the first two minutes, Gershwin has thrown away the rule-books on how to start a piano concerto. There is an abundance of musical ideas in this opening (or 'exposition') section, one of them a broad melody on the strings whose yearning second strain pre-echoes *But Not For Me* by five years. When he comes to his loosely-defined 'development' section, he not only introduces a skittish, pentatonic, new idea on the piano, but combines it with a counter-melody on the strings – which proves be a speeded-up version of the first notes from that expressive string melody. This is typical of the man who said: 'What I don't know about music is enough to keep me occupied for the rest of a normally long life'. It is the very not-knowingness of what is expected in a concerto that somehow manages to hold everything together, because the material is itself refreshing and original.

Gershwin described the second movement as conveying 'a poetic nocturnal atmosphere which has come to be referred to as the American blues, but in a purer form than that in which they are usually treated'. The opening is wonderfully evocative, a lazy tune on a solo trumpet curling its way through blue notes and jazzy inflections. Gershwin worked on this movement during the summer of 1925; we might imagine him standing at his apartment window overlooking a spectacular view of downtown Manhattan, inspired by a crimson sunset offsetting the myriad lights of New York on a sultry evening. He referred to himself as 'a modern romantic', and this music

proves his point. As in the first movement, the piano enters with something entirely different, a snappy dance tune which is pacified by a touch of blue, 'klezmer' fiddling from a solo violin. After a return of the trumpet soliloquy, a piano cadenza leads to the heart of the movement: one of Gershwin's passionate, swelling melodies that, as it grows to its climax, momentarily resembles one of César Franck's Symphonic Variations for piano and orchestra. After a brief reprise of the trumpet theme, now played on the flute, the movement closes peacefully with four simple notes played in octaves on the piano – four fateful notes, as it would transpire, for Gershwin.

The finale is, in his words, 'an orgy of rhythms, starting violently and keeping to the same pace throughout'. Practically nothing that happens in this spiky, hyperactive movement could have come out of a textbook. The key of the concerto is supposed to be F major. Defying traditional harmonic analysis, we are thrust at the start into G minor, swerve with difficulty into F minor twenty bars later, and only achieve the 'proper' key of F major after another 110 bars. And the tunes pile in one after the other, cross-referencing to the earlier two movements with lightning speed in a terse example of 'cyclic form' (themes from one movement reappearing for some fresh working-out in a later one).

Towards the end, a huge stroke on the gong silences everything. This theatrical gesture was probably learned from Broadway rather than from anything symphonic, but if Gershwin had chanced to hear the 'Little Russian' Symphony by Tchaikovsky (No. 2), he would have found the same dramatic card being played at the same point in Tchaikovsky's finale. After a gong-stroke and a pause, a composer can go anywhere he likes because the hiatus effectively destroys the tonality. Where Gershwin goes is to an overwhelming statement of the piano's initial blues melody from the opening movement, before hurtling the music to a bombastic finish with pentatonic scales pounded out at the keyboard. (Dvořák set a precedent, closing the 'New World' with stamping, pentatonic scales in the lower instruments.)

Even by Hollywood biopic standards, an unusual degree of tackiness was achieved in an extract from this finale in the film *Rhapsody in Blue*. During the gong's reverberations, a messenger walked on to the platform and handed a note to the conductor, who turned solemnly to the audience, announced Gershwin's death, then

briskly finished the concerto. Party to this absurdity was Oscar Levant at the piano, whose private opinion of this *coup de théâtre* Hollywood-style can easily be imagined.

The concerto's première was on 3 December 1925, in a packed Carnegie Hall. Whether or not the audience realized how effectively Gershwin had deconstructed the piano concerto form and re-assembled it in his own image, they loved it. The critics, predictably, were divided. On the positive side was Samuel Chotzinoff in *The World*: 'Gershwin is an instinctive artist who has the talent for the right manipulation of the crude material he starts out with that a lifelong study of counterpoint and fugue never can give to the one who is not born with it.' Lawrence Gilman, the *Tribune* critic who had panned *Rhapsody in Blue* with the words 'trite and feeble', had not changed his mind about Gershwin; the concerto was 'conventional, trite, at its worst a little dull'.

In the *New York Times*, Olin Downes – who had enthused about the rhapsody – did not take to the concerto either. 'Gershwin has tried earnestly and sincerely to compose a work of symphonic dimensions. He has not succeeded because the form he employs is not native to a composer of his experience. Another rhapsody or one-movement concerto – Liszt wrote one-movement concertos – might have been a marked step in advance.' Downes was a perceptive critic, but it seems puzzling that, compared with *Rhapsody in Blue*, the wealth of thematic variety in the concerto had made no impression. He felt the rhapsody 'had a cheerful Broadway insouciance and a certain raciness and ginger in its principal ideas. Moreover, these ideas were well contrasted. There is no such effective contrast in the themes of the concerto.'

Years later, Gershwin said that adverse reviews had to be taken in his stride. 'I am one of those who honestly believe that the majority has much better taste and understanding, not only of music but of any of the arts, than it is credited with having. It is the judgement of the great mass that finally decides.' He certainly needed this defence mechanism against Paul Rosenfield, who reflected on the concerto seven years after the première. 'The second movement begins with an interesting, muted treatment of a blues theme; but the impulse of the beginning is entirely let down. Though the last movement begins vigorously with a good scherzando theme for the xylophone [this

critic is not even reading the score – the xylophone only briefly colours the theme, and not until three minutes in] one is not surprised to find the movement largely a recapitulation of old material. If the main honours for the symphonic exploitation and idealization of jazz have gone to Milhaud for *La Création du monde*, to Honegger for his Piano Concertino, and to Copland for his Piano Concerto, he at least stands almost gigantically among the other sons of Tin Pan Alley – Bennett, Levant, Grofé – who have grappled with more or less symphonic forms.'

Rosenfield charitably puts Gershwin well ahead of his three Broadway friends. But in no way can the Milhaud, Honegger and Copland pieces be said to have established their place in the concert repertoire in comparison with Gershwin's concerto. Even the supreme Sviatoslav Richter played it, albeit with an unnerving studiousness devoid of 'swing'. More than any of Rosenfield's 'main honours' candidates, Ravel's G major Piano Concerto, begun four years after Gershwin's, has found a regular place in the concert hall. It was a favourite on Bernstein's concert tours, when he would direct the orchestra from the keyboard. With exquisite Gallic taste, it combines elements of 1920s jazz with a circus-like gaiety, contrasted with tender passages as in the Gershwin. Ravel did not conceal his admiration for Gershwin's fusion of jazz with symphonic procedures, and greatly admired his improvisatory wizardry at the piano.

Copland, a benevolent giant in American music, seemed to have a problem with Gershwin. He returned to New York from his studies at Fontainebleau under the legendary teacher Nadia Boulanger in June 1924, not long after the rhapsody première. He had done what Gershwin hankered after, but missed while he was song-plugging and subsequently earning a fortune: he had left Brooklyn for musical studies under a world-famous teacher in Europe. In 1926, the year after Gershwin's concerto (which he must have heard), Copland wrote his own, full of jazz influences. Compared with the clarity of Gershwin's instrumentation, many pages are over-scored to the extent that the soloist is drowned out. 'I was interested not so much in jazz,' said Copland, 'as in trying to write a music in the serious field which would be as American in quality as the jazz boys had been able to manage in the light field. I wrote a piano concerto in which I used actual jazz elements. That was considered very daring at the time. Jazz

was all right in its place but, my heavens, what is it doing in Symphony Hall, Boston?'

Not a word about Gershwin. Asked about him by a student in the 1970s, Copland remarked: 'He was a good Broadway composer.' Copland, not a malicious person, used to rever Ives, Ruggles and other 'tough' American composers in his teaching sessions and in his writings. So his attitude towards Gershwin's non-Broadway music only helped perpetuate the disappointment Gershwin bore all his life, in that his success with the public did not bring with it the recognition he craved from the American musical establishment.

At least he could find comfort in the fulsome programme note Damrosch had written for the concert. 'Various composers have been walking around jazz like a cat around a plate of hot soup, waiting for it to cool off. Lady Jazz, adorned with her intriguing rhythms, has danced her way around the world. But she has encountered no knight who could lift her to a level that would enable her to be received as a respectable member in musical circles. George Gershwin has accomplished this miracle. He has done it boldly by dressing this extremely independent and up-to-date young lady in the classic garb of a concerto.'

Between the 1925 concerto and the writing of his next concert piece, *An American in Paris*, in 1928, Gershwin made two enhancements to his personal life, away from the hurly-burly of his Broadway projects. He took up painting as a hobby. And he at last found a woman who came closest to his exacting ideal.

Gershwin had long been one of America's most eligible bachelors. But he continued to be wary of forming a long-term relationship, let alone contemplating marriage. It was one of the many contradictions in his psyche that, at one moment, he would ask his friends why he should limit himself to only one woman 'when I can have as many as I want', and at the next bemoan his inability to find a permanent partner, despairing that all the artistic and financial success life had bestowed on him still left him feeling 'all mixed up'. The quandary was largely of his own making, because he habitually idolized his woman friends, then became disillusioned when they fell short of his ideal. His mother had been emotionally distant, his father a proud parent but passive in his own marriage and ineffectual in female company. It was therefore unlikely that George and Ira would form

successful relationships easily, and putting their work first seemed to provide a deep-seated compensation. Ira had at least found, in the words of one of his lyrics, 'someone to watch over me' – a very domineering watcher at that.

S. N. Behrman told how he began hearing about 'Dream Girl'. She was a physical-culture teacher who gave George workouts. (He was always keen on exercise and eventually employed his own trainer. He loved walking, tennis and golfing. The diet-fad hypochondriac with the 'composer's stomach' inside a strong body was one further contradiction in Gershwin's make-up. He would complain that sitting down writing music was basically against his outdoor nature.) Behrman learned that George had become infatuated with her, but time passed and no engagement was announced. Eventually Behrman was begged by Ira to take on the disagreeable chore of visiting George to tell him that Ira had discovered 'Dream Girl' was married. Gershwin was at work on the concerto when Behrman called on him. 'His brown eyes showed a flicker of pain,' recalled Behrman. 'Finally he spoke. "Do you know, if I weren't so busy I'd feel terrible."'

One of George's close friends, Mabel Schirmer, surmised that 'maybe he had too many women. They followed him all over the place. He came home usually with about two or three women from a party. They just followed him home.' Another, Kitty Carlisle, observed that 'people felt very protective about him. He was successful, he was good-looking, women adored him, he had money. He had everything, but yet there was something vulnerable, childlike. He needed approval. I know he wanted to get married.'

There was another reason Gershwin had not gone to pieces at the news about 'Dream Girl'. Three months before starting work on the concerto, he had met Kay Swift at a party she was giving for Jascha Heifetz. She was then married to James Warburg, a banker she later divorced – probably hoping this would lead to a marriage proposal from Gershwin, though she would not admit it. Their friendship blossomed into the most fulfilling of all his relationships with women.

Kay Swift had been a gifted musician since childhood; she wrote the hit song *Can't We Be Friends* and the score for the 1930 musical *Fine and Dandy*. She had the critical discernment to discuss his music and could play it over with him, four hands on one piano. She proof-read his scores and copied out orchestral parts. She had a remarkable musical memory, and was able to recall in detail every page of *Porgy*

Actress Kitty Carlisle, resplendent in satin for a Paramount Studios publicity shot; she was among the many glamorous women Gershwin dated.

Kay Swift, whose devotion to Gershwin did not yield a marriage proposal. Oscar Levant used to quip: 'There goes Mr George Gershwin with the future Mrs Kay Swift.'

and Bess and other Gershwin compositions long after he died. In his turn, Gershwin had at last found a cultured, witty and highly-musical soulmate with enormous charm and social refinement. Yet, as always, there was to be no tying of the knot. When he refused to make a commitment she advised him to undergo psychoanalysis. He did, but the result was the opposite of what she had hoped for. Their friendship remained intact but the passion had cooled.

Kay was the mother of three daughters. One of them, April, was still in her teens and had grown to resent Gershwin as being, in her view, the main cause of her parents' divorce. He struggled to weigh up his attraction to Kay, her family situation, and the prospect of giving up his bachelor life to take on marital responsibilities. It was a dilemma he could not resolve. In the end they agreed a year's separation. One month before it had run its course, Gershwin died without forming a relationship with anyone else. He had phoned her from Hollywood saying 'I'm coming back for both of us.'

Perhaps it was as a means of escaping the inner turmoil over his symphonic ambitions and his perplexing love-life that he turned to painting. He had always shown a talent for sketching. His rehearsal scripts were covered with caricatures of people involved in the production, and not long before his death his valet realized that even

his doodlings on the phone-pad were worth saving, so he collected them to give to Ira. Indeed, Ira initiated his brother's new pastime. His childhood sketches and drawings had been more advanced than George's, but when one day he brought home some watercolours and brushes it proved to be the start of a joint hobby, and George made rapid progress.

He was helped by a cousin who was a professional artist, Henry Botkin. Although Ira gave up painting, George became 'hooked' and continued to produce canvases until his death. Working both in oil and watercolour, he preferred portraits to landscapes and his paintings of his parents, DuBose Heyward, Kern, and Schoenberg (his last canvas) are all excellent likenesses. *My Grandfather* is an imaginative vision of his smartly-attired paternal grandfather in a street in old Russia with, significantly, a synagogue painted into the background. He became as passionate about his new hobby as about composing, and in his wilder fantasies talked about concentrating on art rather than music and about going on a painting trip to the Middle East with Botkin.

Two of his most striking paintings are self-portraits. In *Self-Portrait in an Opera Hat* (1932) he painted the reflection of himself at the easel as seen in a mirror, dressed in white tie, top hat and tails. *Self-Portrait in a Checkered Sweater* (1936) is probably the best-known of his paintings through its frequent use on publicity material and compact discs. In both paintings, Gershwin looks towards us with a solemn seriousness that is not present in his photographs.

Apart from finished canvases, Botkin counted over a hundred drawings in which he said Gershwin showed 'an amazing skill as a draughtsman'. His involvement did not stop at guiding Gershwin's brush. From 1926 he spent much time in Europe and scoured art dealers for paintings and sculptures which Gershwin, with his generous income, could purchase and ship back to his apartment. The result was a valuable collection of nearly 150 works of art which showed the combined taste of Gershwin and Botkin to be impeccable. Paintings by Utrillo, Picasso, Kandinsky, Modigliani, Gaugin, Derain and Chagall were among this treasure-trove, along with rare watercolours and lithographs. In his choice of art, as in his music, Gershwin preferred the modern to the traditional. Above all other painters he adored the French expressionist Rouault, who had initially specialized in stained-glass windows and whose paintings seemed to be

Gershwin's *Self-Portrait in an Opera Hat* (1932). Later that year, Ira painted *My Body*, a self-portrait dressed only in vest and underpants – a droll comment on his brother's canvas.

bathed in an ecstatic light, his figures accentuated by black outlining similar to the leaded framing that holds such windows together. The bold lines and translucent richness of his palette struck a chord in a composer more than ever fascinated with orchestral colour. 'If only I could put Rouault into music,' he said. His art collection was exhibited several times after his death and remains the property of the Gershwin estate.

Gershwin's piano concerto was given its European première in Paris in May 1928. The soloist was Dimitri Tiomkin (later to compose numerous Hollywood scores including *High Noon* and *The Guns of Navarone*), and Gershwin was present to hear him launch the new concerto and also perform Liszt's Piano Concerto No. 2, under the

baton of Vladimir Golschmann. (Either one of these works is a sufficient evening's work for a concert pianist). Despite the rage for jazz and ragtime in Paris at the time, during rehearsals the conservative trumpeters of the Théâtre de l'Opéra orchestra had only agreed to use derby hats as mutes (for the essential 'wah-wah' sound) when the rims were cut off and the hats painted gold, thereby resembling normal trumpet mutes.

As in New York, a Gershwin première generated an audience dotted with celebrities, this time including Maurice Chevalier, Diaghilev, Honegger and Prokofiev. Diaghilev described the new concerto as 'good jazz but bad Liszt'. To Prokofiev, it was not much more than 'a succession of thirty-two-bar choruses ineptly bridged together'. He was, however, intrigued by 'some of the pianistic invention' and invited Gershwin to his apartment the next day, accompanied by Vernon Duke, who reported that Gershwin 'played his head off' and that Prokofiev assured him he would go far if he left dollars and dinners alone.

Gershwin also met Ravel, at a party honouring his fifty-third birthday. Eva Gauthier had asked Ravel what he wanted as a present, and his request had been to meet Gershwin and listen to him play. A subsequent visit to Ravel gave rise to the perennial story that Gershwin asked him for lessons, to which the French master had replied: 'Why be a second-rate Ravel when you are a first-rate Gershwin?' It was almost as if Gershwin could not meet an international figure in music without asking to become a pupil. Most of the time his insecurity about his lack of musical training was compensated by his outward self-assurance. But he never knew when it might rise sharply to the surface, and in the presence of world figures in symphonic music he could be reduced to feeling he was the perpetrator of a fraud.

The final work on the programme at the New York première of his concerto had been Glazunov's Fifth Symphony. Several years later Gershwin was thrilled to meet this distinguished Russian composer after giving a performance of *Rhapsody in Blue* with the New York Philharmonic, a concert which Glazunov attended. They might have talked about almost anything except Gershwin's longing for tuition. Typically, he brought it up. When Glazunov's interpreter translated his urgent remark, 'tell him it has been the dream of my life to go to Russia to study orchestration under him', Glazunov's reply was so

The party to celebrate Maurice Ravel's fifty-third birthday: left to right, conductor Oscar Fried, party hostess Eva Gauthier, Ravel, Tedesco (conductor of the San Carlos Orchestra), George Gershwin

dismissive his interpreter had not the heart to relay it. 'He wants to study orchestration? He hasn't the slightest knowledge of counterpoint.' The awkward silence was broken when Glazunov managed to summon enough English to tell Gershwin he could not possibly give him orchestration lessons until he had mastered basic theory.

He asked Nadia Boulanger, but she advised him to concentrate on the type of music at which he was best. Without hurting his feelings by expressing it, she perceived that his restless personality – let alone his frenetic lifestyle – precluded the rigorous formal study for which she was renowned. He put the same question to Stravinsky, who – having asked how much Gershwin earned and being told the annual figure was 100,000 dollars – replied: 'Then maybe I should be taking lessons from you'. Stravinsky was the last composer to be ashamed of earning a good living from composing, but his remark (which he denied for years but was witnessed by a composer called Richard Hammond) emphasizes the guarded jealousy with which a majority of serious composers regarded the huge material success of this former song-plugger.

There was an underlying naïvety in Gershwin's obsession with seeking technical betterment from famous people, and it is difficult to see why world figures such as Glazunov, Ravel or Stravinsky should

take time out to give him lessons. They were full-time composers, not professors of composition. He did arrange counterpoint tuition from a lower-profile musician, the prolific American composer Henry Cowell, whose music explored ultra-modern techniques (such as tone-clusters played with the fist, and using 'prepared' pianos) which were developed further by his pupil, John Cage. Cowell said that when he called at Gershwin's apartment he might well find him wearing a silk dressing gown and giving instructions to his secretaries. When it came to doing some musical theory, 'Gershwin's fertile mind leaped all over the place' and he would suddenly insert 'juicy ninth chords' into an exercise meant to be in the strict style of Palestrina, the sixteenth century master of polyphony.

Gershwin's approaches to illustrious musicians could never have borne fruit because deep down he could not surrender to the long-term discipline needed – any more than he could truly surrender himself to the long-term responsibilities of marriage. Not until 1932 did he settle down to some productive training – not from a European celebrity, but in New York. It came from Joseph Schillinger, a Russian-born theorist who had evolved a mathematical approach to musical structure which Gershwin used to some advantage in his concert music after *An American in Paris*, and especially in his opera.

During his Paris visit in 1928 for the concerto's première he shopped around for a selection of taxi-horns to take home. In his mind was the idea for an orchestral piece that would feature the sound of Parisian traffic. He began to sketch it during his stay, but put it on one side while he completed what was to be his last European visit, a whirlwind tour in company with Ira and Leonore. In Berlin he met Kurt Weill and Franz Lehár, and in Vienna the orchestra of the famed Sacher Café struck up *Rhapsody in Blue* as the Gershwins entered, escorted by the operetta composer Emerich Kalman. Alban Berg honoured him at his home with a private performance of his *Lyric Suite*. When it had finished, Gershwin commandeered Berg's piano and performed some of his Broadway songs. Then he turned to the Austrian atonalist to ask how he could possibly like such wildly different music. Berg replied: 'Music is music.' Gershwin took home a portrait photo of Berg inscribed to him with a quotation from the *Lyric Suite* and hung it proudly among his art treasures. In 1931 he would make a point of interrupting a busy schedule to attend the

American première of Berg's opera *Wozzeck* in Philadelphia, conducted by Stokowski.

Taxi-horns were not the only items Gershwin put into his luggage. He bought the complete works of Debussy in eight volumes. As ever, he had no intention of playing Debussy, or any music apart from his own, in public. But his searching, often capricious mind compelled him to try and keep abreast of modern developments. He enthused about a Hindemith string quartet at a time when Hindemith was little-known in America. He was proud of a copy of the *Lyric Suite* score which Berg had autographed and given him in Vienna, and after hearing *Wozzeck* he bought the score for his library.

Back in New York in June 1928, he returned to the sketches begun in Paris. Despite work on *Treasure Girl* and its dismal box-office failure, within five months he had completed his first orchestral composition not to include a solo piano. The wording on the manuscript title-page is significant:

An American in Paris
A Tone Poem for Orchestra
Composed and Orchestrated by George Gershwin
Begun early in 1928, finished November 18, 1928

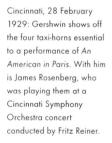

Cincinnati, 28 February 1929: Gershwin shows off the four taxi-horns essential to a performance of *An American in Paris*. With him is James Rosenberg, who was playing them at a Cincinnati Symphony Orchestra concert conducted by Fritz Reiner.

There is a sense of pride about this. He was clearly fed up with the insinuations about his inability to orchestrate. His use of 'tone poem' shows he is presenting a large-scale, one-movement work – the province of Liszt, Saint-Saëns, Richard Strauss, Elgar – that will tell a story rather than follow a purely musical discourse. Interviewed in *Musical America*, Gershwin declared that 'this new piece, really a rhapsodic ballet, is written very freely and is the most modern music I've yet attempted. The opening part is developed in typical French style, in the manner of Debussy and "Les Six", though the themes are all original.' But there is hardly a 'typical French style' of developing material; in addition, the opening is so American-sounding that Debussy would have been incapable of writing a bar of it, and 'Les Six' (the group of young French composers comprising Auric, Durey, Honegger, Milhaud, Poulenc and Tailleferre) were in fact anti-Debussy (though their music can show the breezy jauntiness Gershwin captures so well at the outset of his piece).

His outline of the story behind the music was more precise. 'My purpose is to portray the impressions of an American visitor in Paris as he strolls about the city, listens to the various street noises and absorbs the French atmosphere.' Freed from the previous responsibility of organizing his material in concerto form, Gershwin was back in his element as regards concert music – a freely-flowing 'rhapsodic' structure that could be full of tunes but not dependent on thematic development. That the overall shape of *An American in Paris* is indeed balletic rather than symphonic was effectively shown by Gene Kelly and Leslie Caron in the ballet sequence that ends the eponymous 1951 film musical. As a purely concert piece, it was once described by a BBC radio announcer as being 'in five sections held together more or less by intuition'.

Bernstein, for all his love of Gershwin's music, had no illusions about its diffuse construction. 'You rejoice in the first theme, then sit and wait through the "filler" until the next one comes along. In this way you sit out about two-thirds of the composition. The remaining third is marvellous because it consists of the themes themselves; but where's the composition?' A critique which, statistically, is unduly harsh but which did not prevent Bernstein from performing and recording the piece with sparkling *élan*. His first recording was early enough in his career to be on 78rpm discs, with the RCA Victor Symphony Orchestra.

An American in Paris is 'programme music' – that is, music which tells a story, in the sense that Richard Strauss had used the symphony orchestra to relate the exploits of the mischievous scamp *Till Eulenspiegl*, or Elgar to picture episodes from the life of Sir John Falstaff. Gershwin's 'tone poem' is a marked advance on his previous concert scores; in a good performance it does not seem to be bolstered by as much 'padding' as either *Rhapsody in Blue* or the first movement of the piano concerto. In place of the masterly treatment of themes Strauss or Elgar could bring to bear on their programme music, Gershwin's newly-found command of orchestral colour (including four saxophones) guarantees a kaleidoscope of effects that help sustain one of the jauntiest pieces in the repertoire.

It was first performed at Carnegie Hall on 13 December 1928, with Damrosch conducting the New York Philharmonic. The critic Deems Taylor had written a detailed programme note which went much further than the brief description Gershwin had provided, a storyline so picturesque that Gershwin gave it his enthusiastic approval. Taylor asks us to imagine, at the start, a visiting American swinging down the Champs Élysées. This is conveyed by the first of three 'walking themes' during which our tourist gets to various locations in the city. Gershwin's four real taxi-horns come into their own to suggest the mayhem of Parisian traffic. The American visitor subsequently passes a restaurant from which the strains of a popular song, *La Sorella*, are heard (on trombones), slackens his pace to pass a church (or maybe the Grand Palais), then crosses the Seine to the Left Bank for a leisurely drink on a café terrace.

Taylor now coyly suggests that a bridge-passage on solo violin represents a lady addressing the American visitor 'in the most charming broken English' in what he terms 'an unhallowed episode' – then hastens to add that maybe 'the whole episode is simply a musical transition'. In his two-piano version of the piece prior to orchestrating it, Gershwin had indeed written 'sees girl ... meets girl ... strolling flirtation'. Whatever the preferred storyline, the episode does serve as a transition. Just as in the slow movement of the piano concerto, Gershwin reaches for the strains of the orchestra leader's violin – momentarily echoing the 'klezmer' fiddling he heard in Brooklyn as a boy – improvising a bluesy solo on the first 'walking theme'.

Gene Kelly as an American
painter living in Paris, with
Oscar Levant at the piano –
a scene from Vincente
Minnelli's 1951 film musical,
An American in Paris

This plaintive solo leads to an attack of homesickness. Our tourist literally has the blues, and Gershwin presents one of the most memorable tunes he ever devised – a swooning, twelve-bar blues on a solo trumpet, stricter in its shape than the extended trumpet solo in the concerto, supported by cooing saxophones and jazz-style percussion (he originally thought of importing a jazz-style drum-kit as part of the instrumentation, then held to his symphonic ideals and assigned the percussion parts to regular orchestra personnel). The music seems to sink into a haze of nostalgia for things back home, then suddenly springs into life with a bouncy Charleston featuring two trumpets. Taylor's programme note suggests 'our hero must have met a compatriot. A wise-cracking orchestra proceeds to demonstrate that it's always fair weather when two Americans get together.' After a huge, elaborately-orchestrated climax of the blues theme, 'the orchestra, in a riotous finale, decides to make a night of it. It will be great to get home; but meanwhile, this is Paris!'

Gershwin faced the usual barrage of mixed reviews; he must have
come to expect them. They ranged from 'nauseous claptrap, vulgar
and inane; pitifully futile and inept' (Herbert Peyser in the *Telegram*)
to Olin Downes, who acknowledged 'a material gain in workmanship
and structure'. As Gershwin said, the judgement of the great mass
finally decides. The piece holds a secure place in the orchestral
repertoire regardless of its formlessness, or whether listeners are aware
of the 'programme'.

It received the ultimate accolade when Toscanini – who never
conducted any Gershwin during the composer's lifetime – performed
it in 1943. Later he made a highly-charged recording of it with the
NBC Symphony Orchestra. In 1942 he had made his Gershwin début
conducting *Rhapsody in Blue*, with Benny Goodman playing the
clarinet solo and Earl Wild the piano. (Earl Wild went on to compose
and perform transcendentally difficult *Virtuoso Etudes* on some of
Gershwin's songs, and a *Grand Fantasy on Airs from 'Porgy and Bess'*).
At that first attempt Toscanini was clearly not at home in Gershwin's
jazzy style. But he was entirely won over by 1944, when he partnered
Oscar Levant in the concerto. 'Gershwin's music is the only real
American music,' pronounced the Italian maestro who had achieved
god-like status on the American musical scene.

Lasting about eighteen minutes, *An American in Paris* has rounded-
off concerts as a generous and unexpected encore (launched into) by
the American conductor Lorin Maazel, on tour with the Pittsburgh
Symphony Orchestra. The most unusual rendering of it, however,
must surely be a piano-roll cut in 1933 and now available on compact
disc. The piano-roll industry had virtually collapsed by then due to
the Depression, but the Aeolian Company still issued a limited
number, and they kept in employment one of their outstanding 'roll
editors', Frank Milne. He had worked closely with Gershwin and was
so skilled at overdubbing holes in the punched paper rolls that he had
gone beyond the need for a pianist actually to sit down and play.
Drawing lines on a kind of graph paper, he painstakingly punched in
every note of a piano-duet arrangement of *An American in Paris*. It is a
tour de force of a lost art, made all the more poignant because the roll
was labelled as being played by 'Milne and Leith' ('Leith' was one of
Milne's pseudonyms). The Aeolian Company felt the public had to
believe such a complex sound could only be the result of two real

pianists at one keyboard. As the note-packed roll threaded through their pianola at home, few listeners could have realized it was the work of one tenacious technician with a ruler and a hole-punch.

Gershwin was not particularly interested in cinema and would rarely 'go to the movies'. But in 1930 he could not resist an invitation for himself and Ira to spend a few months in Hollywood providing the music for a film called *Delicious* – particularly when Fox Studios offered him 70,000 dollars and a coach on the New York–Hollywood train reserved entirely for the Gershwins and their associates. After the frenzy of New York, the sunshine and easy living in the film capital suited the easy-going Ira, but although George at first liked it his cynicism was to increase.

Even on this first visit during the winter of 1930, he saw how the balmy Californian climate and the huge fees negotiated for little artistic effort might easily seduce a workaholic such as himself into taking things easy. Borrowing from material he had already written, he spent seven unpressured weeks on the score only to find that four songs, a 'dream sequence' and one minute from a six-minute orchestral sequence were all that would be incorporated in the film. The old urge never to waste good manuscript came to the fore. Why not work-up that six-minute sequence into a concert score?

By the time he arrived back in New York in February 1931 he had sketched the new work. Hollywood was good for his bank balance but far too shallow for his musical goals. He was plain about it in a letter to Isaac Goldberg. 'I wanted to write a serious composition and found the opportunity in California. Nearly everybody comes back from California with a western tan and a pocket full of motion picture money. I decided to come back with both these things and a serious composition. The old artistic soul must be appeased every so often.'

By May he had completed a fourteen-minute piece for solo piano and orchestra. As usual he wavered between various titles. The film sequence had pictured the noise and activity of Manhattan, giving rise to an obsessive 'riveting' motif in Gershwin's music that was meant to suggest construction work on a skyscraper. After initially labelling his sketch *Rhapsody in Rivets*, he could not decide between *New York Rhapsody* and *Manhattan Rhapsody*. Finally – as with the concerto – city names were discarded and it became plain *Second Rhapsody*. The rest of the title was 'for orchestra with piano', a curious reversal of

normal terminology which also applies to *Rhapsody in Blue* and the
'*I Got Rhythm' Variations*.

The *Second Rhapsody* has never enjoyed anything approaching the
popularity of its predecessor. Ironically, its construction is far more
'symphonic' (the word Gershwin liked to use) and the whole
conception is more ambitious, not least because he has moved a long
way from handing Grofé his piano sketches and seeing him nimbly
adapt them for Whiteman's band. His own use of the orchestra is
assured, with bright and jazzy effects he certainly did not get out of
Forsyth's *Orchestration*, and more concentrated interplay between
soloist and orchestra. The 'riveting' rhythm chugs away in various
departments, and at one climactic moment is banged out on one of
the timpani. The piano sets off with a series of 'rivets' hammered in by
both hands, the first eight of them on one note. From then on
Gershwin makes this a genuinely unifying motif, syncopated against
cross-rhythms that give the music his usual 'pep'.

When we arrive at the romantic central section, the tempo slows
just as it did in *Rhapsody in Blue*, and the violins introduce a
beautifully caressing melody that is technically finer than the famous
one in the earlier rhapsody (with which it shares the feature of an
octave leap downwards). In this melody the phrases do not keep
coming to a halt; it has a breadth of line and a soaring, vocal quality
that pre-echoes *There's a Boat Dat's Leavin' Soon* in *Porgy and Bess*.
Compared with the simple chords that lie under the *Rhapsody in Blue*
tune, here the harmony is constantly shifting. The energetic music of
the first part returns (essentially the piece is a big ABA structure) and
at the very end, as in his concerto, Gershwin 'signs off' with his
beloved pentatonic scale in loud octaves on the piano.

He gave a scintillating account of the very difficult solo part at the
Boston première under Serge Koussevitsky on 29 January 1932. This
was eight months after its completion, an unusually long time for
Gershwin to get his new work before the public, and the result of
vainly awaiting confirmation that Toscanini might give a prestigious
première in New York, where he was music director of the
Philharmonic. Koussevitsky, however, proved an ideal collaborator
because he had consistently championed new American music as
conductor of the Boston Symphony Orchestra since 1924, and was
bedazzled by Gershwin's pianism.

As was becoming the norm, the packed audience loved the piece but press criticism was lukewarm. Inevitably, reviewers compared the two rhapsodies and most of them decided that, although Gershwin's technical advancement was plain to hear, the spontaneous swagger of the first rhapsody was missing. The new piece seemed contrived and too long for its material. Above all, the tunes were not as catchy or memorable. When the same forces gave the New York première a few days later its reception was much warmer, with the critic W. J. Henderson coining a phrase that could easily be applied to so much of Gershwin at his best: 'It is full of youth and recklessness, it is America of untrammelled manners and cocktail energy.' The public has made the final decision – although the piece produces a striking impact in the concert hall it is the tunes from the first rhapsody the world will go on humming.

A few months after the première, Gershwin got together with a few friends and took a carefree holday in Havana. When he had been a youngster and hearing a piece of music for the first time, this instinctive melodist was more likely to be attracted by the tune above all else. But the fully-fledged composer was alert to new harmonies and especially to new rhythms, and in Havana it was the rhythmic

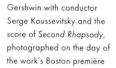

Gershwin with conductor Serge Koussevitsky and the score of *Second Rhapsody*, photographed on the day of the work's Boston première

aspect of Latin-American music that caught his ear. Moreover, the rhythmic pulse was created by a selection of exotic percussion instruments not normally associated with a symphony orchestra: claves (short wooden sticks), maracas (modern versions of a pair of hollowed-out fruits called gourds, containing beads or other objects that rattle when shaken), the guiro (a serrated gourd scraped with a stick) and bongos (small drums rapped with the fingers). He was fired with the idea of putting these sounds into a new orchestral piece. Just as he had bought taxi-horns in Paris, he took home samples of these four instruments and began to write a piece named *Rumba*.

He spelled out his intentions in a formal programme note for its first performance. 'I have endeavoured to combine the Cuban rhythms with my own thematic material. The result is a symphonic overture which embodies the essence of Cuban dance. It has three main parts.' He went on to summarize the three parts in almost exclusively technical terms, as though he was out to impress his readers with musical jargon. This seems all the more inappropriate given that its first performance was not in a concert hall before musical *cognoscenti*, but at the Lewisohn Stadium, a huge outdoor venue in New York where all-Gershwin concerts would become a regular feature after the success of this first one. Five thousand people had to be turned away for lack of space; the remaining 18,000 applauded him with the kind of enthusiasm generated at the 'Three Tenors' concerts of the 1990s.

Examples of composers visiting a foreign country and bringing back inspiration for a concert overture are legion, one of the most famous being the overture *The Hebrides* which sprang from a visit Mendelssohn made to Scotland. But when Gershwin uses the words 'symphonic overture', he is not getting involved in the old bug-bear 'sonata form', which Mendelssohn used brilliantly to contain his impressions of 'Fingal's Cave' in the Hebrides, and which had been the principal basis for overtures since Mozart and Rossini (Bernstein managed to use it to great effect in his Glinka-inspired, 'pastiche' overture for *Candide*). But overtures have long grown out of their classical straight-jacket, and composers such as Tchaikovsky, Berlioz, Elgar and William Walton used the term very flexibly. Gershwin revisits the overall shape of the *Second Rhapsody* – two energetic sections framing a much slower one.

Gershwin drew little pictures of the Cuban instruments on the title page of his manuscript, explaining they should be positioned in front of the orchestra near the conductor. He was disappointed that they lost their impact at the première in the open-air acoustic. The capacity audience could not have found the piece as easy to take on first hearing as the other Gershwin favourites on the programme. The beginning sounds unsettled – a Cuban carnival that careers through various keys before settling into the 'home' one, and even then not for very long. Gershwin had been taking advice from Schillinger as regards orchestration, and although the piece is 'busy' with notes he did achieve more clarity and expertise than ever before. The central episode is in sultry, dreamy contrast to the riotous goings-on around it, and Gershwin leads into it with an unexpectedly Yiddish turn of phrase rather than a Latin-American one. Over a soft timpani roll, a 'klezmer-style' clarinet solo provides the only moment of stillness.

At the stadium, William Daly shared the conductor's podium with the English conductor Albert Coates, who was in charge of *Rumba*. Not the first name to come to mind for Gershwin's music, Coates was nevertheless a respected guest conductor in America. Born in Russia and formerly principal conductor at St Petersburg's Mariinsky theatre, he could claim that the first British performances of Prokofiev's Third Concerto and Rachmaninov's Fourth were conducted by him, with their respective composers at the piano. The next performance of *Rumba* was at the Metropolitan Opera House, when Gershwin himself conducted. By then he had decided to give it a new title that actually used the word 'overture', since he felt Rumba had too much of a dance-band connotation. As *Cuban Overture*, it has held its place in the orchestral repertoire.

In 1933 Gershwin moved to what proved to be his last New York address, a fourteen-room duplex on East 72nd Street styled with a traditional elegance, rather than the 1920s chrome and glass of 33 Riverside Drive. There was a gymnasium and an artist's studio, and ample space to display his magnificent art collection and his own paintings. The apartment was commensurate with the lifestyle of one of America's highest-paid musicians. As always, Ira was not far away; he and Leonore moved to an address across the street. On a special composing desk George himself designed, he completed what was to be his final concert piece, *Variations on 'I Got Rhythm'*.

It would be gratifying if this premature farewell to the concert hall showed Gershwin enlarging his command of thematic development and consolidating his symphonic ambitions. But although the variations are witty, always showing the sense of fun he had when improvising around his show tunes, the overall impression is that he wrote them quickly as a diversion (especially since he was about to start a month-long concert tour and needed an alternative to the inevitable first rhapsody or the piano concerto, which concert managers kept on requesting). In any case, the tour featured a 'pick-up' ensemble called the Leo Reisman Orchestra, conducted by Charles Previn, and at around thirty musicians it was necessary to scale down his normal orchestral forces – though he made sure there was room for the four saxophones that so effectively coloured *An American in Paris*. (The published 1953 score, doctored by Schoenfeld, indicated that saxophones were optional and generally made unwarranted 'improvements' to Gershwin's transparent instrumentation.)

Any hope of us knowing what he would have made further of 'sonata form' – which he had avoided since paying homage to it in the opening movement of the concerto – is now abandoned. At least, this last concert piece, in its variation form, does get away from the three-part ABA form of *Lullaby*, the *Second Rhapsody* and the *Cuban Overture*, and the intuitive patchwork that manages to hold *Rhapsody in Blue* and *An American in Paris* together.

A solo clarinet eases in the first four notes at the start, extends them, and is answered by the piano. This all sounds innocent, but belies the intensity with which Gershwin was by now in thrall to Schillinger. The notes in these opening bars are first an expansion then a contraction of Gershwin's tune. The intervals between the notes are derived with such meticulous numerical logic that, in his treatise 'The Schillinger System of Musical Composition', the distinguished professor quotes them under the label 'Geometric Expansions of George Gershwin's *I Got Rhythm*'. It might even be that Schillinger came up with these bars and Gershwin put them in as a deliberate tribute. Underneath its carefree surface, many more applications of Schillinger's mathematical procedures can be discovered throughout the piece. Gershwin, according to Schillinger, got so excited that he exclaimed, 'You don't have to compose any more. It's all there.' This is merely typical of the boyish enthusiasm he

Gershwin at the piano with the Reisman Orchestra during their strenuous 1934 tour, for which he wrote *Variations on 'I Got Rhythm'*

never lost. No amount of methodology could have made Gershwin's music live had he not been so prodigiously musical in the first place.

After a rousing climax on the orchestra, the piano plays the whole song, before flying into a tricky series of embellishments two octaves apart while the tune stays with the accompanying players. For the second variation the tempo changes to waltz time, the piano seeming to sigh with pleasure as the orchestra slowly breathes the theme. After some Lisztian fireworks, Gershwin goes into what he called 'a Chinese variation in which I imitate Chinese flutes played out of tune, as they always are'. This cheekiness is accomplished by having the pianist splash around the pentatonic scale as though his fingers are too big for the keys. Once and for all, Gershwin's pentatonic leanings are positively identified with the Orient (we had a taste of this in *Rhapsody in Blue*), since the scale is the backbone of Chinese music and, using only the black keys of the piano, anyone can make up a Chinese-sounding tune. The next variation sounds like 'stripper music', with the basses slapping their strings, the jazz drummer

brushing his cymbals, and bluesy variants of the theme on the woodwind. At the start of the exuberant final section the piano's repeated chords were described by Gershwin as 'the rhythmic variation in which the left hand plays the melody upside down and the right plays it straight, on the theory that you shouldn't let one hand know what the other is doing'.

Plainly, Gershwin had a lot of fun dashing off this piece (most of it was done during a three-week vacation in Palm Springs), and it is also fun to play. Despite the methodology, the variations work as music. On the published two-piano arrangement, though not on the full score, he wrote the dedication: 'To my brother Ira' – the only instance in any of his compositions. If we have regrets that his last contribution to concert music was distinctly lightweight, they can be tempered by the realization that, three months before its première in Boston, Gershwin had signed a contract with the Theatre Guild for an opera based on Heyward's novel *Porgy*. His mind was already full of grander things, which would draw on the consummate talents of both Gershwin brothers.

The epigrammatic Three Preludes for piano solo, published in 1927, had a very convoluted history. As early as 1917 Gershwin was experimenting with little piano pieces he called 'Novelettes'. Two years later, still little known as a composer, he managed to persuade his piano-roll company to issue his performance of one of them, *Novelette in Fourths*. Although at the time he did not rate these pieces highly, he came to realize they could be worth promoting. In 1925 he gave permission to the violinist Samuel Dushkin – a child prodigy who had studied with the great violinists Leopold Auer and Fritz Kreisler – to join *Novelette in Fourths* on to another *Novelette* and transcribe the resulting piece for violin and piano. It was given the title *Short Story*.

Subsequently, Gershwin took the original piano versions of those two *Novelettes* and added three more, performing this set of five 'Preludes' in 1926. The following year, he published these three added pieces under the title Three Preludes, in the form they are known to us. But Gershwin played six preludes in a Boston recital in 1927. What happened to number six? It is assumed he improvised on a melody called *Sleepless Night*, which can be found in a 1924 sketchbook. He returned to this fragment in 1936, shortly after he and Ira arrived in Hollywood to work on *Shall We Dance?*, and turned the sketch into a

'song without words'. After George's death Ira tried to write a lyric, considering it to be his favourite unpublished Gershwin tune, but in the end decided that *Sleepless Night* was ideally left as a piano solo.

Gershwin talked of composing a complete set of twenty-four piano preludes under the title *The Melting Pot*. This would inevitably be compared with the twenty-four preludes by Chopin, spanning all the major and minor keys. Nothing came of this project except the three published ones, which he dedicated to William Daly and which show Gershwin's preference for ABA structure. Not only is each individual prelude in this pattern, but – considered as a set – two athletic preludes frame a moody, blues-laden slow one. They are so well-contrasted and the three pieces seem to belong so happily together that, had Gershwin been inclined to write a tiny Sonata, he might easily have come up with this triptych.

The first and third preludes are both marked Allegro ben ritmato e deciso (quick, very rhythmic and decisive), and they need strong hands and a firm technique. The driving rhythm of the first prelude seems to be a mix of Charleston and Rhumba (Gershwin spelled his original *Cuban Overture* title without the letter 'h'). In Gershwin's own recording, made by Columbia in London in 1928, he comes off the rails towards the end, but neither he nor his recording producer went for a better 'take' – strange, since the last prelude is dashed off brilliantly. The main theme of this third prelude shows a close resemblance to *Rialto Ripples*, his 1917 piano rag. He marked the middle one to be played Andante con moto e poco rubato (moving along, with some flexibility within the tempo).

There are two interesting aspects to his use of these tempo markings. For all his trail-blazing, Gershwin conservatively marked his concert pieces with traditional Italian terms, as though to give their Americanism an extra air of respectability. Later American composers, in common with European ones, would use colloquial English when it helped make the meaning clearer. Secondly, his recording of the middle prelude is an outstanding example of how he could disregard his own indications, leaving others to find more tender interpretations. He plays it faster than anyone would today, in strict tempo (so much for rubato – that is, 'robbed time'), devoid of sentiment and with a matter-of-factness that to our ears seems to go against the soulful quality of the music. Almost perversely, the playing

sounds as though Gershwin is oblivious to the beauties he has put on paper.

He was content to offer his own playing as a straightforward blueprint, almost a pianola roll, and he enjoyed hearing other pianists bringing their personal view to the music. If played romantically, the very opening of this prelude turns into 'blue Chopin'. Even on the page, the rocking left hand figuration looks like the start of Chopin's Impromptu No. 2 in F sharp. In both pieces the right hand soon joins with a flowing melody that cries out for the subtle rubato inflections Gershwin pointedly avoids. His melody combines the blues with Jewish nostalgia; many Yiddish lullaby-tunes have a rocking motion between two notes a third apart, which characterises this lovely theme and which is prominent in the title-song from *Funny Face* and in *'S Wonderful.*

The preludes lend themselves to all manner of transcriptions. Heifetz arranged them for violin and piano and played them as encores. The middle prelude in particular has attracted arrangements good and bad. One by Irwin Kostal for two pianos (recorded by the Labèque Sisters) inexplicably adds an extra twelve bars of mock 'improvisation' to Gershwin's central blues section, destroying the symmetry for no artistic purpose. The arranger Dave Grusin, on the other hand, shows the limitless possibilities inherent in this second prelude when approached imaginatively. Using clarinet, keyboards, bass guitar, string bass and drums, he extends the music and creates a world of colour in an almost 'funky' style – worlds away from Gershwin's straight-faced interpretation. Whereas Gershwin ends on a sustained blue chord, Grusin slowly fades into the stratosphere, affectionately quoting reminiscences of *Rhapsody in Blue.*

Gershwin's no-nonsense approach to his own music is again apparent in the recordings he made of various songs. They give a good idea of his pounding style and the way he effortlessly changed key as he improvised chorus after chorus. The pianola and Remick's cubicle never seem far away because – unlike his playing in his recordings of *Rhapsody in Blue* and the Finale of his concerto (we do not have the other two movements) – the music ploughs on in a crisp, relentless mezzo forte with scarcely a change of dynamic. This was an effective kind of pianism for playing at rehearsals of his shows, when the producer might be shouting instructions to the dancers – or at parties,

where it would survive any amount of nearby chatter and laughter. It seems out of place in the intimacy of a recording studio, but Gershwin was clearly uninterested in subtle effects for posterity.

Greatly reduced versions of these improvisations are crystallized in *George Gershwin's Song Book*, a collection of eighteen of his best-known Broadway tunes which his publisher persuaded him to arrange for piano solo, and which he dedicated to Kay Swift. They are tantalizingly short – mostly two pages of score that encapsulate the melodic and rhythmic tricks he would embroider around his tunes by the hour. The publishers asked Isaac Goldberg to 'ghost write' a preface. Gershwin rejected it, saying it did not sound like his own style of writing. He made them print his own, complete with a chauvinist swipe at girl pianists.

The publishers cannot be blamed for getting out simplified versions of songs, since the majority of the purchasers of popular music are little girls with little hands, who have not progressed very far with their study of the piano. Gradually, with the general increase of technical skill at the piano, there has arisen a demand for arrangements that shall consider that skill. Hence, in this book, the transcriptions for solo piano of each chorus. Some of these are very difficult; they have been put in for those good pianists, of whom there is a growing number, who enjoy popular music but who rebel at the too-simple arrangements issued by the publishers with the average pianist in view.

Gershwin goes on to summarize the evolution of America's popular pianistic style, from the introduction of ragtime just before the Spanish–American War to the culminating point in the jazz era that followed the Great War. He lists a roster of names that crowd into his memory (some forgotten today), proving how assiduously he had sought out the most influential pianists in Harlem clubs and noted aspects of their style that he could use for himself.

... Mike Bernard, Les Copeland, Melville Ellis, Luckey Roberts, Zez Confrey, Arden and Ohman, and others. There was the habit Les Copeland had of thumping his left hand onto a blurred group of notes, from which he would slide into a regular chord. Then there was Bernard's habit of playing the melody in the left hand, while he wove a filigree of

counterpoint with the right. To all of these predecessors I am indebted;
some of the effects I use in my transcriptions derive from their style of
playing the piano.

And not only in his transcriptions. They became an integral part of
his writing for piano generally. He ends by explaining why his own
playing is so 'stencilled' – a good choice of word.

To play American popular music most effectively one must guard
against the natural tendency to make too frequent use of the sustaining
pedal. Our study of the great romantic composers has trained us in the
method of the legato, whereas our popular music asks for staccato effects,
for almost a stencilled style. The rhythms of American popular music are
more or less brittle; they should be made to snap, and at times cackle. The
more sharply the music is played, the more effective it sounds. Most
pianists with a classical training fail lamentably in the playing of our
ragtime or jazz because they use the pedalling of Chopin when
interpreting the blues of Handy [W. C. Handy, famous for St. Louis
Blues *among others]. The romantic touch is very good in a sentimental*
ballad, but in a tune of strict rhythm it is somewhat out of place.

As for the music itself, the over-riding impression given by these
highly-condensed transcriptions is how consistently interesting each
one is. He seems to be looking at the tunes as if they are brand-new
and seeing what he can do with them. Although the piano textures
change every few bars, showing a wealth of invention, in a larger
sense each song seems to have its own set of rhythmic motifs and
accompaniment figurations that distinguishes it from its neighbours.
He cannot just sit down and write something ordinary. *Who Cares*,
for example, emerges as an example of George deliberately
undercutting Ira's lyrics. This was a Depression song, with lines such
as: 'Who cares what banks fail in Yonkers / As long as we've got a love
that conquers.' The song is usually heard as a typically brassy,
showbiz number. But, adapting it for piano solo, he marks the tempo
as 'Rather slow' and gives the left hand loping, jerky interjections
that seem to be trying to derail the melody. The words said love is
going to conquer; shorn of them, the baleful music gives the lie
to that.

Golf – one of Gershwin's favourite sports – was a release from intensive periods of composing, and proved well-suited to his energetic, competitive nature.

Gershwin's piano transcriptions of his songs show his masterly use of complex, colourful chords and harmonic progressions that are equally at home in Debussy's music, although the two composers were using a similar harmonic vocabulary for different expressive purposes. There is a story that Debussy was given two months to deliver a finished manuscript. 'Two months? It takes me that long to decide between two chords!' For Debussy, each chord was an emotional experience in itself, a colouring of the melodic line; he would use chords not to progress from one harmonic centre to another, but for the gorgeous sounds they provided in themselves. His well-known prelude, *La Cathédrale engloutie* ('The Submerged Cathedral') is a typical example. Chains of chords create wistfulness and nostalgia

simply because they are 'unresolved'; that is, a sense of progression from one harmonic point to another is almost entirely lost. For Gershwin, these same highly-coloured chords (we might call them 'juicy') are used in a more functional way, supporting the melody line in ways we can analyse according to the basics of chromatic harmony. When he does become highly-chromatic, there still remains an underlying discipline. A good example is his note-packed transcription of his song *Liza*, written in the key of five flats (D flat major, a Debussy favourite) and stuffed with sliding 'passing-notes'.

Gershwin said that Hambitzer made him 'harmony-conscious'. There is no doubt that, compared with the simplistic harmonization of the popular, commercial tunes the young boy was hearing at every turn, exploring music by the great masters with Hambitzer opened up tantalizing avenues. But, despite his lifelong desire to take formal instruction from musicians he admired, Gershwin relied heavily on an instinctive response to chords and other musical features. His was an acute ear, and if he liked some detail he heard in another composer's music, he had an uncanny knack of knowing how to use it without necessarily being able to explain what he was doing in a technical sense. Isaac Goldberg wrote that Gershwin, even at the time of *Rhapsody in Blue*, 'knew as much harmony as could be found in a ten-cent manual'. If this seems harsh, we have the composer's own admission that many of the chords he used throughout his career 'were set down without any particular attention to their theoretical structure. When my critics tell me that now and then I betray a structural weakness, they are not telling me anything I don't know.' Pieces with complex harmonization such as the *Liza* transcription are therefore a triumph of instinctive harmonic awareness, because they can be analysed according to established rules and still pass the test.

The Austrian theorist Heinrich Schenker (1868–1935) developed a unique method of converting musical scores into graphical sketches, to show how all music of any value has a rigorous inner logic. He became a cult figure, and in 1995 Steven Gilbert – a professor at California State University – published a book meticulously analysing Gershwin's entire output according to Schenker's methods, which were never intended for music later than Brahms. This unusual enterprise does impress, with its complicated proofs demonstrating the inner musical logic of Gershwin's melodies and of his contrapuntal

and harmonic structures. The fact remains that, having fed Gershwin through Schenker's musical atom-splitter, the resultant fallout would surely have left George chuckling and speechless at his own latent ingenuity. He once remarked: 'I wrote a whole thirty-two bar chorus in canon' (one melodic strand of music imitating another, following at a distance), 'and if someone told me it was a canon, I'd laugh in his face.' Despite his self-doubts, he became wonderfully competent at his craft. But there is no question of inordinate technical prowess; rather, the best of his music has an organic coherence that was partly intuitive, partly due to his voracious appetite for trying to learn how other composers put well-structured pieces together, and partly the result of unending experimentation at the keyboard.

Gershwin's remaining non-Broadway music consists of material too brief for concert performance but thankfully rescued from oblivion and available on compact disc. *Merry Andrew* is his arrangement of a dance from the musical *Rosalie*, and its pentatonic tune skips along merrily. *Violin Piece* and *For Lily Pons* were found among his sketches after his death and have been realized for performance by Michael Tilson Thomas. The former was given its title by Ira in remembrance of the young violinist Max Rosen, and the latter because the three-page sketch seemed to be written with a separate melody above the piano part. Ira decided it could have been a song George had started to write for the French soprano Lily Pons. Finally, two tiny sketches show Gershwin playing around with matters which the jazz pianist/composer Dave Brubeck would turn to years later. *Impromptu in Two Keys* reveals Gershwin flirting with bitonal harmony in 1929; from about the same period, *Three-Quarter Blues* has him putting the four-square blues structure into three-four waltz time.

There was a driving force behind Gershwin's concert music: the aspiration of a largely self-taught song-plugger to establish his credentials as a 'serious' composer, without compromising his obsession with integrating elements of jazz and popular American music within what he called 'symphonic' structures. Gershwin, a child of immigrants to a new country, inherited his parents' drive to be more American than anybody, and children born with his degree of toughness and ambition needed to be Number One in their field. Ira could have settled for being a book-keeper. For George to be Number One, his name had to be outside Carnegie Hall as well as on the

placards of Broadway. Naked ambition propelled him to write fugues and ask Stravinsky for lessons.

The critics, at first bewildered by what he was doing, split into those who saw things beneficial to American art music and those eager to jump on the 'crudities' and 'triteness' in his scores. These failings have always worried the critics more than the public, for whom Gershwin had a not-so-secret weapon: his tunes. One of the ironies he never resolved was that the more technically proficient his music became, the harder it had to work to gain acceptance. The *Second Rhapsody* is, in terms of construction and execution, superior to *Rhapsody in Blue*. But, when it comes to the tunes, there is no contest. *Cuban Overture* is more intricately designed and more contrapuntally challenging than *An American in Paris*, but its themes are elusive to the memory once the piece has finished, compared with the jaunty 'walking' tunes and the inspired trumpet blues that accompany our tour around the French capital.

The ideal balance seems to have been achieved only once, in the *Concerto in F*, where the all-American Gershwin grabbed the classical concerto by the throat and poured tune after tune into his metamorphosis of a respected, European art-form. Effects such as the gong stroke, putting a stop to the mad whirl of recollected themes and rising sequences which Gershwin has got himself into, and giving him a pause for breath to work out how on earth he is going to end the piece, have no right to 'work'. But in performance they do. The force of his personality and the sincerity of his intent nearly always manage to overcome the deficiencies in his technique.

Gershwin's non-Broadway music spread the sound of America throughout the world's concert halls as no previous American composer had ever done. His contemporaries in the serious music field who derided his efforts were not entirely innocent of jealousy. Here was a young Broadway songwriter of enormous glamour and wealth, going around talking about rhapsodies and 'symphonic sound' while they were perhaps locked into unrewarding teaching and journalistic chores – or, if composers, maybe struggling to maintain themselves between commissions.

Meanwhile Gershwin kept on worrying about how he could measure up to his symphonic peers. If he had looked at the score of Elgar's *Cockaigne* overture – the work of another largely self-taught

musician – he would surely have marvelled at the technical expertise with which the Englishman conducts us through Edwardian London, compared with his own orchestral picture of 1920s Paris. Did he ever hear Dohnányi's *Variations on a Nursery Song* (composed in 1914), in which the Hungarian pianist-composer took the simplest of tunes and wrought a marvellous set of variations for piano and orchestra? If he did, could he perhaps admit to himself how far they out-distanced what he had done with *I Got Rhythm*? In the same year that *Cuban Overture* was first performed, Copland visited Mexico and brought back the inspiration for his witty and brilliantly-scored *El salón México*, a direct parallel to Gershwin's piece in its use of exotic rhythms and Latin-American percussion. Could Gershwin ever achieve the sense of structure which makes Copland's more extended piece hold so well together, or his translucent orchestration? All of this does not alter a simple fact: a concert of the Gershwin pieces will sell out faster than one offering the Elgar, the Dohnányi and the Copland.

Gershwin's lack of academic training – and his yearning to correct it – does not trouble his listeners. It was his own problem, and to a chronic degree. It is a pity the psychoanalysts he came to rely on towards the end of his life could not reinforce something he felt deep-down anyway: that the very process of learning the academic rules of counterpoint to perfection would go against his innate musical personality and spoil, rather than enhance, the products of his inspiration. Down the ages, every worthwhile composer takes what he needs from inherited tradition and adapts it to suit his own voice. A student who could resist putting a juicy ninth chord into a Palestrina-style exercise would be able eventually to turn out perfect specimens of sixteenth century Italian counterpoint. Whether he could go on to write *Concerto in F*, let alone *Porgy and Bess*, is another question.

6

Gershwin working on the
piano sketch of *Porgy and
Bess*

*Do you think that now I am capable of grand
opera? Because, you know, all I've got is a lot of
talent and plenty of 'chutzpah'.*

George Gershwin,
quoted by Jerome Kern in 1938

Porgy and Bess

Porgy and Bess is the most successful American opera of the twentieth century. Gershwin had always aspired to write a full-length, American musical drama, and although it was not until the mid 1930s that his compositional technique was equal to the task, he had always been searching for the right story. He told his biographer Isaac Goldberg in 1931: 'I'd like to write an opera of the melting pot, of New York City itself, with its blend of native and immigrant strains.' (*The Melting Pot* had been the title of his projected twenty-four piano preludes.) The score would allow the inclusion of many musical types – Eastern and Western, black and white – and he would attempt a fusion of this diversity into an artistic unity. 'Here is a challenge to a librettist, and to my own muse. I'd rather fail at this than achieve a passable duplication of an already consecrated style.' He referred to New York as 'a rendezvous of the nations', and he wanted to catch the rhythms of these interfusing peoples. 'I'd especially like to blend the humour of it with the tragedy of it.'

When he used the term 'chutzpah' to describe his ambition to step from Broadway into grand opera, it was no exaggeration. Hebrew for 'brazen audacity', the word has by tradition defined the attitude of an imaginary character who slays his parents then applies to the court for clemency as an orphan. Twice in his career, Gershwin had come close to writing a theatre piece about Jews rather than blacks. He would have put his hand to something akin to a Jewish operetta as far back as 1915, when the impresario Boris Thomashevsky tried to organize a collaboration between Remick's teenaged song-plugger and Sholom Secunda, a musician four years older than George with extensive knowledge of Jewish music. He had studied at what is now the Julliard School of Music, and had already published a Yiddish counterpart to the hit-song *Home! Sweet Home!*. Thomashevsky reckoned their combined talents would ensure a hit for his National Theatre. Secunda would hear none of it. It was beneath him to work with someone who had not published anything and who, apparently, played the piano mainly by ear.

In the contract Gershwin signed with the New York Metropolitan Opera in October 1929 'to compose the music for a new opera, the libretto and title of which are to be known as Dybbuk', he undertook to supply the score by April 1931, allowing eighteen months – exactly the time he would take to complete *Porgy and Bess*. (In Jewish folklore a 'dybbuk' is the malevolent, disembodied spirit of a deceased person which enters a living being and has to be painfully exorcized.) The serious nature of this agreement proves that, even though he had read *Porgy* in 1926 and had talked to DuBose Heyward about his operatic ambitions for it, three years later he was none the less ready to clear his desk for an opera on a Jewish subject commissioned by America's most prestigious opera company. Gershwin, Jewish-born and thoroughly assimilated into American society, was at this point turning to his own roots rather than to those of black music, or to the multi-racial melting pot of New York.

He had already shown a degree of 'chutzpah' over the Met commission. He would need to orchestrate the opera himself, since the Met would not have been satisfied with a Gershwin piece orchestrated by another name, as was the practice on Broadway. The agreement stipulated the delivery of a full orchestral score and chorus parts. Gershwin must have felt as confident about this in 1929 as he did six years later orchestrating *Porgy*. Michael Feinstein recalls visiting Ira with the actress Lauren Bacall shortly after the première of Stephen Sondheim's musical *Sweeney Todd* in 1979. A devoted fan of Sondheim's work, she remarked that his new piece was more like an opera than a Broadway musical. Ira asked if the orchestrations were Sondheim's, and Feinstein replied that they were not. 'Then it's not really an opera. George worked for eight months on just the orchestration of *Porgy*. Unless a composer orchestrates it himself, it's not a true opera.'

Gershwin planned to use Shlomo Ansky's 1914 play *The Dybbuk* as the basis of his opera for the Met, but in the event, the rights to the play were found to be already held by an Italian composer, Lodovico Rocca. He was actually setting the story to music between 1928 and 1930, and his *Il Dibuk* had its première in Milan in 1934. In the words of *Grove's Dictionary of Music and Musicians*, the score 'juxtaposes modality, orientalisms, stark parallel 2nds and other dissonances, while the orchestration is sometimes bizarre, even macabre.' A far cry from Gershwin even at his most adventurous. Rocca's ownership having

been established, the Met had no option but to annul the contract. Typically, Gershwin had already got busy on some sketches, which, unfortunately for posterity, have disappeared.

In 1928 Gershwin had said that two plays particularly appealed to him as operatic possibilities – one being DuBose Heyward's *Porgy*, the other *The Dybbuk*. Two years later Isaac Goldberg reported that, on a visit to Gershwin's apartment, '[Gershwin] picked up one of his notebooks. He glanced at the notes and was soon constructing not only a music but a scene. The room became a synagogue and this was the indistinct prayer of those to whom prayer has become a routine such as any other. The lilt had acquired animation; it was the swaying bodies of the chanters. An upward scratch in the notebook suddenly came to life as a Chasidic dance.' (The Chasidic sect developed in Europe in the eighteenth century, praising the Almighty with songs and dances; rabbinical authorities denounced them as frivolous.)

Almost word for word, we could apply Goldberg's impressions to the prayers of the tightly-knit black community in *Porgy and Bess*. That these twin plays – *Porgy* and *The Dybbuk* – should be finalists on his list of potential opera subjects shows Gershwin clearly heading in one direction: to portray in music the lives of an oppressed, religious, isolated minority whose day-to-day existence is being threatened by changing times. In the case of *Porgy*, this includes the magical effects of 'happy dust' (cocaine) and the lure of a new life in far-away New York. Gershwin's *Dybbuk* score would not have been thoroughly Jewish music, any more than *Porgy and Bess* is thoroughly black music. His trademark blue notes and minor-key melodies would have permeated whichever story he chose, and these are at home in the folk music of both peoples.

Ira said that George's attraction to the *Dybbuk* play stemmed from his sympathy for minority groups – 'a keen feeling for them as people'. A few weeks before George died and with his nerves on edge through illness, he abruptly left the dinner table with a bitter remark about the plight of Germany's Jews, the conversation having turned to the Nazi regime. His sympathies were with the fortunate Jewish émigrés he had met who were now starting new lives in America, as much as with those suffering Hitler's menace in Germany.

It would be another American-born Jew, Leonard Bernstein, who would set music to Ansky's folk tale. His *Dybbuk* ballet of 1974,

choreographed by Jerome Robbins, included sung Hebrew texts which Bernstein retained in the first of two suites he compiled for concert performance.

In 1932, with the *Dybbuk* prospect out of the way, Gershwin returned to the idea of a black American opera that had been burrowing away in his mind ever since *Blue Monday* had briefly flickered into life a decade earlier. He wrote to DuBose Heyward confirming that he had not forgotten their meeting to discuss *Porgy*, and that 'it is still the most outstanding play that I know about coloured people.' Heyward's reply, in March 1932, typified the politeness and mutual respect that would characterize the collaboration between Gershwin, the son of immigrants – dubbed by Isaac Goldberg 'the Jew of the North', who would 'take up the song of the Southern Negro and fuse it into a typically American product' – and Heyward, the church-going Southerner born of an aristocratic

DuBose Heyward and Ira autographed this photograph on the day *Porgy and Bess* received its première in Boston, 30 September 1935.

family. 'I would be tremendously interested in working on the book with you. I have some new material that might be introduced, and once I got your ideas as to the general form suitable for the musical version, I am pretty sure that I could do you a satisfactory story.'

Having raised new expectations in Heywood, Gershwin found himself exceptionally busy. Apart from his usual concert schedule, *Pardon My English* and *Let 'Em Eat Cake* were in preparation. (This was also to be the year of *George Gershwin's Song Book* and the *Cuban Overture*.) It took him until 20 May to reply, the delay being partly because he was in mourning for his father. Morris Gershwin had been suffering from leukemia and had died the previous week, causing George to cancel a European tour as soloist under Albert Coates. (His father's sense of humour had never deserted him. An hour before he died, he had removed his oxygen mask and said to his wife: 'Well Rose, when you marry again, will you marry a tall man?' Rose liked tall men. She never re-married.) George was deeply affected, and it was small wonder that further prevarication set in. He told Heyward there was no possibility he could start on *Porgy* before January 1933, but in the meantime he would read the book several times to see what ideas he could evolve.

Suddenly, a major figure in Gershwin's life reappeared to propel matters forward: Al Jolson. Heyward alerted Gershwin that the superstar was trying to clear the rights to *Porgy* in order to appear in his own adaptation. The financial implications for Heyward could hardly have been more different than those for Gershwin, who had no money worries and whose royalties from his longest-running musical, *Of Thee I Sing*, were pouring in. Heyward was doing badly because of the Depression. He admitted: 'I evidently have an asset in *Porgy*, and in these trying times this has to be considered.' Gershwin was sympathetic; he was still in no hurry to start work, and did not even have a producer for the opera. 'If you can see your way to making some ready money from Jolson's version, I don't know that it would hurt a later version done by an all-coloured cast.' This shows Gershwin not only content to let Jolson get in first, but also determined to have his own version sung by real Negroes. Jolson's blackface make-up, and the burnt-cork impersonations of *Blue Monday*, were outside his concept. 'The sort of thing I had in mind for *Porgy* is a much more serious thing than Jolson could ever do. It

would be more a labour of love than anything else.' Even when it emerged that Kern and Hammerstein – creators of the phenomenally successful *Show Boat* – were set to write Jolson's musical for the Theatre Guild (which had produced the original *Porgy*), Gershwin remained calm. He told Heyward that Jolson would probably just add some songs to the existing play, and reiterated that he himself would not stand in the way of Heyward making some money out of *Porgy*, which was after all his property.

The gentlemanly gavotte continued in a letter that, for the first time, Heyward headed 'Dear George' (having progressed from ' Dear Mr. Gershwin' to 'My Dear Gershwin'). 'It is not my idea to work in' any way upon a possible Jolson musical, but merely to sell the story. It makes me all the more eager to work with you some day, some time, before we wake up and find ourselves in our dotage.' Gershwin was pleased to read further how Heyward found his attitude to be 'simply splendid', and he immersed himself in his current projects. Within a year the situation resolved itself. Jolson and his associates had lost interest. The way was clear for the Theatre Guild to sign up Gershwin and Heyward to make an opera out of *Porgy*, and a contract was at last signed on 26 October 1933.

In signing the Theatre Guild contract, Gershwin was highlighting the improbability of any successful collaboration with the Metropolitan Opera, for whom he would have been delighted to write his Jewish opera a few years earlier. First, the white-dominated Met would have found it difficult to guarantee an all-black cast. (Gershwin's stipulation that this be honoured has remained an integral condition of theatre performance maintained by the Gershwin estate. Black singers from America helped form the cast for the first staging by a British opera company – the outstanding Glyndebourne production of 1986 conducted by Simon Rattle.) Secondly, as Gershwin explained: 'The reason I did not submit this work to the usual sponsors of opera in America was that I hoped to develop something in American music that would appeal to the many rather than the cultured few.' Even though the Guild was taking a gamble on venturing into opera, he knew that a Met production would only result in a few performances during the season. If successful, the Guild could keep an operatic *Porgy* running nightly on Broadway, just like any musical.

At last Heyward could get to work on turning his novel into an opera libretto. This needed to be significantly different from the adaptation he and Dorothy had made for the stage (although it had included some Negro spirituals to heighten the action). Within a few weeks of signing the contract he mailed the first scene to Gershwin, and soon learned that the composer would be very much in charge. Heyward eagerly suggested that 'recitatives', the sung dialogue customary in opera, should be jettisoned in favour of spoken dialogue. 'This will give the opera speed and tempo ... with such music (singing) as grows out of the action.' Gershwin replied that he had not yet started, and needed time to think and to gather thematic material.

In truth the *Variations on 'I Got Rhythm'* must have been his main concern, since he was about to holiday in Florida and compose the variations there in time for his January 1934 concert tour with the Reisman Orchestra. On his way to and from Florida he fitted in two short visits to Heyward to get the feel of Charleston. He had asked 'to hear some spirituals, some real singing, and perhaps go to a coloured café or two'. Already he was telling Heyward he did not agree about having spoken dialogue. For him, the staging would only work if music accompanied all the action and dialogue, with recitatives in the manner of traditional grand opera. Later, he hit on the idea of giving spoken dialogue only to the story's white characters; their distance from and threat to the black community are thereby brought into sharper focus.

Once back in New York, he told the press: 'Though of course I will try to keep my own style moving in the opera, the Negro flavour will be predominant throughout.' Casting singers for the opera lay some way ahead, but he let it be known he hoped the magnificent Paul Robeson – indelibly associated with Kern's *Show Boat* after playing the lead in the 1928 London production – would accept the role of Porgy. He also turned his mind to the important matter of helping the Theatre Guild raise money for their expensive foray. Though personally wealthy, Gershwin did not like his projects to be financially unsound and he was smarting from the cash failure of the Reisman tour. Despite sold-out concerts there had been too many small venues, and 12,000 miles of costly travelling. Even as a partner in the enterprise he had only received expenses, and ended up contributing 5,000 dollars towards the deficit.

This time, radio would provide some solid finance. During 1934 he hosted two series of informal radio programmes from New York studios, earning 2,000 dollars a week as star performer and introducing a galaxy of visitors including Irving Berlin, Cole Porter and Richard Rodgers. Inevitably titled 'Music by Gershwin', the guest appearances of these and many other composers actually meant that Gershwin, for once, was at the piano performing other people's music (including some by his brother Arthur – though nothing by Kay

George hosting his half-hour CBS radio show, 'Music by Gershwin', September 1934; extracts from his earlier fifteen-minute shows for NBC have survived, available on compact disc.

Swift, who attended all the sessions). His arrangers and instrumentalists were of the highest calibre. But he complained that radio, compared with concert tours, was rapacious in exhausting his repertoire.

Heyward, who was meanwhile earning a living writing screenplays, saw the funny side of a situation whereby their opera was in effect being subsidized by the programme's sponsor, 'Feenamint' – the product being a laxative chewing-gum.

At no other time has it been possible for a writer to earn by hiring himself out as a skilled technician for, say, two months, sufficient income to sustain him for a year. I decided that the silver screen should be my Maecenas and George elected to serve radio. Statistics record the fact that there are 25,000,000 radios in America. Their contribution to the opera was indirect but important. Out of them for half an hour each week poured the glad tidings that Feenamint could be wheedled away from virtually any drug clerk in America for one dime – the tenth part of a dollar. And with the authentic medicine-man flair, the manufacturer distributed his information in an irresistible wrapper of Gershwin hits, with the composer at the piano. There is, I imagine, a worse fate than that which derives from the use of a laxative gum. And, anyhow, we felt that the end justified the means.

Coincidentally, one of the screenplays Heyward wrote was for the film *The Emperor Jones*, based on Eugene O'Neill's 1920 play about Negro life. The same play was turned into an opera by Louis Gruenberg, a Russian-born American composer much inspired by Negro music. It was staged two years before *Porgy and Bess* – by the Metropolitan Opera.

A week after launching his radio shows Gershwin wrote to Heyward, who had been mailing to New York more of his libretto. Heyward had worked at condensing the play's dialogue, suggesting where songs could be inserted and rewriting those sections as song lyrics. Gershwin said:

I really think you are doing a magnificent job with the new libretto and I hope I can match it musically. I have begun composing music for the First Act and I am starting with the songs and spirituals first. I am

hoping you will find some time to come up North and live at my apartment, if it is convenient for you.

This was not what Heyward had in mind. He was getting concerned about 'effecting a happy union between words and music across a thousand miles of Atlantic seabord'. His next letter, on 2 March, reported that he was at a sort of deadlock. 'The storm scene must stand about as it is, with very few cuts in dialogue. Musically it must be done when we are together.' He added a friendly note of impatience:

I have been hearing you on the radio, and the reception was so good it seemed as though you were in the room. In fact the illusion was so perfect I could hardly keep from shouting at you, 'Swell show, George, but what the hell is the news about PORGY!!!!' I am naturally disappointed that you have tied yourself up so long in New York. I believe that if you had gotten down for a reasonably long stay and gotten deep into the sources here you would have done a bigger job. I know well what an enormously advantageous arrangement the radio is ... only I am disappointed.

The sting was not lost on Gershwin; he resolved to arrange a 'long stay' in Charleston as soon as the first radio series finished at the end of May. Meanwhile Heyward made a visit to New York and realized to his delight that one more collaborator had become part of the team: Ira. No one had planned this. Ira was busy on a show with fellow-lyricist Yip Harburg and composer Harold Arlen when work on the opera got under way. But George had drawn him into adapting the lyrics Heyward had been sending. With years of writing for the musical theatre behind him, Ira was superbly qualified to add inspirational touches. Thanks to Ira working alongside his brother in time-honoured fashion, Heyward's libretto would be refined into just what George needed.

Never one to stir himself unnecessarily, Ira laboured away in New York and succeeded in conjuring up the flavour and dialect of Charleston without actually visiting the region. Ultimately his involvement was so crucial that he is rightly credited as the co-lyricist. Heyward observed that 'Ira's gift for the more sophisticated lyric was exactly suited to the task of writing the songs for Sportin' Life, the

DuBose Heyward wields a pencil and Ira a cigar, as they transform Heyward's play *Porgy* into a libretto for George.

Harlem gambler who had drifted into Catfish Row.' Heyward used the spelling 'Sportin' Life' in his novel, but in the play and in Gershwin's score the spelling is 'Sporting'. The name 'Catfish Row' came from a tenement slum near Heyward's childhood home called Cabbage Row. After the songs, Ira proceeded to most of the lyrics and some portions of the recitative. On his own he wrote some of the prayers and several of the songs including *It Ain't Necessarily So, There's a Boat Dat's Leavin' Soon for New York* and *Oh, Where's My Bess?*. Working with Heyward he wrote *I Loves You, Porgy, My Man's Gone Now* and *I Got Plenty o' Nuthin'*, and adapted lines from the libretto to create *Bess, You Is My Woman Now*. So closely did Ira and Heyward match their skills that it is impossible to detect where the New Yorker leaves off and the Charleston man takes over.

Heyward's pleasure during his several visits to see George and Ira at work in New York made up for his earlier frustrations. 'We evolved a system by which, between my visits North, or George's dash to Charleston, I could set scenes and lyrics. Then the brothers Gershwin, after their extraordinary fashion, would get at the piano, pound, wrangle, swear, burst into weird snatches of song and eventually emerge with polished lyrics.'

For his intensive work period in South Carolina, George was joined by his cousin Henry Botkin. Botkin was specializing in

painting Negro subjects at the time. George's paints and easel went along too – ideal recreation between bouts of composing. They hired a sparse beach cottage near the waterfront at Folly Island, ten miles from Charleston; Heyward and his wife took a summer home close by. Botkin wrote: 'The appointments were not of Waldorf Astoria level. Gershwin had a crudely decorated room furnished with a primitive iron bed, a small washbasin and an old-fashioned upright piano imported from Charleston.' There was no tap water and no telephone. Sand crabs were everywhere, and at night the chirping of crickets drove Gershwin to distraction. But away from the social diversions and the pressures of New York, all his energies could go into creating his Negro opera in the most appropriate setting. For six weeks he relished the freedom of not shaving for days and working in swimming shorts.

Reaching the end of Act 1 by 18 June, he wrote to Ira in high spirits: 'There was quite a bit of writing on the Promise' Lan' song but it will be finished today and then I'll go on to Act 2. This is a place for a complete rest as there isn't even a movie on the island. But – believe it or not – there is a Jewish delicatessen store.' A journalist from the *Charleston News and Courier* spent a day with Gershwin and captured his exhilaration. 'I've never lived in such a back-to-nature place. At home, I get up about noon. Here, I get up at 7. Well, at 7:30 anyway.' When the reporter left after dark, Gershwin was still rattling away merrily at his battered old piano, with a crowd of local islanders swaying to the beat. 'Don't know who that man is,' said one. 'But that man can really play!'

Heyward was able to observe Gershwin closely during these weeks of intense creativity in the Carolina sunshine. He said afterwards that the quality in Gershwin that had produced *Rhapsody in Blue* in New York, America's most sophisticated city, found its counterpart in the impulse behind the music and bodily rhythms of the simple Negro peasant of the South. Gershwin soaked up the sights and sounds of Folly Beach, taking a special interest in the Gullah Negroes, who lived on nearby James Island. Compared with the black people living on the mainland of Georgia and Charleston, the Gullahs had led an isolated life resistant to outside influences. Gershwin saw in them striking counterparts to the fictional residents of Catfish Row. Their dialect, their prayers, their superstitions, their singing and dancing all combined to serve as models for the kind of ensemble numbers he was

turning over in his mind, which would culminate in some of the most
vivid scenes in the opera.

Heyward recalled two memorable evenings that brought Gershwin
face to face with these inspirational models, prompting the
observation that for George – who had been writing music influenced
by blacks since his teens – these encounters were 'more like a
homecoming than an exploration'. The first happened when they took
a boat across to a distant island:

> *The Gullah Negro prides himself on what he calls 'shouting'. This is a*
> *complicated rhythmic pattern beaten out by feet and hands as an*
> *accompaniment to the spirituals, and is indubitably an African survival.*
> *I shall never forget the night when, at a Negro meeting on a remote sea-*
> *island, George started 'shouting' with them. And eventually to their huge*
> *delight, stole the show from their champion 'shouter'. I think that he is*
> *probably the only whte man in America who could have done it.*

Gershwin's use of the chorus is one of the opera's most outstanding
accomplishments, and joyful moments such as the Act 2 chorus *Oh, I
Can't Sit Down*, or *Good Mornin', Sistuh!* in the final scene, hark back
to his exciting contest with the 'shouters'. Another evening visit at
Folly Island, to a dilapidated cabin being used as a meeting house by a
group of Negro Holy Rollers, was the direct inspiration for the scene
in Act 2 where the terrified occupants of Catfish Row pray for
deliverance from a raging storm. Six separate solo lines move freely
against each other (Gershwin omitted bar-lines in the score) against a
humming, sustained background from the chorus. Heyward described
the moment this idea came to Gershwin:

> *George caught my arm and held me. The sound that had arrested him*
> *was one to which, through long familiarity, I attached no special*
> *importance. But now, listening to it with him, and noticing his*
> *excitement, I began to catch its extraordinary quality. It consisted of*
> *perhaps a dozen voices raised in loud rhythmic prayer. ... while each had*
> *started at a different time, upon a different theme, they formed a clearly*
> *defined rhythmic pattern, and ... this, with the actual words lost, and the*
> *inevitable pounding of the rhythm, produced an effect almost terrifying in*
> *its primitive intensity. Inspired by this extraordinary effect, George wrote*

six simultaneous prayers producing a terrifying invocation to God in the face of the hurricane.

In July 1934 Gershwin returned to New York with a deep sun-tan and an enormous portfolio of music manuscripts. His second series of radio shows began on 30 September, the pressure eased by working on one half-hour broadcast each week rather than two of fifteen minutes. Every available moment went into finishing the composition of *Porgy* and getting on with the orchestration. It was time to cast roles, choose a conductor and decide upon a stage director.

Assembling an almost completely Negro cast was a tough prospect, since at that period very few Negroes had been lucky enough to gain any experience in the opera house. Hundreds of auditions were arranged. We can only guess at what Paul Robeson would have made of the complete role of Porgy – some of Porgy's songs naturally became part of his repertoire later. But he was unavailable. Olin Downes had heard a gifted baritone singing in an all-black production of *Cavalleria rusticana*, and suggested he audition for Porgy. His name was Todd Duncan, and he was Professor of the Music Department at Howard University in Washington. He was not particularly fond of popular vocal music or jazz, but he was intrigued that the word 'opera' was being bandied about in relation to Gershwin. So he turned up, without an accompanist, at George's apartment. Gershwin stopped playing when they were halfway through an aria by an obscure Italian composer, which Duncan had brought along as a refreshing change from the likes of Kern's *Ol' Man River*. 'Will you be my Porgy?' he asked. Duncan's rich, strong voice would be ideal, if not for Porgy then for the role of Crown. A lengthy second audition, before Theatre Guild board members, clinched his engagement as Porgy. The novelty of that first audition stayed in Duncan's memory: 'Imagine a Negro, auditioning for a Jew, singing an old Italian aria.'

Of the other two prime roles, a twenty-year-old student at the Juilliard School, Anne Brown, was chosen for Bess, and John Bubbles – half of a popular vaudeville team called Buck and Bubbles – became Sporting Life. He could not read a note of music, but Gershwin regarded him as his personal 'discovery' and decided to take a calculated risk because of his ebullient stage personality.

Baritone Todd Duncan, the first Porgy; Gershwin gave him forty dollars after auditioning him in New York, so he could afford a second trip from Washington to be assessed by the Theatre Guild.

Gershwin put the music in the charge of an experienced conductor, Alexander Smallens. He had recently heard Smallens conduct *Four Saints in Three Acts*, an unconventional opera by Virgil Thomson to an intractible libretto by Gertrude Stein. Staged at a Broadway theatre – not at the Met – one of its main features was that, like *Porgy*, it had an all-black cast. As far as Gershwin was concerned, there the resemblance ended, describing the libretto as being 'entirely in Stein's manner, which means that it has the effect of a five-year-old child prattling on. Musically, it sounded early nineteenth century, which was a happy inspiration and made the libretto bearable.' In the event, Gershwin not only raided Thomson's opera for its conductor but also for a singer called Edward Matthews, who became Jake the fisherman.

John Bubbles, the unpredictable vaudeville star who created the role of Sporting Life

This could not have helped when Thomson sat down to write a particularly nasty review of Gershwin's opus.

Gershwin hired as vocal coach Alexander Steinert, a former pupil of Vincent D'Indy in Paris. The stage direction was in the hands of Rouben Mamoulian, an innovative figure in both film and theatre who had directed the Heywards' original play for the Guild; he was also a tremendous admirer of Gershwin. He signed his contract in Hollywood without having heard a note of the music, and arrived in New York for a play-through at Gershwin's apartment:

George sat down at the piano while Ira stood over him like a guardian angel. George's hands went up in the air about to strike the shining keys. Halfway down he changed his mind, turned to me, and said: 'Of course, Rouben, you must understand, it's very difficult to play this score. As a matter of fact it's really impossible! Can you play Wagner on the piano? Well this is like Wagner!

Gershwin's knowledge of Wagner was limited, but there is something endearing about the way he could invoke the great master at the moment of plunging into his own opera. Shortly after arriving at Folly Beach he had told the press: 'If I am successful it will resemble a combination of the drama and romance of *Carmen* and the beauty of *Meistersinger.*' Singling out Wagner's opera only for its 'beauty' does not betray an intimate acquaintance with its historical, comedic and philosophical aspects; he was much closer to the mark with *Carmen*, as would be apparent when he came to answer his critics.

When Mamoulian had heard the opening 'piano music' in the opera, he interrupted the performance to enthuse over the music.

Both brothers were as happy as children to hear words of praise. They both blissfully closed their eyes before they continued with the lovely 'Summertime' song. George played with the most beatific smile on his face. He seemed to float on the waves of his own music with the Southern sun shining on him. Ira sang – he threw his head back with abandon, his eyes closed, and sang like a nightingale. In the middle of the song George couldn't bear it any longer and took over the singing from him. So it went on. George was the orchestra and played the parts. Ira sang the other half. It was touching to see how he, while singing, would become so

Rouben Mamoulian, director
of both stage and opera
versions of *Porgy*, was a
leading Hollywood figure;
this 1933 photograph
shows him with German
stars Marlene Dietrich (left)
and Dorothea Wieck,
before the filming of
Mädchen in Uniform.

overwhelmed with admiration for his brother, that he would look from
him to me with half-open eyes and pantomime with a soft gesture of the
hand, as if saying: 'He did it. Isn't it wonderful? Isn't he wonderful?

Finishing the opera and completing the orchestration took Gershwin
months of unremitting labour. The pre-Broadway trial in Boston was
set for 30 September 1935, and with his lifelong flair for meeting
deadlines virtually 'on the nail', he dated the last page of his full score
2 September. It amounted to seven hundred pages of beautifully-
written manuscript, the final section being furiously pounced upon by
a battery of copyists and proof-readers, including the devoted Kay
Swift, to have the parts ready in time for rehearsal.

Joseph Schillinger was part of the household when the Gershwins
rented a summer home near New York in 1935, fuelling speculation as
to how much he had to do with the instrumentation. Gershwin had
written to him: 'I am working on the second act scoring, but it goes
slowly. Would like to see you one of these days and perhaps continue
to take some lessons as I am planning to stay in New York all
summer.' After Gershwin died, Schillinger claimed he had supervised
Porgy three times a week over eighteen months. Ira sensibly remarked

that such lessons broaden musical horizons 'but they don't inspire an opera like *Porgy*'.

My belief is that Gershwin did not need Schillinger for the actual composition of the opera, but that the professor was on hand in an advisory capacity during its composition and orchestration. Gershwin must have known exactly which sounds he wanted from the orchestra, labouring over every bar to write them down. His seven hundred pages are a stunning achievement from a former song-plugger who, a decade earlier, watched Grofé deftly orchestrate *Rhapsody in Blue* and who, since then, had written only five other concert pieces, none of them providing experience in the skills of balancing vocal soloists, chorus and orchestra. (André Previn, as devoted a Gershwin-lover as his distant relative Charles, was hired to 'arrange' the score when Samuel Goldwyn filmed the opera in 1959. He won an Academy Award for doing so – a typical Hollywood irony.)

It was Mamoulian again who left us the most telling recollection of how Gershwin felt after rehearsals began:

The first day of rehearsing a play is always difficult. It is like breaking mountains of ice. The end of it leaves one completely exhausted and usually a little depressed. That's the way I felt after the first day of Porgy and Bess. *Suddenly the phone rang. George's voice came glowing with enthusiasm: 'I am so thrilled and delighted over the rehearsal today. Of course I always knew that* Porgy and Bess *was wonderful, but I never thought I'd feel the way I feel now. I tell you, after listening to that rehearsal today, I think the music is so marvellous – I really don't believe I wrote it!'*

As ever, there were no self-doubts about his achievement. But Mamoulian saw in Gershwin's excited phone call an objectivity that was apt to be misunderstood by people who did not know him well. Rather as a parent praises a gifted child, Gershwin assessed his work 'without any self-consciousness or false modesty. Conceit is made of much sterner stuff.'

Porgy rehearsals stretched all concerned to their limits. Many of the cast were at home in vaudeville but entirely new to the world of opera, which is how Gershwin was determined they should approach his score. The stage was filled with black people, but everybody on the

production side was white. Heyward and the Gershwin brothers agonized over agreeing cuts, and in getting everyone to use an authentic, Charleston dialect. Rehearsing as Sporting Life, John Bubbles was a special problem. He was so laid-back as to be often absent when needed. At one session this was too much for Smallens. He threw down his baton and shouted to Mamoulian: 'I'm sick of this waiting. We'll have to throw him out and get somebody else.' Gershwin, constantly hovering over rehearsals and nervously chewing peanuts, emerged from the darkened stalls. Frantically mixing up his musical categories, he cried: 'You can't do that! Why, he's – he's the black Toscanini!' Eventually Smallens resorted to teaching Bubbles his vocal rhythms by tap-dancing them. Todd Duncan remembered that, during the New York run, 'this individual would hold a particular note two beats on Monday night but on Tuesday night he might sustain that same note through six beats.' Gershwin called him 'my Bubbles' and forgave him everything on account of his marvellous dancing and his sheer star quality.

Even before finishing the scoring, Gershwin hired an orchestra for a day and conducted selected passages with the principal singers, so that he could check how they sounded. Some of this is preserved on a recording which includes Gershwin giving instructions and joining in the singing. As a final test before the try-out in Boston, a private run-through of the complete opera was arranged at Carnegie Hall. Only Gershwin's closest friends and colleagues were present. No scenery, no acting, no costumes. Henry Botkin said: 'In some ways it was the most beautiful performance I ever heard. Without the distractions of the stage, the music itself became a profound and moving experience that stirred everybody listening to the very depths of their being.'

The plot centres around the inhabitants of Catfish Row in Charleston, 'a former mansion of the aristocracy, now a Negro tenement', and the love that springs up all too briefly between a crippled beggar, Porgy, and a young woman of easy virtue – Bess – who becomes torn between her attraction to Porgy and her involvement with Crown, a bullying stevedore who drinks heavily and is her pimp. During a crap-game, Crown is unable to see the dice properly because he has been plied with drugs and alcohol by the manipulative drug-peddler, Sporting Life. Crown picks a fight with a fisherman, Robbins, and kills him with a cotton-hook. He flees to

avoid the police, and Bess is left among the hostile inhabitants of the Row. She has nowhere to hide, but Porgy lets her take shelter in his primitive little house.

She begins to fall in love with him and is slowly assimilated into the community. She joins them at a picnic on Kittiwah Island (Heyward took the name from Kiawah, an island off the Carolina coast). But Crown has been hiding there; he suddenly appears and abducts her. She escapes, and returns to Porgy. A terrifying hurricane blows up, and it is assumed Crown must have perished in it. But he reappears in Catfish Row to claim Bess. Porgy, despite being a cripple, has very strong arms and summons up the strength to kill Crown. While he is away being questioned by the police, Bess succumbs to the temptations of Sporting Life and the alluring picture he paints of a new life together in New York. Released from jail, Porgy returns and realizes Bess has been taken from him. He vows to make his way to the big city and find her – an ending both poignant and inconclusive.

The corruptive influence of the big city presents itself straight after the opening flourishes on the orchestra, which give way to a lone jazz pianist on stage jangling through a highly-syncopated, low-down blues. This is music of the urban North and the player is Jasbo Brown, making his sole appearance in the opera (he was not in the original play). The stage directions describe 'half a dozen couples dancing in a slow, almost hypnotic rhythm'. It is a direct statement of two cultures, the unworldly Charleston community seduced by popular dance music. Heyward said he chose the name Jasbo because, according to one tradition, jazz took its name from this itinerant Negro who started off along the Mississippi and ended up playing in the cabarets of Chicago.

Gershwin called this section *Jasbo Brown Blues*, and it was one of many casualties of the savage cutting process the opera had to undergo, starting before the Boston try-out and with additional cuts before its opening in New York. The Carnegie Hall run-through had revealed a total of over three hours of music – unsustainable for a Broadway audience. By the time *Porgy and Bess* arrived in New York the score was about forty-five minutes shorter. After Jasbo had been dropped, the scissors excised parts of the Act 1 crap-game and two of the peak moments in Act 2: the Buzzard Song, which the British composer and writer Wilfred Mellers described as 'the turning point

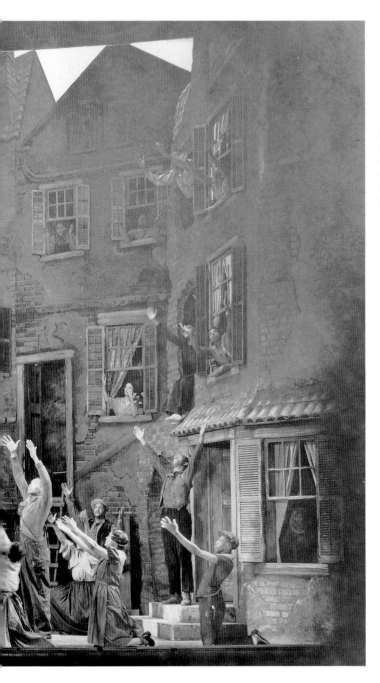

Porgy (Todd Duncan, centre) with the residents of Catfish Row in the 'Buzzard Song' from Act II, scene 1, in the original 1935 production of *Porgy and Bess*

of the opera ... Porgy's realization of the significance of his love ... a victory for love/life over death', and the very section inspired by the arresting moment when Gershwin heard the Gullahs chanting – the six-stranded prayer, *Oh, Doctor Jesus*. Act 3 lost passages from Porgy's fight with Crown and the music to which Bess seeks shelter, together with most of the intensely dramatic trio between Maria, Serena and Porgy, leading to his anguished cry, 'You ain' mean Bess dead?' (These cuts were not fully restored until 1976, the year the Houston Grand Opera mounted an unabridged production, and also the year Lorin Maazel conducted the Cleveland Orchestra in the first complete version on record, with Willard White and Leona Mitchell in the title roles.) Understandably, every cut hurt Gershwin. But he himself suggested some of them, and as a Broadway professional he took them in his stride. As Jasbo Brown was torn out of the running-order, he said: 'Okay, that means we start with the lullaby. And that's some lullaby.'

'Some lullaby' was, of course, *Summertime*, sung by Clara, wife of the fisherman Jake, to her baby. Every socialite in New York wanted a piece of Gershwin. Among them was the writer Kay Halle, whose piano appealed to Gershwin. She gave him free access, and arrived home late one night to hear him playing. 'I knew he had been working very hard to get the lullaby and that he had done several versions. He sang in this wailing-wall voice ... "Summertime", and it was exquisite. We looked at each other and the tears were just coursing down my cheeks and I knew that this was going to be beloved by the world.' Her response may sound over-emotional but in essence she was right. The lullaby recurs at key points in the opera, pointing up the need for tenderness and protection among people constantly under threat from outside forces. Along with *Bess, You Is My Woman Now*, it is one of the most inspired vocal melodies of not only this opera but of the twentieth century.

When Porgy makes his first entrance it is to a five-note 'blue' motif that identifies him throughout the work. In true operatic fashion, Gershwin allotted specific musical motifs to the main characters – except Bess. Not to allocate her one is a device of some subtlety. Willard White, who played the lead in the Glyndebourne production with Cynthia Haymon as Bess, points out that Bess is a 'confused lady'. Her happiness depends on the man she is able to attach herself

to, and her value of herself is dependent on whom she is with. So her music is structured according to her encounters with the three men in her life – Porgy, Crown and Sporting Life. Anne Brown – the first to sing Bess – missed this point to the extent that she wrote to Gershwin a year after the première asking whether he could insert a distinctive solo number for her to sing in future productions.

Porgy's opening music includes the line 'When Gawd make cripple, he mean him to be lonely'. It is the key to his dependence on Bess, the first woman to show love for him. But, in the Glyndebourne production, Willard White took an independent view regarding the goat cart in which Porgy travels about, agreeing with the stage director Trevor Nunn that it should be dispensed with. White had always wanted to change the nature of Porgy's disability (and to avoid the discomfort of spending a whole evening on his knees). The cart was replaced by two rough-hewn crutches of uneven length. In a dramatic break with tradition, he threw the crutches aside at the final moments, when the scenery pulled back to let him start his long journey to New York, no longer hobbling and with a new-found strength. (Heyward had based Porgy on a real cripple, a beggar named Samuel Smalls, known as 'Goat Sammy' because of his goat-drawn cart. He accumulated a police record and was jailed pending trial for an attempted shooting, but somehow disappeared; a body with his name tag was eventually found buried on an island off Charleston.)

The second scene opens with one of the opera's many songs in the style of a Negro spiritual, *Gone, Gone, Gone*, as the residents of Catfish Row mourn Robbins. They are in the house of his widow, Serena, and his body is laid out with a saucer on his chest; unless enough money is dropped into it for burial, the medical students will claim him. Gershwin gives Serena her own haunting aria, *My Man's Gone Now*. When the undertaker agrees to the burial even though only fifteen dollars has been put into the saucer, a joyful chorus number with a distinctly Broadway flavour – *Headin' for the Promis' Lan'* – ends Act 1.

Act 2 begins with Jake and the other fishermen mending their nets. By now Gershwin's use of the chorus is crucial to the action, and his writing for them is skilful and idiomatic. 'It take a long haul to get there' is followed by the word 'huh!', a rhythmic exhortation that Heyward and Gershwin would have heard among the Gullah workers. When Porgy enters, it is to the most famous song in the score apart

from *Summertime*: his celebration of poverty, *I Got Plenty o' Nuthin'*. A strumming banjo connects Gershwin's mid-1930s opera with the earliest roots of the minstrel show.

The Buzzard Song is one of the main hinges of the action, since it is the point where the superstitious fatalism of Porgy and the community is most passionately sung out. The bird can only mean trouble. Porgy makes an impassioned plea for it to 'Pack yo' things an' fly from here'. Porgy, whom the bird 'used to feed on', does not live here any more; there are 'two folks livin' in this shelter ... ain' no such thing as loneliness.' It is baffling that the opera was performed minus these crucial pages for so many years. After Porgy gets rid of Sporting Life, mincingly trying to peddle his 'happy dust' to Bess, he is left alone with her for the opera's great love-duet.

As with *The Man I Love*, not a note of *Bess, You Is My Woman Now* can be improved. There are wide leaps and an almost conversational urgency in the melody lines; sometimes the lovers seem on the point of breaking into speech, so natural is the word-setting. The blue note on the first syllable of 'woman' has the same potency as those in the first two phrases of *The Man I Love*, but here the emotion is heightened when Porgy's melody in the first refrain is taken over by Bess as she begins singing. He counterpoints in ardent phrases, assuring her that at last she has a man to rely on. At the end the music is suffused with an exquisite tenderness, Porgy's 'We is happy now' intertwined with 'Porgy, I's yo' woman now'. The song fades into silence with high, major/minor caresses from the orchestra that resonate in the very last bars of Bernstein's *West Side Story*.

The idyllic love-duet could not give way to a greater contrast than the picnic on Kittiwah Island. The stage directions read: 'General gaiety – all well-fed – some few well-liquored.' Everyone is in a particularly receptive mood as Sporting Life sings and dances his blasphemous way through a revisionist view of the Bible, *It Ain't Necessarily So*. Like a legitimate Negro preacher, he has his flock hanging on to every word, joining in after each line and twice erupting into 'scat' singing. Gershwin improvised the scatty words 'Wa-doo, Zim bam boodle-oo, Hoodle ah da wa da, Scatty wah' when he first came up with the tune at the piano. Ira put them into his lyrics, and they punctuate the scepticism which Sporting Life weaves around some vivid Old Testament stories: David and Goliath,

Jonah, Moses, Methuselah. The crowd at the picnic love these
Bible tales, but now they are being invited to take them 'wid a grain
of salt'.

The sinuous melody line perfectly captures Sporting Life's
subversiveness, and has been claimed as particularly Jewish by hearers
who are only hearing part of what they want to hear. The blue note is
a constituent of both black and cantorial music, and lies at the heart
of a Negro opera by a Jewish composer. The rocking interval of a
minor third – sung six times to the syllables 'Li'ble to read in de Bible
it ain't nece ...' is the most insistent chanting of blue notes anywhere
in Gershwin. Minor thirds are pounced upon by writers eager to prove
the Jewishness of his melodies. But to be really Jewish, the song would
need a sprinkling of augmented 2nds, which cast their Hebraic spell if
one sounds the notes E, D flat, C a few times (E to D flat being the
augmented 2nd). Augmented 2nds, a life-force of synagogue
cantilation and Yiddish folk-songs, are nowhere to be found in
Gershwin's hit songs. We shall never know whether they would have
come into their own in *The Dybbuk*. It was Mussorgsky, orchestrated
by Ravel (neither of them Jewish), who put authentic-sounding
cantilation into the popular concert repertoire. His portrait of wealthy
Samuel Goldenberg preening himself in *Pictures at an Exhibition* is
convincing just because of its augmented 2nds; there is nothing in
Gershwin that sounds so Jewish. When augmented 2nds do turn up
on Broadway they make their mark – as in Tevye's cantorial insertion
during *If I Were a Rich Man* (from Jerry Bock's *Fiddler on the Roof*) or
in Porter's *My Heart Belongs To Daddy*.

Through this ingenious song Sporting Life achieves a more
rounded character than he had in the play. Gershwin described him as
a 'dancing villain who is likeable and believable and at the same time
evil'. Whereas minor thirds gave Sporting Life his bluesy persistence,
rising and falling major thirds are effortlessly linked by Gershwin to
produce a second, soaring love-duet, *I Loves You Porgy*. Bess has
returned to Catfish Row after her encounter with Crown on the
island, and this is her last moment of closeness with Porgy and the last
time we see them alone together.

After the wildness of the hurricane (expertly scored considering the
noise the orchestra is required to make) come the hushed moments of
Crown's reappearance, and the fateful attack by Porgy, with his

triumphant cry: 'Bess, you got a man now, you got Porgy!' The crap-game fugue is not the only one in the opera. Gershwin now supercharges this Baroque procedure with jagged, violent music which animates the murder scene. (Morton Gould and Gunther Schuller were among later American composers who relished the possibilities of jazz fugues, as did Bernstein in *Prelude, Fugue and Riffs*.) Gershwin gleefully played the contrapuntal crap-game scene to songwriter Vernon Duke. Overwhelmed by how far a one-time Remick's keyboard-slave had outstripped his peers, George exclaimed: 'Get this – Gershwin writing fugues! What will the boys say now!'

Benjamin Britten used an incisive motif similar to Gershwin's 'murder' fugue subject for the storm in *Peter Grimes* (1945). There are striking parallels between the operas' stories, centering as they do on tiny fishing communities resisting violent events, raising morale through uniting in traditional songs, and having among them a purveyor of drugs (in *Grimes* it is Ned Keene selling laudanum), a headstrong fisherman (Bob Boles) and a central male character who is set apart from the rest (Peter Grimes).

Parallels can be made with a second English composer, Frederick Delius. Gershwin's harmonic language in his choruses mirrors that in *Appalachia*. Delius's *Hassan* has, in its closing scene, a tenor soloist whose wordless phrases over a drone bass suspend time in the same way as do the Strawberry Woman and Crab Man selling their wares. The epilogue in *Sea Drift* shares its yearning (and its key) with Porgy's *My Bess! I Want Her Now*. While an orange planter in Florida, Delius became fascinated with Negro spirituals; like Gershwin, he spent months composing *Appalachia* in a primitive shack.

Ironically, it is Porgy's slaying of Crown that leads not to his winning Bess, but to losing her. Sporting Life is the one witness to the murder, and – trading on superstition – he reminds Porgy that Crown's wound will bleed if his murderer views the body. Unable to endure that, Porgy is jailed for contempt of court, and Sporting Life seizes his chance to take Bess on 'a boat dat's leavin' soon for New York'. However, Porgy's final song, *I'm On My Way*, never mentions New York. So we have a finale that moves the story from the particular to the universal – the start of a journey not to a specific place, but to 'a Heav'nly Lan'. Even if he never finds Bess, Porgy will make himself a bigger man.

The Boston try-out performances went well, one of them earning Gershwin a fifteen-minute ovation. 'He has travelled a long way from Tin Pan Alley to this opera,' said one reviewer. 'He must now be accepted as a serious composer.' On 10 October came the challenge of the New York opening. The papers sent along their music and their drama critics, and the former were not as impressed as the latter. Early in their association, Todd Duncan had told Gershwin that he had worked on his vocal craft for years, 'waiting for a serious work like this, open to the serious Negro artists'. The critic Paul Rosenfield (who had poured cold water on the Piano Concerto) felt very differently. 'It would seem as if Gershwin knew chiefly stage Negroes and that he very incompletely felt the drama of the two protagonists.' One of Gershwin's staunchest allies, Samuel Chotzinoff, had to admit that 'it is a hybrid, fluctuating constantly between music drama, musical comedy, and operetta.' Many commentators felt Gershwin had made a mistake by going against Heyward's concept and insisting on a 'through-composed' opera with sung recitative, which they felt slowed down the action. (When the heavily-abridged 1942 version took to the stage, supervised by Gershwin's mother, almost all the recitative music had been cut, and thereby most of the plot and

The sheet music cover for *Summertime*, issued in 1959 in association with Goldwyn's film starring Sidney Poitier as Porgy, Dorothy Dandridge as Bess and Sammy Davis Jr as Sporting Life

Virgil Thomson, prolific
American composer and
outspoken music critic,
whose black opera *Four
Saints in Three Acts* failed to
win public acclaim

development of character. Inconceivable today, this version resulted in
considerably more success at the box office.)

In *Modern Music*, the quarterly of the musical establishment, Virgil
Thomson wrote: 'With a libretto that should never have been
accepted on a subject that should never have been chosen, a man who
should never have attempted it has written a work that is of some
power and importance. I like its lack of respectability, the way it can
be popular and vulgar.' But the barbs were driven home. 'Gershwin
does not even know what an opera is. At best it is a piquant but highly
unsavoury stirring-up together of Israel, Africa and the Gaelic Isles.
His lack of understanding of all the major problems of form, of
continuity, and of serious or direct musical expression is not surprising
in view of the impurity of his sources and his frank acceptance of
same. I do not like fake folklore, nor fidgety accompaniments, nor
bitter-sweet harmony, nor six-part choruses, nor *gefilte* fish
orchestration.'

'Gefilte' fish is a traditional Jewish recipe; the word is Yiddish for
'stuffed'. Subsequent printed versions of Thomson's review changed
the phrase to 'plum-pudding orchestration'. He presumably felt better
for getting this anti-Semitic swipe out of his system. If *Porgy* is stuffed
with notes, so are colourful post-Romantic scores such as Stravinsky's
Petrushka and Strauss's *Salome*, which he would not have condemned
in the same terms.

The Gershwin brothers did not react publicly to thinly-veiled
prejudices of this kind, but in the climate of the mid 1930s they did
not go unnoticed. In 1934, the year Gershwin started *Porgy*, the
English composer Constant Lambert published a provocative survey
of contemporary trends called *Music Ho! – a Study of Music in Decline*.
His most popular work, *The Rio Grande*, had demonstrated in 1927
his affection for jazz and Negro music. Levant, who wrote about
Lambert, must have mentioned the book to Gershwin. On reading it
Gershwin would have been confronted with the observation that
Rhapsody in Blue was 'that singularly inept albeit popular piece', and
that 'the importance of the Jewish element in jazz cannot be too
strongly emphasized. But although the Jews have stolen the Negroes'
thunder, although Al Jolson's nauseating blubbering masquerades as
savage lamenting, although Tin Pan Alley has become a
commercialized Wailing Wall, the only jazz music of technical

importance is that small section of it that is genuinely negroid. The blues have a certain austerity that places them far above the sweet nothings of George Gershwin.' The Gershwins would have regarded Thomson and Lambert as being among a minority of public figures who were unable to take on board the simple truth that popular songwriting was, and always will be, not merely an American art form but a Jewish one.

Gershwin, wounded particularly by the Thomson review, answered his critics. The *New York Times* printed a feature entitled 'Rhapsody in Catfish Row', in which he explained: 'It was my idea that opera should be entertaining. When I chose *Porgy and Bess* ... I made sure that it would enable me to write light as well as serious music and that it would enable me to include humour as well as tragedy. It is true that I have written songs for *Porgy and Bess*. I am not ashamed of writing songs at any time so long as they are good songs. The recitative I have tried to make as close to the Negro inflection in speech as possible.'

Valid though this was, it did not answer two fundamental questions: whether Gershwin had indeed produced a real opera (not just a string of hit numbers linked by sung dialogue) and whether his white man's view of American blacks patronized them or paid them tribute. On the 'real opera' issue, he did not help matters by saying that 'I decided against the use of original folk material because I wanted the music to be all of one piece. Therefore I wrote my own spirituals and folk songs. But they are still folk music, and therefore, being in operatic form, *Porgy and Bess* becomes a folk opera.' This is a definition which proved problematical for years, and which was no answer to Olin Downes's criticism that Gershwin did not 'utilize all the resources of the operatic composer'. Mamoulian, seeing how the critics were labouring over the fact that it seemed to be neither an opera nor a musical, simply said: 'You give someone something delicious to eat and they complain because they have no name for it.' Todd Duncan remembered Gershwin being 'caught between', worrying that opera-lovers would stay away because they did not believe he could write one, while Broadway thought: 'Georgie's gone high-hat on us.'

To some extent Gershwin confused the second issue – his portrayal of blacks – by stating that the opera 'deals with Negro life

in America'. In fact Catfish Row represented an isolated Negro community in a particular area of the South, in many ways a world away from the lives Negroes were living in 1930s New York. When Porgy is told that Bess has gone to New York, he has never heard of it. Criticisms aimed at Gershwin were in effect directed at Heyward too. The opera was subjecting the characters he had invented to unprecedented public view. Had he delineated them sensitively, or were they the same old black stereotypes with their naïve superstitions, their whoring and their gambling? In truth, Heyward was the first white author to attempt, for a predominantly white readership, such a dignified and realistic portrait of an authentic black community. Most American Negroes did appreciate that he had gone to unusual lengths to investigate their culture and present a fair picture.

This did not deter widespread black opposition to what the Gershwin brothers had produced. The most illustrious black complainer was Duke Ellington, who had started composing a black opera called *Boola* in 1930 (never completed). He condemned Gershwin's work for being 'black on stage, white everywhere else', and said it was time to 'debunk Gershwin's lampblack Negroisms. No Negro could possibly be fooled by *Porgy and Bess.*' A black journalist, James Hicks, was vitriolic when the opera was revived on Broadway in 1953. He found it 'the most insulting, the most libellous, the most degrading act that could possibly be perpetrated against coloured Americans of modern times' – words that starkly echo criticism of *Blue Monday.* Of all people, Gershwin – the roller-skating Jewish boy from the tenements of Brooklyn – was no stranger to racial stereotyping or to discrimination. He and Ira had struggled with the racist problems inherent in their subject, in addition to the purely musical and dramatic ones of creating a viable piece for the Broadway stage in an operatic format.

Porgy and Bess remains the single outstanding American theatre piece of the twentieth century. In the 1940s and 1950s it was seen on tours in America, the USSR and Europe, enjoying a resounding success at La Scala, Milan. But its canonization came in 1985, fifty years after the première, when it finally arrived on the stage of the Metropolitan Opera, with Simon Estes and Grace Bumbry in the title roles. Bumbry had to be coaxed into playing Bess:

I resented the role at first, possibly because I really didn't know the score, and I think because of the racial aspect. I thought it beneath me, I felt I had worked far too hard, that we had come too far to have to regress to 1935. My way of dealing with it was to see that it was really a piece of Americana, of American history. Whether we like it or not, whether I sang it or not, it was still going to be there.

A year after its sold-out début season at the Met, the opera 'raised the roof' at Glyndebourne. One British reviewer noted that a radical theatre piece about poor, working-class American blacks triumphed in front of the most socially élitist, conservative, overwhelmingly-white opera audience in the country. The same production gained standing ovations in 1992 amid the red-plush and gilded mirrors of the Royal Opera House. All this was too late for Gershwin. He saw the New York production close after 124 performances. Box-office receipts, including a short tour that followed, earned him 10,000 dollars in royalties – less than he had spent on having the music copied. Although individual songs from the opera soon became hits, he never

Willard White (Porgy) and Cynthia Haymon (Bess) in Trevor Nunn's outstanding Glyndebourne production, 1986

saw another production. He put together an orchestral suite from *Porgy and Bess* to help promote the opera, rescuing some of the music that had been eliminated. Even this suffered something of a jinx, disappearing from the repertoire. When rediscovered in 1958 it had to be renamed, because in 1943 Robert Russell Bennett had fulfilled a commission from the conductor Fritz Reiner to make his own suite (an effective *Symphonic Portrait* which has become the standard version, and less of a 'scissors-and-paste' job than Gershwin's). Ira retitled his brother's suite *Catfish Row*.

Gershwin had vigorously defended the notion of an opera containing song hits. He said: 'Nearly all of Verdi's operas contain what are known as "song hits". *Carmen* is almost a collection of song hits.' His comparison with Bizet's masterpiece did not go on to recall that *Carmen* was also a box-office failure, and that its heartbroken composer died at thirty-six – the same age as Gershwin at the time he was writing *Porgy*. After Gershwin's death, residuary values were assigned to his manuscripts – understandably kept as low as possible for inheritance-tax purposes. *Rhapsody in Blue* was appraised at 20,125 dollars. The lovingly-crafted 700 pages of *Porgy and Bess* were given a nominal value of 250 dollars.

In the audience for the final performance of his opera, Gershwin was seen to be moved to tears. He may be reproached for the moments when he could have been more sensitive to others, for the egocentricity that was part of his nature. But to appreciate the deep sincerity of his artistic intentions, it helps to imagine him there in the darkness, sharing with the audience the glorious outpouring of melody that is *Bess, You Is My Woman Now*, his eyes moist at the beauty of what he had created.

7

The Gershwin brothers
leaving Newark airport for
Hollywood on 10 August
1936; George would never
see New York again.

*I had to live for this ... that Sam Goldwyn
should say to me: 'Why don't you write hits like
Irving Berlin?'*

George Gershwin, 1937

Hollywood and Final Curtain

Taking stock of his situation early in 1936, Gershwin would have
admitted that Broadway was not treating him kindly. He had been
working harder than at any time in his life, yet had scored three
failures in succession: *Pardon My English* and *Let 'Em Eat Cake* in 1933,
and now, *Porgy and Bess*. The 'Great White Way' of Broadway had lost
much of its glitter and much of its creative talent, and the debilitating
effects of the Depression were causing loss-making shows to close in
alarming numbers. It was clear where much of that talent was
heading. George saw his fellow songwriters – Kern, Berlin, Porter,
Rodgers, Arlen – practically commuting from New York to
Hollywood, where the climate was balmy and where film studios were
able to offer golden rewards for a mere handful of songs – provided
composers and lyricists were realistic enough to let control of their
work pass into the hands of studio executives, rather than fuss and
worry protectively about their songs as on Broadway.

By the middle of the year he had also become aware of falling
audiences at his concerts. Some critics wanted him to find something
new to play – year after year it had been *Rhapsody in Blue* and
Concerto in F, his other two concerted pieces having failed to win the
same popularity. Two all-Gershwin evenings at the Lewisohn Stadium
made headlines of the wrong sort. On 10 July the *New York Times*
reported: 'It was George Gershwin night at the Lewisohn Stadium,
and there were empty seats. That is news.' Only 7,000 turned up, and
the audience was sparse again on the following night. The previous
year, 17,000 had filled the stadium. He was especially disappointed
because, along with the usual concert favourites, he had put excerpts
from *Porgy and Bess* on the programme. When his friends pointed out
that the hottest weather in the city's records must have kept thousands
away, his mood brightened. But generally his spirits seemed low. In
March he had told the young American composer David Diamond
that he was getting severe headaches. It seemed a good idea to get
away from New York for a while.

Porgy and Bess had given the wrong signals to Hollywood producers. They knew Gershwin had not enjoyed a 'smash hit' since *Of Thee I Sing* in 1931, and now his operatic pretensions were eyed with suspicion. Maybe he had lost the common touch. Ira knew that Hollywood really didn't want him. The brothers' agent told Ira: 'They think George is too highbrow. Can't he write a few words and explain to them?' George duly wired: 'Rumours about highbrow music ridiculous. Am out to write hits.'

It had been six years since the Gershwins had worked briefly in the film capital, on the less-than-successful *Delicious*. After striking a hard bargain with RKO studios to write songs for *Shall We Dance*, George left for Hollywood with Ira and Leonore. They hired a creamy-white, Spanish-style house in Beverly Hills with its own tennis court. Living not far away was Schoenberg, as fanatical a tennis-player as Gershwin. Having come to terms with his exile from Nazi Germany (he had left in 1933), Schoenberg had settled into a rewarding teaching post at the University of California. Gershwin insisted he used the tennis court whenever he liked. Another German composer who was now an émigré in Los Angeles, Albert Heink Sendrey, described the scene in

Leonore and Ira at their Hollywood home. After Ira's death she promoted and funded many performances of Gershwin's music, and made generous donations to the Library of Congress to preserve his manuscripts.

the Californian sunshine the day he visited 1019 North Roxbury
Drive:

> *There they were, separated by a mere net, perhaps the two greatest and
> certainly the most discussed musicians of this decade. On one side the
> younger one who had succeeded in making a respectable woman out of
> that little hussy, Jazz ... on the other side of that separating net the older
> man, agile, small of stature but immense of mind, who is beating new
> paths for music through the wilderness of the unknown, over which we are
> as yet unable to follow him. There they were, those two contrasting giants
> of modern music, George Gershwin and Arnold Schoenberg, united in one
> common thought to make a little ball scale the top of the net, as though
> nothing else mattered.*

Schoenberg was much impressed by Gershwin's genius, although there
must have been times when the younger man's naïvety about aspects
of classical music took his breath away. Oscar Levant remembered
how, during one of their tennis games, George referred to a
performance of one of Schoenberg's string quartets he had heard, then
said: 'I'd like to write a quartet some day. But it will be something
simple, like Mozart.' After all those years steeped in music, he was still
wide of the mark when it came to appreciating the supreme structural
and harmonic craftsmanship beneath Mozart's melodies.

Predictably, he saw Schoenberg not just as a tennis partner but as
a potential composition teacher. The old compulsion to study with
somebody notable, preferably with European credentials, had not
subsided. Two months after arriving in Hollywood he was writing –
on 'RKO Studios' notepaper – a letter to Joseph Schillinger. 'I've
been considering doing some studying with either Schoenberg or
Toch.' (Ernst Toch, an Austrian-born composer now in California,
who was on record as saying that composition cannot be taught.) 'I
haven't gotten down to making the decision yet, but it might be a
good idea for me to keep working a little.' He seemed to be assuring
the esteemed professor that earning huge fees by writing songs for
the movies could not be regarded as 'working'. He continued: 'I'm
very anxious to begin thinking about a symphonic composition ...
I'm leaning towards the idea of a bright overture.' Schillinger replied

Gershwin completed this starkly realistic portrait of friend and tennis partner Arnold Schoenberg in December 1936.

– with a sardonic touch – that he should take lessons from both, doing four-part fugues with Schoenberg and submitting his symphonic efforts to Toch. He certainly knew Gershwin by now.

Gershwin's cynicism over the Hollywood lifestyle was greater than it had been during his first trip in the winter of 1930. 'Look at this place – desert,' he said to Henry Botkin. 'Here they drill four holes and plant palm trees. Then they drill a bigger hole and install a swimming pool. Finally, they build a still larger, deeper hole and put up a house. It's unbelievable.' But despite his reservations about life in Hollywood, George resolved to make the most of it. He wrote to New York arranging for a selection from his art collection to be sent over, together with his own painting materials and 'two hundred cigars'. He enjoyed strenuous hikes in the warm sunshine; in the evenings he met up with songwriting friends and theatre colleagues who had made the break to California. He wrote: 'Hollywood has taken on a new colour since our last visit six years ago. There are many people in the business today who talk the language of smart showmen and it is therefore much more agreeable working out here.' He and Ira retuned their work ethic. They would commit themselves to a handful of songs then stay out of the way and let the producers take over. On top of the pleasure of working again with their old friends Astaire and Rogers, nothing in Hollywood could compare with the care and professionalism lavished by the studio on

On the set of the film *Shall We Dance*, Fred Astaire joins George in a spontaneous duet. Ira, who had given up the piano as a boy, looks on.

an Astaire movie. The film star enjoyed collaborating with composers and lyricists and had control over editing the dance footage. The uncomfortable path that lay ahead for Gershwin was not Astaire's doing, but resulted from attitudes higher up, in the 'front office'.

As with most of Gershwin's stage musicals, the film plots were thin and the situations unlikely. What mattered were the songs and the incomparable dance sequences, meticulously choreographed then rehearsed for hours on end. The plot of *Shall We Dance* was typical: Fred and Ginger play two American dancers who have been working in Paris. He contrives to be on the same boat when they return to New York, and sets about wooing her (partly through *Walking the Dog*, which became the short piece for piano, *Promenade*). Three songs – *They All Laughed, Let's Call the Whole Thing Off* and *They Can't Take That Away from Me* – survived the film's transience to join the canon of Gershwin standards.

The changes in George's music for the theatre in the 1930s were reflected in the tunes he was now writing for the movies, and Ira's lyrics had become ever more sophisticated and conversational. *They All Laughed* starts straight off with George's adored pentatonic scale – all five notes of it. But each time it comes round, it leads somewhere else. The key changes rapidly, yet nothing could seem more natural. Ira had taken his cue from an advert for a music correspondence-school, headed: 'They all laughed when I sat down to play the piano.' His lyric tosses the names of great pioneers – Columbus, Edison, Wilbur Wright, Marconi, Henry Ford – into a virtuoso word-display that makes this one of the cleverest of modern love songs. *Let's Call the Whole Thing Off* features the dilemma between a couple who cannot agree how to pronounce 'Eether, eyether, neether, nyther', the dogged insistence of which George humorously captures by setting each word to the interval of a falling fifth. The casual lyricism of *They Can't Take That Away from Me* belies the wonderful construction that went into both words and music. Nowhere else did Gershwin begin a song refrain with five repeated tonic notes ('The way you wear your ...') – which come round again and again as the singer spells out for his loved one some of the things he finds enchanting about her. The title-song *Shall We Dance*, and *Beginner's Luck*, never achieved the same popularity. *Slap that Bass* saw Astaire dancing amid the machinery of the ship's engine room; it recalls the nervous fidgeting of *Fascinating Rhythm* without attaining that song's exceptional status.

The little extract from the film, *Promenade*, exists in a twilight world – too interesting to remain lost on the soundtrack of an Astaire–Rogers movie and too slight to be programmed at concerts except as part of a Gershwin selection or as an encore. For such a simple piece, it had a chequered history before reaching its restored state. The Gershwins wrote eight songs for the film (two were unused), then were told by RKO Studios that George's old colleague Nathaniel Shilkret would do the 'background music'; the composer of a film musical did not have to bother with that. Gershwin retorted that he wanted to bother, and he proceeded to supply four ballet sequences and this *Walking the Dog* sequence to accompany a scene where Fred and Ginger were walking a little pet dog on the promenade deck of a ship.

Gershwin entertains the *Shall We Dance* team: left to right, Hermes Pan (dance director), Fred Astaire, Mark Sandrich (film director), Ginger Rogers, George, Ira, Nathaniel Shilkret (conductor).

Ira could not find the manuscript score after his brother's death. Fortunately Hal Borne, who had been the film's rehearsal pianist, was able to remember the whole piece and Ira published it in 1960 for piano solo, calling it *Promenade*. Not until 1978 did George's original arrangement turn up in a box of scores at the studio warehouse. The instrumentation casts a personal comment on the inflated Hollywood scores of the time. Whereas RKO would have provided Shilkret with the usual big studio orchestra, Gershwin 'walks the dog' via a tiny chamber orchestra plus two pianos. The tune literally walks through one key after another, then – just as it seems we might never find the home key – a blue-note cadence drops us back with a shake of the tail. It recalls Prokofiev in the Gavotta of his 'Classical' Symphony, where the theme switches from one key to another only to arrive home at the last bar.

Hermes Pan, the film's choreographer, remembered how easily Gershwin's acute observation could translate action into music. While Fred and Ginger rehearsed the walk, 'he watched them and wrote this

wonderful ditty. He sort of caught the tempo of the way they walked, and the way the dog was trotting along. And he did it right there on the set. Just like that. Pure inspiration. He was very dance-wise, you might say.' His sister Frances remembered him as 'a beautiful dancer. George used to come home after rehearsals with Fred Astaire and show me the steps he'd learned from Fred. He did it beautifully because he was so well co-ordinated.' (During rehearsals for *Lady, Be Good!* in 1924 Fred and Adele Astaire had been having trouble finding an 'exit step' to dance themselves off the stage after their *Fascinating Rhythm* routine. It was George who got up from the piano and showed them how to 'travel with that one'. Fred recalled that it was 'the perfect answer to our problem, this suggestion by hoofer Gershwin, and it turned out to be a knockout applause puller'.) The Gershwins had at last proved themselves in tinsel town. 'George and I were pretty proud of *Shall We Dance*,' Ira said. 'We thought it had a smart score. Maybe that was a mistake, to put so many smart songs in one picture.' George was as clear-sighted as ever about what was happening to his music, complaining that 'the picture does not take advantage of the songs as well as it should.' It irked him to lose control of his work the moment he handed it over to the studio. In 1941, Ira summarized his brother's eleven months in Hollywood: 'After writing "the Great American Opera" George wrote some of the best hits he ever did in his life. He met the boys at their own game. He went back to his first love and did that better than ever before.'

RKO were quick to take up options on a further two Gershwin scores, but neither of the films – *A Damsel in Distress* and *Goldwyn Follies* – were up to the standard of their predecessor. *Damsel* was set in England, giving George the chance to write two pastiches in English madrigal style, *The Jolly Tar and the Milkmaid* and *Sing of Spring*. He was not just having fun showing off his Elizabethan part-writing (Schillinger's recent supervision of *Porgy* had given him extra confidence in writing for chorus); after losing control of his songs in *Shall We Dance* he announced that 'we have protected ourselves ... so the audience will get a chance to hear some singing besides the crooning of the stars.' His edginess about Hollywood was getting hard to conceal. The 'stars' included no less than Astaire, Joan Fontaine, George Burns and Gracie Allen, but the undistinguished movie is only

remembered for two superb songs, *Nice Work if You Can Get It* and *A Foggy Day (in London Town)*, a tune extraordinary for its rising, probing intervals and the major/minor ambivalence that really does give the impression of peering through a fog.

By the time he started work on *Goldwyn Follies* in the spring of 1937, Gershwin's disillusionment with the movie business was complete. Todd Duncan recalled how they sat up until five in the morning at the Gershwin house in Beverly Hills. George told him how unhappy he was, though he was making a lot of money. 'Todd, I'm not the kind of composer where a man tells me I need five songs for this film, now compose. I can't do that any more. I'm dying to get back to New York to compose when I want to.'

He had come to refer sarcastically to his employer as 'The Great Goldwyn'. Samuel Goldwyn (1881–1974) was one of Hollywood's most powerful figures, who could make or break the people he hired. For

Gershwin smiles at conductor Alfred Newman during a recording session for *Goldwyn Follies*, while an intense Goldwyn lends a critical ear via headphones. Ira, as always, keeps a watchful eye.

Producer Samuel Goldwyn doubted whether Gershwin could come up with 'hits' for *Goldwyn Follies*. The film is all but forgotten, but two of its songs are immortal.

George, the last straw came when Goldwyn summoned him and Ira to a humiliating 'audition'. In his magisterial office they had to perform their five new songs in front of the great man and, as Levant quipped, 'his full staff of loyal, well-paid amanuenses (stooges)'. The film turned out to be a shapeless throwback to vaudeville, its lame comedy routines and overdressed production numbers rubbing shoulders with a gaudy excerpt from Verdi's *La traviata*. The music had been mutilated, but from this sorry episode came two Gershwin songs of the highest quality: *Love Walked In*, and the last George ever wrote, *Love Is Here To Stay*.

Early in 1937 Frances Godowsky visited her brother in Hollywood. She found him full of vitality and 'coming into his own as a rounded person'. He had again been seeing Dr Gregory Zilboorg, a Russian psychoanalyst he had first been prevailed to call upon by Kay Swift in 1934. Zilboorg impressed Gershwin with his erudition in many fields besides analysis, and had joined him on a vacation in Mexico after the strain of completing his opera. Now George seemed in a positive mood, telling his sister: 'I don't feel I've scratched the surface. I'm out here to make enough money with movies so I don't have to think of money any more. Because I just want to work on American music: symphonies, chamber music, opera.'

The real picture was different. Surrounded by stimulating people,
he nevertheless became lonely and depressed. When long-standing
friends of his found a marriage partner, he asked hopelessly: 'Why can
they get married and I can't?' He had an affair with the French actress
Simone Simon. Later he became totally bewitched by another
vivacious film star, Paulette Goddard, and believed he had at last
found 'dream girl'. Snapshots and home movies show them happily
together by the swimming pool at Roxbury Drive. But as so often, the
dream fell apart. Goddard had been Charlie Chaplin's protégé, and
they had married in 1935. Gershwin wrote to a friend: 'She is married
to the "famous Charlie" and under such circumstances I am not
allowing myself to become too involved.' But he did. Her refusal to
leave Chaplin plunged him into renewed despair.

Henry Botkin recalled that George would ring him and ask him
over for dinner, which seemed not much more than 'a dab of sour
cream' because of his diet fads. 'If I hadn't come,' said Botkin, 'he
would have been all alone. You kept wondering why is a guy like this
in this particular condition? George wanted the most beautiful gal,
the most marvellous hostess, someone interested in music. What he
wanted and demanded just didn't exist.' To Alexander Steinert,
George made the most pitiful remark of those darkening months: 'I
am thirty-eight, famous, and rich, but profoundly unhappy. Why?'

One of the players who had been in the Reisman Orchestra, oboist
Mitch Miller, recalled following Gershwin down the steps of the train
that had pulled them into Detroit for the next concert in their tour.

'He looked back at us and said: "I smell burning garbage."' Miller remembered thinking that was strange, since neither he nor anyone else leaving the train noticed it. The tour schedule shows the date to have been 21 January 1934. Three years later, on 11 February 1937, Gershwin was playing his concerto with the Los Angeles Philharmonic. He stumbled over a simple passage in the first movement, and again over the four notes in octaves which dissolve the slow movement into silence. Afterwards he told Levant he had blacked out for a moment and had smelled burning rubber. For three years at least, a slowly-growing tumour had been taking root on the right temporal lobe of Gershwin's brain; the olfactory sensation was a classic symptom. As late as June 1937, after Gershwin had been examined by a doctor and a neurologist, Levant asked him what they thought. 'Well, before they told me anything they wanted to rule out the possibility of a brain tumour.' But they made no such diagnosis. He was relieved of the awesome prospect and resolved to get on with his work.

This was only one of several medical checkups that month, culminating in three days of tests at the Cedars of Lebanon Hospital. When he was sent home on 26 June the medical report stated: 'most likely hysteria.' This was a curt way of suggesting Gershwin was in the throes of 'Hollywooditis', disillusioned with the movie industry and upset at his treatment by Goldwyn. One morning Ira phoned the studios to say George was ill with a severe headache. Goldwyn ordered him off the payroll till he was ready for work. It is sad that relations between the two sank to this, considering Gershwin offered Goldwyn *An American in Paris* without payment to use in *Goldwyn Follies*, an offer he did not take up.

X-ray technology of the time was far below modern standards. During the hospital tests one doctor had noted photophobia (extreme sensitivity to light) indicating abnormal pressure in the brain. He suggested a 'spinal tap', a test which would have revealed a tumour. In rejecting this painful procedure, Gershwin probably threw away his last chance of survival. His fate was further sealed when Zilboorg sent him to another psychoanalyst, Dr Ernest Simmel. He was not a neurosurgeon, and neurosurgery was the key to Gershwin's condition, not analysis. Gershwin had invested in a patented contraption, a kind of metal helmet connected to a pump which was supposed to invigorate the scalp and slow down hair-loss. Now he persuaded himself it was good for his headaches. But they grew more frequent and severe, and he

would collapse in the street with the pain. Sometimes he could not play the piano. He would spill his food or drop his knife and fork. One terrible evening, Leonore banished him from the dinner table. Ira helped him upstairs, and their eyes met. 'I'll never forget that look as long as I live,' Ira said later.

Simmel moved Gershwin to the nearby house of the lyricist Yip Harburg. Harburg was leaving for New York with his wife to work on a musical, and Simmel felt it would be a better place to isolate his patient from 'Hollywood's parlour psychiatrists'. George's eyes could not bear the light. Leonore sent him chocolates, which in his unbalanced state he kneaded together and applied to his body in a rage – they were from someone who had removed a sick man from her elegant table, who had described his falling down in the street as just another way of getting attention.

Late on 9 July he awoke from a long sleep and was helped by Simmel's assistant into the bathroom, where he collapsed. He was rushed to hospital in a coma and the following day a spinal tap confirmed all that had been feared. He died at 10.35 am on Sunday 11 July, never recovering consciousness after five hours of surgery to remove a deeply-embedded tumour. Earlier detection might have led to removal before it turned malignant, but it may have recurred. He would almost certainly have been seriously paralysed had he survived. Walter Dandy, an outstanding neurosurgeon whom the hospital frantically tried to contact to perform the operation (he was on a private yacht), believed that nothing more could have been done. 'I think the outcome is much the best for himself. For a man as brilliant as he with a recurring tumour would have been terrible. It would have been a slow death.'

Henry Botkin said: 'Who could have known? And once we knew, it was too late. It was nobody's fault. Not the doctor's, not the psychoanalyst's. Not anybody's. But it is preposterous and unbelieveable.' 3,500 people attended the funeral service at the Temple Emanu-El on Fifth Avenue. As the crowds left, Todd Duncan spotted someone walking, head down in the pouring rain, in the road between the traffic. 'I looked at the man and saw that it was Al Jolson, and I watched him keep on walking, oblivious to all around him.'

For Ira, his brother's death was devastating. He wondered whether the tumour had originated in their boyhood days, when George had escaped from a fight between young Irish and Jewish gangs by roller-skating into a building under construction. He had fallen down an

elevator shaft, landing on his head. There were many such
unanswered questions for Ira to agonize about, including feelings of
guilt – could he have done even more to trace the source of his
brother's illness? Michael Feinstein heard him talking to George in his
sleep, and he would awake from nightmares believing his brother to
be still alive. Looking at the only colour photos ever taken of George,
during his Mexico holiday in 1935, Ira remarked: 'Can you believe that
somebody who looked like that, so healthy, died so young?'

George had died before completing the verse section of *Love Is
Here To Stay*. His distraught brother, with help from Levant, somehow
finished both the lyrics and the music to meet the studio deadline.
(The song was truncated on the soundtrack, and only became famous
after Gene Kelly's sensitive performance in the 1951 film *An American
in Paris*.) In the years ahead, Ira found comfort in supervising his
brother's musical legacy and publishing rediscovered pieces. But
Feinstein considered there were 'so many emotional issues that he
hadn't dealt with'. Leonore was a steel-willed woman who had not
allowed Ira to cry after George died – ironic, given that he had just
written a song called *Stiff Upper Lip* for *A Damsel in Distress*. The
Jewish custom of Yahrzeit ('year's time') involves lighting a memorial
candle on the anniversary of the deaths of close family members, and

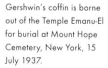

Gershwin's coffin is borne
out of the Temple Emanu-El
for burial at Mount Hope
Cemetery, New York, 15
July 1937.

people said Ira became a human Yahrzeit candle for the rest of his life. Eventually recovering from the worst of his depression, he went on to write lyrics for another two decades. His greatest commercial hit proved to be not something he had written with George, but *Long Ago and Far Away*, a beautiful Jerome Kern song for the 1944 film *Cover Girl*.

In 1959, an American tabloid magazine ran a story headlined 'I am George Gershwin's Illegitimate Son.' A Brooklyn-born man, Alan Schneider (original name Albert) was claiming that George had been his real father. His mother was said to be Mollie Charleston, a dancer in the Ziegfeld Follies who was already married when Gershwin began a secret affair with her in 1924. Money had apparently changed hands over many years so that Ira could keep his brother free of scandal. The allegations resurfaced in 1993, when further information was published supporting Schneider's claim to be the true heir to the billion-dollar Gershwin fortune. It emerged that, under the name of Alan Shane, he had published several songs of his own. The Gershwin estate (now in the charge of Leonore's nephew Michael Strunsky) has never challenged Schneider's claims in court; on his part, Schneider has never produced hard documentary evidence.

Ira died in 1983 at the age of 86, and Leonore in 1991, aged 90. As he grew increasingly reclusive, Ira's worst moments came when he questioned why he was granted a long life, when fate had taken his brother so young. S. N. Behrman wrote of Gershwin: 'I see that he lived all his life in youth. He was given no time for the middle years, for the era when you look back, when you reflect, when you regret.' Vernon Duke was more bitter: 'Death can be kind and it can be just; but it had no business taking our George.'

Gershwin never made a will. Death was not something to think about. The headaches would stop, and soon he would be back in New York. He had said he would need more than a hundred years to write down all his tunes, and he was only thirty-eight. Just as his deadly illness was poised to strike, he had described a string quartet he wanted to write, using melodies he had heard among the fishermen on Folly Island:

It's going through my head all the time, and as soon as I've finished scoring the next picture, I'm going to rent me a little cabin up in Coldwater Canyon, away from Hollywood, and get the damn thing on paper. It's about to drive me crazy, it's so damned full of ideas!

Epilogue

Gershwin's death was keenly felt across America. Simultaneously with the funeral service at the Temple Emanu-El in New York on 15 July 1937, a service was held at the B'nai B'rith Temple in Hollywood, where famous names in the film industry gathered to pay their last respects. On 8 August the regular all-Gershwin evening at New York's Lewisohn Stadium became a concert in his memory, drawing the largest audience ever assembled there. A further memorial concert was given at the Hollywood Bowl on 8 September. Al Jolson, Fred Astaire and Todd Duncan were among the many distinguished artists; José Iturbi played *Rhapsody in Blue*, and Oscar Levant the *Concerto in F*. Otto Klemperer conducted an orchestral arrangement of Gershwin's Prelude No. 2. The event was relayed by CBS to a worldwide audience on seven short-wave stations, unprecedented for a concert. Excerpts from an off-air recording are now available on compact disc; the sombre atmosphere is almost palpable.

Among the tributes were articles written in 1938 by two eminent musicians Gershwin had revered. The conductor Koussevitsky described him as 'a rare flower which blossoms forth once in a while ... a singularly original and rare phenomenon'. Originality was also the theme behind Schoenberg's words: 'Many musicians do not consider George Gershwin a serious composer. I am not forced to say whether history will consider Gershwin a kind of Johann Strauss or Debussy, Offenbach or Brahms, Lehár or Puccini. But I know he is an artist and a composer; he expressed musical ideas; and they were new – as is the way in which he expressed them.'

During his hectic years on Broadway, Gershwin emerged as a central figure in American popular culture, a dynamic personality who knew the value of his own work. He said: 'I try to put the pulse of my times into my music and do it in a lasting way.' Ira once described his modernity as reflecting American life around him as excitingly as the headline in today's newspaper. In literary terms, F. Scott Fitzgerald was holding up an equally accurate mirror to his times. His novel *The*

Great Gatsby appeared the year after *Rhapsody in Blue*, and is peopled with just the sort of cultivated New York socialites who crowded round George's piano at parties, mesmerized by his improvisations – people among whom Gershwin thrived, and who saw their own audacity and their own aspirations reflected in this handsome, young personification of the Jazz Age. As the more troubled 1930s came in, he adapted to the changes around him and remained in the forefront of developments in the musical theatre.

Gershwin said he was living in 'an age of staccato, not legato – but this does not mean that out of this very staccato utterance something beautiful may not be evolved'. His music had a brash gaiety and a bluesy soul; it was an expression of urban America that no other composer captured more effectively. Nor did anyone else attempt so single-mindedly the hazardous crossover from Tin Pan Alley and Broadway into concert music. The driving force seems to have been as much to do with the perceived longevity of his music as with the need to carve out two parallel careers. I think he was genuinely obsessed with the fear that much of his music might easily disappear once the shows were forgotten. Nor would he always be around to help keep his songs alive with his piano-playing and his natural ability to promote himself. He said in 1935 that when he wrote *Rhapsody in Blue* he had taken the 'blues' and put them into a larger and more serious form. 'That was twelve years ago [eleven, in fact] and the *Rhapsody in Blue* is still very much alive, whereas if I had taken the same themes and put them into songs they would have been gone years ago.'

For this master of the 32-bar song, there was something about putting tunes into 'larger and more serious' form and having them played in concert halls that held a special fascination. Concert music had a future, compared with the fragility of Broadway. Instead of saying his songs would outlive his musicals because they were fine pieces of work, he was suggesting that immortality beckoned once his tunes had 'crossed the tracks'. Small wonder he never gave up his 'symphonic' aspirations. He took on ever more ambitious projects because he knew that harnessing his innate talent to limitless hard work would achieve standards his songwriting peers could not match. As Harold Arlen said: 'There was nothing phoney about him. He knew he had it and he celebrated it.'

We were robbed of so much when Gershwin died at thirty-eight. Apart from a proposed quartet and a symphony, he intended to write some ballet music and to set Lincoln's 'Gettysburg Address'. He talked about various theatre projects, including a George S. Kaufman–Moss Hart musical and a second collaboration with DuBose Heyward. He went so far as to contact Heyward with all the old excitement: 'I am very anxious to start thinking about a serious musical. So, put your mind to it, old boy, and I know you can evolve something interesting.'

He would never have deserted Broadway and the songs would have poured out. But I doubt that, even with his dramatic instinct, he would have become a successful composer of film scores. To judge by his Hollywood experiences his heart was not in it, to the same degree as Copland, Prokofiev or the great movie specialists – Max Steiner, Miklos Rózsa, Erich Korngold – who did not just write a few songs for a disgruntled mogul (Gershwin was perhaps unlucky to come up against Goldwyn) but enjoyed fitting long swathes of music to footage they had carefully studied.

In the wake of Gershwin's death the novelist John O'Hara coined the most oft-quoted tribute: 'George Gershwin died on 11 July 1937, but I don't have to believe it if I don't want to.' It still has a ring to it, not least when an unexpected treasure-trove of about seventy lost songs and the original scores of *Primrose* and *Pardon My English* turn up in a Warner Brothers warehouse in New Jersey, as happened in 1982. When posters went up for 'the new Gershwin musical comedy, *Crazy for You*', the musical theatre of the 1990s had not slipped into a time-warp. But this happy compilation of Gershwin hits, based on *Girl Crazy*, played to sold-out theatres on Broadway for four years and in the West End for three, winning hands-down over much of the current fare. To celebrate his 80th birthday in 1994, Larry Adler recorded arrangements of Gershwin standards in which he was joined not only by the opera singer Willard White but by Elton John, Elvis Costello, Sting and other icons of popular music – a paradigm of 'crossover'. Sales of over two million discs proved Gershwin's lasting appeal (and put Adler into the 'Guinness Book of Records' as the oldest artist in the album charts).

Gershwin was a man of many contradictions. Obsessions about his health and his diet, 'blue' moods, and his constant insecurity about his relationships with women went hand-in-hand with an outwardly self-

confident personality that lit up any room he entered. Kay Swift once remarked that 'under the vibrant and gregarious exterior was a sad Russian'. Isaac Goldberg observed this side too – he called it 'a certain half-puzzled solemnity'. Gershwin responded to Ira's lyrics about the eternal themes of romance, yearning, love and happiness by working tirelessly to produce wonderful songs. But achieving his own emotional stability proved beyond his reach.

He was not alone among artists in giving so much of himself to his muse that areas of his private life were left in some disarray. He knew he was attractive to women and he revelled in their company. He made no attempt to repress his sexual energies and his visits to brothels were known to those close to him. In his later years he yearned for a permanent partner, and he became increasingly depressed as his friends got married while he fell for unavailable film stars. Some people attributed his inability in securing a lasting relationship to homosexual tendencies. But, though his life and his correspondence have been endlessly examined by writers over the years, no evidence has been found.

When he played the piano at parties in New York, the world was in his hands; he was surrounded by friends and admirers, the centre of attention as variations on his show-tunes cascaded from the keyboard. In Hollywood towards the end of his life, things were different. He was clearly unhappy and restless when he found himself invited to a house where there was no piano. Even when there was one, entertaining the company was not as it had been in New York. His sensitive antennae picked up the fact that Hollywood people knew he had experienced a run of failures on Broadway. The guests did not crowd round the piano and lionize his talents as in former days. The music was the same, but his audience was not feeding his ego and it added to his depression.

For another man, this would not have been a problem. But Gershwin was a compulsive performer and he needed the love of an audience. He needed to know that people were moved and excited by his music, that they were enthralled by his gifts. It seems to me that his greatest love affair was not with any of the glamorous women who caught his eye at a party, sang his songs or danced in the chorus. It was with the enormous, family audiences who filled his stadium concerts, the music-lovers who acclaimed his latest concert piece

regardless of the critics, the crowds streaming happily out of another successful première on Broadway.

In return, the public has shown an enduring love for Gershwin. As with Schubert, another born songwriter who died too young, we cannot help lamenting the loss of what might have been. But we can rejoice that, whatever trouble Mrs Gershwin had with that son of hers, he grew up to enrich the music of our century.

Classified List of Works

It is a formidable task to classify every note that George Gershwin put to paper. Detail has had to be omitted in the interests of space, but the title and date of every piece (where known) will be found here. The songs of the Broadway musicals are listed alphabetically, and we have included songs that were added after the opening, and unused items if they were later published (these are marked with an asterisk). Such is the frequency with which Gershwin's individual songs and scores come in and out of print (and many new published items are likely in his centenary year) that any dates of publication occur when date of composition is not known. Information about each show's try-out pre-Broadway is not given, unless the show failed to open on Broadway. Collaborators on music and lyrics in the shows' musical numbers have of necessity been omitted.

In the song section, the music and lyrics were written by the Gershwin brothers unless otherwise indicated. A song did not form part of a show unless the name and date of the show is given. 'fp' denotes first public performance.

Stage Works
(musicals unless otherwise stated)

La, La, Lucille, lyrics by Arthur J. Jackson and B. G. De Sylva after book by Fred Jackson. fp New York, 26 May 1919
Musical numbers: The Best of Everything; From Now On; It's Great To Be in Love; It's Hard To Tell; *The Love of a Wife; Money, Money, Money!; Nobody but You; Oo, How I Love To Be Loved by You; Somehow It Seldom Comes True; Tee-Oodle-Um-Bum-Bo; The Ten Commandments of Love; There's More to the Kiss than the Sound; When You Live in a Furnished Flat

Morris Gest Midnight Whirl, book and lyrics by B. G. De Sylva and John Henry Mears. fp New York, 27 December 1919
Musical numbers: Baby Dolls; Doughnuts; I'll Show You a Wonderful World; The League of Nations; Let Cutie Cut Your Cuticle; Limehouse Nights; Poppyland

George White's Scandals of 1920, lyrics by Arthur Jackson after book by Andy Rice and George White. fp New York, 7 June 1920
Musical numbers: Everybody Swat the Profiteer; Idle Dreams; My Lady; On My Mind; Scandal Walk; The Songs of Long Ago; Tum On and Tiss Me; The Whole Night Long

A Dangerous Maid, lyrics by Arthur Francis after book by Charles W. Bell. Pre-Broadway try-out from March to April 1921. Did not open on Broadway.
Musical numbers: Anything for You; Boy Wanted; Dancing Shoes; Just To Know You Are Mine; The Simple Life; The Sirens; Some Rain Must Fall; True Love

George White's Scandals of 1921, lyrics by Arthur Jackson after book by Arthur 'Bugs' Baer and George White. fp New York, 11 July 1921
Musical numbers: Drifting Along with the Tide; I Love You; She's Just a Baby; South Sea Isles (Sunny South Sea Islands); When East Meets West

George White's Scandals of 1922, lyrics by B. G. De Sylva, E. Ray Goetz and Arthur Francis after book by George White, W. C. Fields and Andy Rice. fp New York, 28 August 1922
Musical numbers: Across the Sea (My Heart Will Sail Across the Sea); Argentina; Blue Monday (opera, withdrawn, including songs Blue Monday Blues, Has Anyone Seen My Joe? and I'm Gonna See My Mother); Cinderelatives; I Can't Tell Where They're From When They Dance; I Found a Four Leaf Clover; I'll Build a Stairway to Paradise; Just a Tiny Cup of Tea; Oh, What She Hangs Out (She Hangs Out in Our Alley); Where Is the Man of My Dreams?

Our Nell, lyrics by Brian Hooker after book by A. E. Thomas and Brian Hooker. fp Nora Bayes Theatre, 4 December 1922
Musical numbers: By and By; The Cooney County Fair; Gol-Durn!; Innocent Ingenue Baby; Little Villages; Madrigal; Names I Love To Hear; Oh, You Lady!; Walking Home with Angeline; We Go to Church on Sunday

The Rainbow, lyrics by Clifford Grey after book by Albert de Courville, Edgar Wallace and Noel Scott. fp London, 3 April 1923
Musical numbers: Any Little Tune; Beneath the Eastern Moon; Good Night, My Dear; Innocent Lonesome Blue Baby; In the Rain; Midnight Blues; Moonlight in Versailles; Oh! Nina; Strut Lady with Me; *Sunday in London Town; Sweetheart (I'm So Glad That I Met You)

George White's Scandals of 1923, lyrics by B. G. De Sylva, E. Ray Goetz and Ballard MacDonald after book by George White and W. K. Wells. fp New York, 18 June 1923
Musical numbers: Garden of Love; Katinka; Laugh Your Cares Away; Let's Be Lonesome Together; The Life of a Rose; Little Scandal Dolls; Lo-La-Lo; Look in the Looking Glass; ('On the Beach At') How've-You-Been?; There Is Nothing Too Good for You; Throw 'Er In High!; Where Is She?; You and I

Sweet Little Devil, lyrics by B. G. De Sylva after book by Frank Mandel and Laurence Schwab. fp New York, 21 January 1924
Musical numbers: Hey! Hey! Let 'Er Go!; Hooray for the USA!; The Jijibo; Just Supposing; *Mah-Jongg; The Matrimonial Handicap; *Pepita; Quite a Party; The Same Old Story; Someone Who Believes in You; Strike, Strike, Strike; System; Under a One-Man Top; Virginia (Don't Go Too Far)

George White's Scandals of 1924, lyrics by B. G. De Sylva after book by William K. Wells and George White. fp New York, 30 June 1924
Musical numbers: I Love You, My Darling; I'm Going Back; I Need a Garden; Just Missed the Opening

Chorus; Kongo Kate; Lovers of Art; Mah-Jongg; Night Time in Araby; Rose of Madrid; Somebody Loves Me; Tune In (to Station J.O.Y.); Year after Year

Primrose, lyrics by Desmond Carter and Ira Gershwin after book by George Grossmith and Guy Bolton. fp London, 11 September 1924
Musical numbers: Ballet Music; Beau Brummel; Berkeley Square and Kew; Boy Wanted; The Countryside (This Is the Life for a Man); Four Little Sirens; I Make Hay While the Moon Shines; Isn't It Terrible What They Did to Mary Queen of Scots; Isn't It Wonderful; It Is the Fourteenth of July; Leaving Town While We May; The Mophams; Naughty Baby; Roses of France; Some Far-Away Someone; That New-Fangled Mother of Mine; Till I Meet Someone Like You; Wait a Bit, Susie; When Toby Is Out of Town

Lady, Be Good!, lyrics by Ira Gershwin after book by Guy Bolton and Fred Thompson. fp New York, 1 December 1924
Musical numbers: Buy a Little Button from Us; Carnival Time; The End of a String; Fascinating Rhythm; The Half of It, Dearie, Blues; Hang on to Me; I'd Rather Charleston; Juanita; Leave It to Love; Linger in the Lobby; Little Jazz Bird; Oh, Lady, Be Good!; *The Man I Love; Rainy Afternoon Girls; So Am I; Something about Love; Swiss Miss; Weather Man; We're Here Because; A Wonderful Party

Tell Me More!, lyrics by B. G. De Sylva and Ira Gershwin after book by Fred Thompson and William K. Wells. fp New York, 13 April 1925
Musical numbers: Baby!; Have You Heard; How Can I Win You Now?; In Sardinia; Love, I Never Knew; Love Is in the Air; Mr and Mrs Sipkin; *Murderous Monty (and Light-Fingered Jane); My Fair Lady; The Poetry of Motion; Tell Me More!; Three Times a Day; Ukulele Lorelei; When the Debbies Go By; Why Do I Love You?

Tip-Toes, lyrics by Ira Gershwin after book by Guy Bolton and Fred Thompson. fp New York, 28 December 1925

Musical numbers: It's a Great Little World; Lady Luck; Looking for a Boy; Nice Baby; Nightie-Night; Our Little Captain; Sweet and Low-Down; That Certain Feeling; These Charming People; Tip-Toes; Waiting for the Train; When Do We Dance?

Song Of The Flame, book and lyrics by Otto Harbach and Oscar Hammerstein II. fp New York, 30 December 1925
Musical numbers: Cossack Love Song (Don't Forget Me); Far Away; Midnight Bells; Song of the Flame; Tartar; The Signal; Vodka (Don't Give Me Vodka); Woman's Work Is Never Done; *You Are You

Oh, Kay!, lyrics by Ira Gershwin after book by Guy Bolton and P. G. Wodehouse. fp New York, 8 November 1926
Musical numbers: Bride and Groom; Clap Yo' Hands; Dear Little Girl (I Hope You've Missed Me); Do, Do, Do; Don't Ask!; Fidgety Feet; Heaven on Earth; Maybe; Oh, Kay!; *Show Me the Town; Someone To Watch Over Me; The Woman's Touch

Strike Up the Band (first version), book by George S. Kaufman. Pre-Broadway try-out from August to September 1927. Did not open on Broadway.
Musical numbers: Fletcher's American Cheese Choral Society; The Girl I Love; Homeward Bound; Hoping That Some Day You'd Care; How About a Man Like Me?; The Man I Love; Meadow Serenade; Military Dancing Drill; Oh, This Is Such a Lovely War; Patriotic Rally; Seventeen and Twenty-One; Strike Up the Band!; Typical Self-Made American; The Unofficial Spokesman; The War That Ended War; Yankee Doodle Rhythm

Funny Face, lyrics by Ira Gershwin after book by Fred Thompson and Paul Gerard Smith. fp New York, 22 November 1927
Musical numbers: The Babbitt and the Bromide; Birthday Party; Blue Hullaballoo; *Dance Alone with You (Why Does Everyone Have To Cut In); Funny Face; He Loves and She Loves; High Hat; In the Swim; *How Long Has This Been Going On?; Let's Kiss and

Make Up; Look at the Damn Thing Now; My One and Only (What Am I Gonna Do); Once; Sing a Little Song; 'S Wonderful; Tell the Doc; *The World Is Mine

Rosalie, lyrics by P. G. Wodehouse and Ira Gershwin after book by William Anthony McGuire and Guy Bolton. fp New York, 10 January 1928
Musical numbers (by George Gershwin): *Beautiful Gypsy; Everybody Knows I Love Somebody; Follow the Drum; How Long Has This Been Going On?; Let Me Be a Friend to You; *The Man I Love; Merry Andrew (Dance Music); New York Serenade; Oh Gee! Oh Joy!; *Rosalie; Say So!; Show Me the Town; *Yankee Doodle Rhythm

Treasure Girl, lyrics by Ira Gershwin after book by Fred Thompson and Vincent Lawrence. fp New York, 8 November 1928
Musical numbers: According to Mr Grimes; Feeling I'm Falling; Got a Rainbow; I Don't Think I'll Fall in Love Today; I've Got a Crush on You; K-RA-ZY for You; Oh, So Nice; Place in the Country; Skull and Bones; What Are We Here For?; What Causes That?; Where's the Boy? Here's the Girl!

Show Girl, lyrics by Gus Kahn and Ira Gershwin after book by William Anthony McGuire, based on the novel by J. P. McEvoy. fp New York, 2 July 1929
Musical numbers: 'An American In Paris' Blues Ballet; Black and White; Do What You Do; *Feeling Sentimental; Follow the Minstrel Band; Happy Birthday; Harlem Serenade; Home Blues; How Could I Forget; I Must Be Home by Twelve O'Clock; Liza (All the Clouds'll Roll Away); Lolita, My Love; My Sunday Fella; One Man; So Are You!

East Is West, book by William Anthony McGuire adapted from the play by Samuel Shipman and John B. Hymer. Unproduced, due for presentation in 1929.
Musical numbers (by George and Ira Gershwin): China Girl; Embraceable You; Impromptu in Two Keys (instrumental); In the Mandarin's Orchid Garden; Lady of the Moon; Sing Song Girl; We Are Visitors

Strike Up the Band (second version), lyrics by Ira Gershwin after book by Morrie Ryskind (based on a libretto by George S. Kaufman). fp New York, 14 January 1930
Musical numbers: Fletcher's American Chocolate Choral Society; Hangin' Around with You; He Knows Milk; How About a Boy Like Me?; If I Became the President; I Mean To Say; In the Rattle of the Battle; I've Got a Crush on You; I Want To Be a War Bride; Mademoiselle in New Rochelle; A Man of High Degree; Military Dancing Drill; Soldiers' March (Unofficial March of General Holmes); Official Resumé; Patriotic Rally; Ring a Ding a Ding Dong Dell; Soon; Strike Up the Band!; A Typical Self-Made American; The Unofficial Spokesman

Girl Crazy, lyrics by Ira Gershwin after book by Guy Bolton and John McGowan. fp New York, 14 October 1930
Musical numbers: Bidin' My Time; Boy! What Love Has Done to Me!; Broncho Busters; But Not for Me; Could You Use Me?; Embraceable You; I Got Rhythm; Land of the Gay Caballero; The Lonesome Cowboy; Sam and Delilah; Treat Me Rough; When It's Cactus Time in Arizona; You've Got What Gets Me

Of Thee I Sing, lyrics by Ira Gershwin after book by George S. Kaufman and Morrie Ryskind. fp New York, 26 December 1931
Musical numbers: Because, Because; The Dimple on My Knee; Entrance of Supreme Court Judges; Entrance of the French Ambassador; Garçon, S'Il Vous Plaît; Hello, Good Morning; Here's a Kiss for Cinderella; How Beautiful; The Illegitimate Daughter; I'm About To Be a Mother (Who Could Ask for Anything More?); I Was the Most Beautiful Blossom; Jilted; Love Is Sweeping the Country; Never Was There a Girl So Fair; Of Thee I Sing (Baby); Prosperity Is Just Around the Corner; The Senatorial Roll Call; Some Girls Can Bake a Pie; Trumpeter, Blow Your Horn; Who Cares; Who Is the Lucky Girl To Be?; Wintergreen for President

Pardon My English, lyrics by Ira Gershwin after book by Herbert Fields. fp New York, 20 January 1933
Musical numbers: Dancing in the Streets; The Dresden Northwest Mounted; Hail the Happy Couple; He's Not Himself; In Three Quarter Time; Isn't It a Pity?; I've Got To Be There; The Lorelei; Luckiest Man in the World; My Cousin in Milwaukee; Pardon My English; So What?; Tonight (published without lyrics as one of 'Two Waltzes in C'); What Sort of Wedding Is This?; Where You Go, I Go

Let 'Em Eat Cake, lyrics by Ira Gershwin after book by George S. Kaufman and Morrie Ryskind. fp New York, 21 October 1933
Musical numbers: Blue, Blue, Blue; Climb Up the Social Ladder; Cloistered From the Noisy City; Comes the Revolution; Double Dummy Drill; Hanging Throttlebottom in the Morning; A Hell of a Hole; I Know a Foul Ball; Let 'Em Eat Cake; Let 'Em Eat Caviar; Mine; No *Comprenez*, No *Capish*, No *Versteh!*; On and On and On; Shirts by the Millions; That's What He Did; Throttle Throttlebottom; Tweedledee for President; Union Square; Up and At 'Em; When the Judges Doff the Ermine; Who's the Greatest–?

Porgy and Bess, opera in three acts, lyrics by DuBose Heyward and Ira Gershwin after novel by DuBose Heyward. fp Alvin Theatre, New York, 10 October 1935
Musical numbers: Bess, You Is My Woman Now; *The Buzzard Song; Clara, Don't You Be Downhearted; Crap Game Fugue; Gone, Gone, Gone!; I Got Plenty o' Nuthin'; I Loves You, Porgy; I'm On My Way; It Ain't Necessarily So; It Take a Long Pull To Get There; Leavin' fo' de Promis' Lan'; My Man's Gone Now; Oh Bess, Oh Where's My Bess; Oh, de Lawd Shake de Heaven; Oh, Doctor Jesus; Oh, I Can't Sit Down; Overflow; A Red Headed Woman; Street Cries (Strawberry Woman, Crab Man); Summertime; There's a Boat Dat's Leavin' Soon for New York; They Pass By Singing; Time and Time Again; What You Want With Bess?; A Woman Is a Sometime Thing; Woman to Lady

Miscellaneous Songs

Since I Found You, lyrics by Leonard Praskins (1913)

Ragging the Traumerei, lyrics by Leonard Praskins (c. 1913)

When You Want 'Em, You Can't Get 'Em (When You Got 'Em, You Don't Want 'Em), lyrics by Murray Roth (1916)

The Making of a Girl, music also by Sigmund Romberg, lyrics by Harold Atteridge (for *The Passing Show of 1916*, 1916)

My Runaway Girl, lyrics by Murray Roth (for *The Passing Show of 1916*)

Beautiful Bird, lyrics also by Lou Paley (c. 1917)

When There's a Chance To Dance (c. 1917)

Gush-Gush-Gushing (1918)

When the Armies Disband, lyrics by Irving Caesar (1918)

You-oo Just You, lyrics by Irving Caesar (for *Hitchy-Koo of 1918*, 1918)

The Real American Folk Song (Is a Rag) (for *Ladies First*, 1918)

Some Wonderful Sort of Someone, lyrics by Schuyler Greene (for *Ladies First*)

There's Magic in the Air (for *Half-Past Eight*, 1918, Syracuse, New York)

The Ten Commandments of Love, lyrics by Edward B. Perkins (for *Half-Past Eight*)

Cupid, lyrics by Edward B. Perkins (for *Half-Past Eight*)

Hong Kong, lyrics by Edward B. Perkins (for *Half-Past Eight*)

Good Little Tune, lyrics by Irving Caesar (1918)

Little Theatre of Our Own (c. 1919)

I Was So Young (You Were So Beautiful), lyrics by Irving Caesar and Al Bryan (for *Good Morning Judge*, 1919)

There's More to the Kiss than the X-X-X, lyrics by Irving Caesar (for *Good Morning, Judge*)

O Land of Mine, America, lyrics by Michael E. Rourke (1919)

Something about Love, lyrics by Lou Paley (for *The Lady in Red*, 1919)

Swanee, lyrics by Irving Caesar (for *Capitol Revue* ['Demi-Tasse'], 1919)

Come to the Moon, lyrics by Lou Paley and Ned Wayburn (for *Capitol Revue*)

We're Pals, lyrics by Irving Caesar (for *Dere Mable*, try-out 1920)

Back Home, lyrics by Irving Caesar (for *Dere Mable*)

I Don't Know Why (When I Dance with You), lyrics by Irving Caesar (for *Dere Mable*)

Yan-kee, lyrics by Irving Caesar (1920)

Oo, How I Love To Be Loved by You, lyrics by Lou Paley (for *Ed Wynn's Carnival*, 1920)

Waiting for the Sun to Come Out (for *The Sweetheart Shop*, 1920)

Spanish Love, lyrics by Irving Caesar (for *Broadway Brevities of 1920*, 1920)

Lu Lu, lyrics by Arthur Jackson (for *Broadway Brevities of 1920*)

Snow Flakes, lyrics by Arthur Jackson (for *Broadway Brevities of 1920*)

On the Brim of Her Old-Fashioned Bonnet, lyrics by E. Ray Goetz (for *Snapshots of 1921*, 1921)

The Baby Blues, lyrics by E. Ray Goetz (for *Snapshots of 1921*)

Futuristic Melody, lyrics by E. Ray Goetz (for *Snapshots of 1921*)

Phoebe, lyrics also by Lou Paley (1921)

Something Peculiar, lyrics also by Lou Paley (1921)

Molly-on-the-Shore (c. 1921)

Mischa, Jascha, Toscha, Sascha (c. 1921)

My Log-Cabin Home, lyrics by Irving Caesar and B. G. De Sylva (for *The Perfect Fool*, 1921)

No One Else but that Girl of Mine, lyrics by Irving Caesar (for *The Perfect Fool*)

Tomale (I'm Hot for You), lyrics by B. G. De Sylva (1921)

Swanee Rose, lyrics by Irving Caesar and B. G. De Sylva (1921)

Dixie Rose, lyrics by Irving Caesar and B. G. De Sylva (1921)

Do It Again!, lyrics by B. G. De Sylva (for *The French Doll*, 1922)

Someone (for *For Goodness Sake*, 1922)

Tra-La-La (for *For Goodness Sake*)

The Flapper, music also by William Daly, lyrics by B. G. De Sylva (1922)

The Yankee Doodle Blues, lyrics by Irving Caesar and B. G. De Sylva (for *Spice of 1922*, 1922)

That American Boy of Mine, lyrics by Irving Caesar (for *The Dancing Girl*, 1923)

At Half-Past Seven, lyrics by B. G. De Sylva) (for *Nifties of 1923*)

Nashville Nightingale, lyrics by Irving Caesar (for *Nifties of 1923*)

I Won't Say I Will, But I Won't Say I Won't, lyrics also by B. G. De Sylva (for *Little Miss Bluebeard*, 1923)

The Sunshine Trail (theme song used to promote the silent film *The Sunshine Trail*, released in 1923)

What's the Big Idea (c. 1925)

That Lost Barber Shop Chord (for *Americana*, 1926)

Ask Me Again (late 1920s)

Toddlin' Along (for *Nine-Fifteen Revue*, 1930)

Till Then (1933)

Strike Up the Band for U.C.L.A. (1936)

By Strauss (for *The Show Is On*, 1936)

Film Music

Delicious (Fox Film Corporation), released 3 December 1931
Musical numbers: Blah, Blah, Blah; Delishious; Dream Sequence ('We're from the *Journal*, the *Wahrheit*, the *Telegram*, the *Times* …'); Katinkitschka; New York Rhapsody (part of *Second Rhapsody*); Somebody from Somewhere

Shall We Dance, lyrics by Ira Gershwin (RKO), released May 1937
Musical numbers: (Hi-Ho!); (I've Got) Beginner's Luck; Let's Call the Whole Thing Off; Shall We Dance; Slap that Bass; They All Laughed; They Can't Take That Away from Me; (Wake Up, Brother, and Dance); Walking the Dog (also published as *Promenade*)

A Damsel in Distress, lyrics by Ira Gershwin (RKO), released November 1937
Musical numbers: A Foggy Day (in London Town); I Can't Be Bothered Now; The Jolly Tar and The Milkmaid; Nice Work if You Can Get It; Put Me to the Test; Sing of Spring; Stiff Upper Lip; Things Are Looking Up

Goldwyn Follies, lyrics by Ira Gershwin (Samuel Goldwyn), released February 1938
Musical numbers: (Just Another Rhumba); I Love To Rhyme; I Was Doing All Right; Love Is Here To Stay; Love Walked In; Spring Again (music by Vernon Duke)

Orchestral

An American in Paris, tone-poem (1928). fp New York, 13 December 1928

Cuban Overture (originally *Rumba*) (1932). fp New York, 16 August 1932

Catfish Row, suite from *Porgy and Bess* (Catfish Row; Porgy Sings; Fugue; Hurricane; Good Morning, Brother) (1936). fp Philadelphia, 21 January 1936

Piano with Orchestra

Rhapsody in Blue, for jazz band and piano, orchestrated by Ferde Grofé (1924). fp New York, 12 February 1924. Two further orchestrations by Grofé in 1926 and 1942.

Concerto in F, for piano and orchestra (1925). fp New York, 3 December 1925

Second Rhapsody, for orchestra with piano (1931). fp Boston, 29 January 1932

Variations on 'I Got Rhythm', for orchestra and piano solo. fp Boston, 14 January 1934

Solo Piano

Tango (1914)

Rialto Ripples, in collaboration with Will Donaldson (published 1917)

Preludes for Piano (1926). fp (five preludes) New York, 4 December 1926; (these, plus an additional prelude) Boston, 16 January 1927

Merry Andrew, from *Rosalie* (1928)

Impromptu in Two Keys (1929)

Three-Quarter Blues (1929)

George Gershwin's Song Book, transcriptions of eighteen songs (published 1932)

Two Waltzes in C, from *Pardon My English* (1933)

For Lily Pons, unpublished sketch (1933), transcribed by Michael Tilson Thomas (1983)

Sleepless Night, melody (1936)

Promenade, piano transcription by Hal Borne of 'Walking the Dog' sequence from the film *Shall We Dance*, published 1960

Violin Piece, sketch (date unknown), transcribed by Michael Tilson Thomas (1984)

Instrumental

Lullaby, movement for string quartet (1919)

Short Story, for violin and piano, arranged by Samuel Dushkin from two unpublished Gershwin *Novelettes* for piano. fp New York, 8 February 1925

Miscellaneous

Sutton Place, *Three Note Waltz*, *Romantic* (an unpublished song from *Oh, Kay!*) and *Machinery Going Mad* are among dozens of unpublished, undated piano sketches (some awaiting lyrics) given numbers or titles by Ira.

Further Reading

Published material on Gershwin is virtually limitless, taking into account press reviews, magazine articles, programme notes and an unending stream of biographies, of which the very first – by Isaac Goldberg in 1931 – was supervised by the composer and therefore remains of interest. Many of the books recommended here have extensive bibliographies inviting further exploration. I have selected a wide range. Some are content to portray his celebrity-filled life without getting to grips with the music. At the other extreme, Stephen Gilbert's analytical study presupposes the reader's understanding of musical notation and arcane terminology. Inevitably, some titles are out of print; they are included because they are outstanding contributions to Gershwin literature and are worth tracking down via libraries or book dealers.

Armitage, M. *George Gershwin* (New York, Da Capo Press, 1995)
Merle Armitage, a publisher who shared Gershwin's love of modern art, edited and designed this anthology in 1938. A treasury of tributes by Gershwin's friends and colleagues, it includes a chapter by Ira and two articles by George.

Behr, E. *Prohibition* (London, BBC Books, 1997)
Originally published to accompany the BBC television series 'The 13 Years that Changed America', this is a compelling study of the Prohibition era, which spanned much of Gershwin's career.

Bernstein, L. *The Joy of Music* (New York, Simon and Schuster, 1959)
Written in Bernstein's inimitable style, this includes an 'imaginary conversation' called 'Why don't you run upstairs and write a nice Gershwin tune?' and the scripts of his 'Omnibus' telecasts 'The World of Jazz' (1955) and 'American Musical Comedy' (1956).

Bordman, G. *American Musical Theatre* (2nd edition, New York, Oxford University Press, 1991)
A vast, encyclopedic chronicle of the American musical.

Brahms, C. and Sherrin, N. *Song by Song* (Bolton, Ross Anderson Publications, 1984)
A lively appraisal of the Gershwin brothers' achievement is among fourteen chapters on great lyric writers.

Ewen, D. *George Gershwin: His Journey to Greatness* (New Jersey, Prentice-Hall, 1970; earlier edition published as *Journey to Greatness*, New York, Henry Holt and London, W. H. Allen, 1956)
An engaging account of Gershwin's life which has long been among the best biographies.

Feinstein, M. *Nice Work If You Can Get It* (New York, Hyperion, 1995)
A spirited book about major names in American musical theatre and cabaret, with revealing glimpses of Ira (to whom Feinstein became archivist and friend) in his final years.

Gershwin, I. *Lyrics on Several Occasions* (New York, Alfred Knopf, 1959; new edition by Limelight Editions, New York, 1997)
Ira's whimsical, erudite essays on life as a lyricist have been reprinted in several editions. He said, 'If nothing else, this book is unique in that the author isn't looking forward to another.'

Gilbert, S. E. *The Music of Gershwin* (New Haven and London, Yale University Press, 1995)
Not for the faint-hearted: biographical coverage takes second place to in-depth technical analysis of Gershwin's scores according to the methodology of Austrian theorist Heinrich Schenker.

Goldberg, I. *George Gershwin: A Study in American Music* (New York, Simon and Schuster, 1931; reprinted New York, Frederick Ungar, 1958)
Gershwin's first biographer, often quoted, is worth reading in the original – especially since this book was sanctioned by the composer himself.

Idelsohn, A. Z. *Jewish Music in its Historical Development* (New York, Dover Publications, 1992)
First published in 1929 – the year Gershwin signed a Met contract for his Jewish opera – this remains a standard work on the elements and characteristics of Jewish music.

Jablonski, E. *Gershwin: A Biography* (New York, Doubleday, 1987)
Jablonski, E. *Gershwin Remembered* (London, Faber and Faber, 1992)
Jablonski, E. with L. Stewart *The Gershwin Years* (3rd edition, New York, Da Capo Press, 1996)
Jablonski's books are the work of a Gershwin *aficionado* – his style is humourless, but the research is meticulous.

Kimball, R. and Simon, A. *The Gershwins* (New York, Atheneum, 1973; London, Jonathan Cape, 1974)
A truly handsome book, unfortunately out of print but worth searching out. Hundreds of illustrations (including colour plates of the brothers' paintings) decorate a fascinating text prefaced by Richard Rodgers.

Kimball, R. (ed.) *The Complete Lyrics of Ira Gershwin* (London, Pavilion, 1994)
Another beautifully presented Kimball book containing over 700 lyrics with alternative versions, production photographs and copious indexes.

Levant, O. *A Smattering of Ignorance* (New York, Doubleday and Doran, 1940; Garden City Publishing, 1942)
Levant's barbed wit is at its sharpest in a chapter he called 'My Life; or The Story of George Gershwin'.

Peyser, J. *The Memory of All That* (New York, Simon and Schuster, 1993)
Structurally wayward, this racy book says little about the music but is brimming with gossip, arguing that Gershwin must have fathered Alan Schneider and possibly a daughter as well.

Rosenberg, D. *Fascinating Rhythm* (2nd edition, University of Michigan Press, 1997)
A thorough and perceptive study of the Gershwin partnership, featuring notated musical analysis that is mostly convincing.

Rosten, L. *The Joys of Yiddish* (Harmondsworth, Penguin, 1971)
Rosten, who died in 1997, wove jokes and fables into his definitive lexicon of Yiddish to produce a best-selling amalgam of wit and learning.

Schiff, D. *Rhapsody in Blue* (Cambridge, Cambridge University Press, 1997)
A concise guide to the many aspects of the Rhapsody (including its influence on other jazz-inspired works), placing Gershwin within the context of Yiddish theatre, Negro music and the Jazz Age.

Schillinger, J. *The Schillinger System of Musical Composition* (New York, Da Capo Press, 1978)
First published in 1941, these two volumes demonstrate the numerical intricacies which intrigued Gershwin.

Schwartz, C. *Gershwin: His Life and Music* (New York, Da Capo Press, 1973)
Despite errors in dates and some unconvincing musical analysis, this is a worthwhile though sometimes long-winded biography with good illustrations.

Steyn, M. *Broadway Babies Say Goodnight – Musicals then and now* (London, Faber and Faber, 1997)
An entertaining, forthright survey of the American musical and its British successors which concludes that the glorious Broadway tradition from Kern to Sondheim has crumbled away.

Struble, J. W. *The History of American Classical Music* (London, Robert Hale, 1995)
Apart from minor errors, this is a work of immense scholarship that includes a chapter on 'George Gershwin's New Synthesis'.

Vail, K. *Jazz Milestones* (Chessington, UK, Castle Communications, 1993)
A fascinating 'Pictorial Chronicle of Jazz, 1900–90', crammed with information and a good introduction for the novice.

Selective Discography

Gershwin is among the most-recorded composers of all time. His music will be found under such diverse headings as Classical, Opera, Musicals, Popular, Easy Listening, Jazz and Nostalgia. In the space available, I felt I could best make selections from the vast catalogue by concentrating on artists who were close to Gershwin, and also on more recent performers who have made enjoyable recordings that demonstrate the limitless range of interpretations. Where appropriate I have suggested several choices. Couplings are not shown since the same pieces reappear in endless combinations. It is interesting to compare Gershwin's piano playing on the Pearl acoustic recordings with the digital piano-roll transfers on Nonesuch. Time limits of the old 78 rpm discs (maximum five minutes per side) explain the cuts Gershwin agreed to make in the Whiteman versions of *Rhapsody in Blue*, and perhaps the fast tempi he adopted on other records. It is exasperating that he did not record the *Second Rhapsody* (apart from a test acetate disc of its first run-through), nor the *Variations on 'I Got Rhythm'* (a lacklustre radio performance survives). Nor did he record the complete *Concerto in F*, and even then, its finale comes from a 'live' Rudy Vallée radio show at which Gershwin was unnerved by the amateurish accompaniment (a band arrangement by Eliot Jacobi). The five reconstructed musicals on Nonesuch are essential listening; sadly, this series has come to a halt. The Glyndebourne *Porgy and Bess* under Rattle will be hard to surpass, but I have also included Maazel's pioneering 1976 version for its warmth and passion, in an excellent transfer from LP.

Stage Works

Lady, Be Good! (1924)
Lara Teeter, Ann Morrison, Jason Alexander, Michael Maguire, John Pizzarelli, Ivy Austin, Michelle Nicastro, Robin Langford, Carol Swarbrick, Steven Blier, conducted by Eric Stern
NONESUCH 75559–793082

Oh, Kay! (1926)
Robert Westenberg, Patrick Cassidy, Adam Arkin, Liz Larsen, Stacey A. Logan, Dawn Upshaw, Kurt Ollmann, Susan Lucci, Fritz Weaver, conducted by Eric Stern
NONESUCH 7559–793612 (2 CDs)

Strike Up the Band (1930)
Brent Barrett, Don Chastain, Rebecca Luker, Jason Graae, Beth Fowler, Charles Goff, Juliet Lambert, Jeff Lyons, Dale Sandish, James Rocco, conducted by John Mauceri
NONESUCH 7559–792732 (2 CDs)

Girl Crazy (1930)
Lorna Luft, David Caroll, Judy Blazer, David Garrison, Vicki Lewis, Eddie Korbich, Stand Chandler, David Engel, Larry Raben, Guy Stroman and Frank Gorshin, conducted by John Mauceri
NONESUCH 7559–792502

Pardon My English (1933)
William Katt, John Cullum, Arnetia Walker, Michelle Nicastro, conducted by Eric Stern
NONESUCH 7559–793382

Porgy and Bess (1935)
Willard White, Leona Mitchell, Cleveland Orchestra and Chorus conducted by Lorin Maazel
DECCA 4145592 (3 CDs) (highlights on 4363062)

Porgy and Bess
Willard White, Cynthia Haymon, Glyndebourne Chorus, London Philharmonic Orchestra conducted by Simon Rattle
EMI 7495682 (3 CDs) (highlights on 7543252)

Porgy and Bess (overture and 14 songs)
Ella Fitzgerald, Louis Armstrong, orchestra conducted by Russell Garcia
VERVE 8274752

Crazy for You (1993)
Kirby Ward, Ruthie Henshall, Chris Langham, Don Fellows, Amanda Prior, Shaun Scott, Robert Austin, Paula Tinker, Vanessa Leigh Hicks, Helen Way
FIRST NIGHT CAST CD 37

Film Music

George and Ira Gershwin in Hollywood
Comprehensive soundtrack anthology, 1937–52,
including rare studio 'takes' previously unavailable
TURNER/RHINO R2 72732 (2 CDs)

A Damsel in Distress – Suite and 'Stiff Upper Lip'
New Princess Theatre Orchestra conducted by John
McGlinn
EMI FORTE 5685892

Promenade (Shall We Dance)
Los Angeles Philharmonic Orchestra conducted by
Michael Tilson Thomas
SONY MK 39699

Orchestral

An American in Paris
NBC Symphony Orchestra conducted by Arturo
Toscanini
AMERICAN CLASSICS VJC 1034

An American in Paris
New York Philharmonic Orchestra conducted by
Leonard Bernstein; with *Grand Canyon Suite* by Grofé
SONY MK 42264

An American in Paris
Cleveland Orchestra conducted by Riccardo Chailly
LONDON (DECCA) 4173262

An American in Paris
Montreal Symphony Orchestra conducted by Charles
Dutoit
DECCA 4251112

Cuban Overture
Cleveland Orchestra conducted by Riccardo Chailly
LONDON (DECCA) 4173262

Cuban Overture
Montreal Symphony Orchestra conducted by Charles
Dutoit
DECCA 4251112

Catfish Row – Suite (by Gershwin)
St Louis Symphony Orchestra conducted by Leonard
Slatkin
VOX 1154832/EMI 7640842

Porgy and Bess – Symphonic Portrait (by Robert Russell
Bennett)
Montreal Symphony Orchestra conducted by Charles
Dutoit
DECCA 4251112

*Overtures: Girl Crazy; Of Thee I Sing; Tip-Toes;
Primrose; Oh, Kay!*
New Princess Theatre Orchestra conducted by John
McGlinn
EMI FORTE 5685892

Piano with Orchestra

Rhapsody in Blue
Oscar Levant (piano), Philadelphia Orchestra
conducted by Eugene Ormandy
SONY CD 42514

Rhapsody in Blue
Earl Wild (piano), Benny Goodman (clarinet), NBC
Symphony Orchestra conducted by Arturo Toscanini
AMERICAN CLASSICS VJC 1034

Rhapsody in Blue
Leonard Bernstein (piano), Columbia Symphony
Orchestra
SONY MK 42264

Rhapsody in Blue
Gershwin (piano roll), Columbia Jazz Band conducted
by Michael Tilson Thomas
SONY SMK 42240

Rhapsody in Blue
Michael Tilson Thomas (piano), Los Angeles
Philharmonic Orchestra
SONY MK 39699

Rhapsody in Blue
Peter Donohoe (piano), London Sinfonietta conducted
by Simon Rattle
EMI 7479912

Concerto in F
Oscar Levant (piano), Philharmonic Symphony
Orchestra of New York conducted by André Kostelanetz
SONY CD 42514

Concerto in F
Oscar Levant (piano), NBC Symphony Orchestra
conducted by Arturo Toscanini
AMERICAN CLASSICS VJC 1034

Concerto in F
Earl Wild (piano), Boston Pops Orchestra conducted
by Arthur Fiedler
RCA 179062

Concerto in F
André Previn (piano), Pittsburgh Symphony Orchestra
PHILIPS 4126112

Concerto in F
Wayne Marshall (piano), Aalborg Symphony
VIRGIN CLASSICS 5614782

Second Rhapsody
Oscar Levant (piano), Morton Gould and his Orchestra
SONY CD 42514

Second Rhapsody
Michael Tilson Thomas (piano), Los Angeles
Philharmonic Orchestra
SONY MK 39699

Second Rhapsody
Wayne Marshall (piano), Aalborg Symphony
VIRGIN CLASSICS 5614782

Variations on 'I Got Rhythm'
Oscar Levant (piano), Morton Gould and his Orchestra
SONY CD 42514

Variations on 'I Got Rhythm'
Wayne Marshall (piano), Aalborg Symphony
VIRGIN CLASSICS 5614782

Solo Piano

Three Preludes
Oscar Levant
SONY CD 42514

Three Preludes
Michael Tilson Thomas
SONY MK 39699

George Gershwin's Song Book
Peter Donohoe
EMI 7542802

Fascinating Rhythm: The Complete Piano Music
Angela Brownridge
HYPERION CDH 88045

Short Story
Violin Piece
For Lily Pons
Sleepless Night
Michael Tilson Thomas
SONY MK 39699

Seven Preludes
Blue Monday
Miniatures
Rhapsody in Blue
Restored and performed by Alicia Zizzo
CARLTON CLASSICS 30366–00052

Instrumental

Lullaby (arranged for string orchestra)
Cleveland Orchestra conducted by Riccardo Chailly
LONDON (DECCA) 4173262

Historic Recordings

George Gershwin Orchestral Works
Includes the first recordings (1924 and 1929) of
Rhapsody in Blue and *An American in Paris*, with
arrangements of *Cuban Overture, Second Rhapsody* and
Concerto in F for the Whiteman Orchestra
PAST PERFECT PPCD 78106

Gershwin Performs Gershwin: Rare Recordings, 1931–1935
Includes long-lost extracts from Gershwin's radio shows,
rehearsals of *Second Rhapsody* and *Porgy and Bess*, and a
radio performance of *Variations on 'I Got Rhythm'*
MUSICMASTERS 50622C

The Piano Rolls, realized by Artis Wodehouse
Vivid reproductions of Gershwin's performances
digitally captured by a computer-driven descendant of
the player-piano. Volume 1 includes Frank Milne's
arrangement of *An American in Paris* punched directly
on to paper.
NONESUCH 7559–792872 (Vol. 1); 7559–793702 (Vol. 2)

George Gershwin Plays George Gershwin
Includes both Whiteman recordings of *Rhapsody in
Blue*, Gershwin playing songs with the Astaires and
Three Preludes, the first *An American in Paris* and *Porgy
and Bess* recordings, and the only recording of
Gershwin in *Concerto in F* (3rd movement)
PEARL GEMM CDS 9483 (2 CDs)

The Original Hits of George Gershwin
18 historic tracks recorded between 1922 and 1931 by top
bands of Gershwin's time
HALCYON DHDL 112

The Radio Years
Off-air recording of extracts from the Gershwin
Memorial Concert at the Hollywood Bowl, 8
September 1937
RADIO YEARS RY 9

Jazz and Modern Interpretations

A Tribute to George Gershwin by the Giants of Jazz
Art Tatum, Dizzy Gillespie, Benny Goodman, Gerry
Mulligan, Sidney Bechet and other jazz stars
GIANTS OF JAZZ 53015

Ella Fitzgerald Sings the Gershwin Songbook
VERVE 8250242 (3 CDs)

Sarah Vaughan: Gershwin Songbook
EMARCY 8468952 (Vol. 1); 8468962 (Vol. 2)

Oscar Peterson: Gershwin Songbook
VERVE 5296982

Dave Grusin: The Gershwin Connection
GRP 20052

Menuhin and Grappelli Play Gershwin
EMI 7692182

Kiri Sings Gershwin
Kiri Te Kanawa with original Broadway orchestrations
EMI CLASSICS 7474542

The Glory of Gershwin
Best-selling 'crossover' album featuring Larry Adler
MERCURY 5227272

100th Anniversary Album

The Very Best of George Gershwin
Produced in association with this biography, a
compilation of twenty-eight tracks spans Gershwin's
Broadway and concert music, featuring artists ranging
from Oscar Peterson, Ella Fitzgerald and Sarah Vaughan
to Lorin Maazel, Arthur Fiedler and Riccardo Chailly.
POLYGRAM 4600022 (2 CDs)

Index

Photographic Acknowledgements

The British Library, London: 39, 77
Corbis-Bettmann, London: 20, 23r,
  139, 165, 182, 199, 214
Corbis-Bettmann/UPI, London:
  13, 50, 137, 182
The George Eastmann House,
  New York: 119 (reprinted with
  permission of Joanna T.
  Steichen)
Glyndebourne Festival Opera: 197
  (© Guy Gravett)
The Hulton Getty Picture
  Collection, London: 54, 55, 57,
  109, 115, 141, 180, 209
Ira and Leonore Gershwin Trusts,
  Beverley Hills, CA: 11, 15, 16,
  17, 43, 201, 211
The Kobal Collection, London:
  79, 146
The Lebrecht Collection, London:
  70, 73, 95 (John Minnion), 126
Photofest, New York: 2, 14, 26, 29,
  33, 35, 48, 59, 62–3, 81, 86, 87,
  89, 90, 92, 96, 99, 102, 107, 110,
  112, 115, 124, 129, 136, 143, 150,
  154, 160, 169, 173, 176, 181, 186–7,
  194, 203, 204, 206, 208, 210
Redferns, London: 23l (photograph
  William Gottlieb)
Warner-Chappell Music, London:
  36, 67, 71 (with permission of
  Adam Gershwin), 193

Text Acknowledgements

Swanee
Music by George Gershwin, lyrics
  by Irving Caesar
© Chappell & Co Inc, New World
  Music Co, Ltd, and Francis,
  Day and Hunter Ltd
Reproduced by permission of
  International Music
  Publications Ltd.

Fascinating Rhythm
Music and lyrics by George and Ira
  Gershwin
© 1924 Chappell & Co, New
  World Music Co Ltd and WB
  Music Corp, USA
Warner/Chappell Music Ltd,
  London W1Y 3FA

The Man I Love
Music and lyrics by George and Ira
  Gershwin
© 1924 Chappell & Co, New
  World Music Co Ltd and WB
  Music Corp, USA
Warner/Chappell Music Ltd,
  London W1Y 3FA

Someone To Watch Over Me
Music and lyrics by George and Ira
  Gershwin
© 1924 Chappell & Co, New
  World Music Co Ltd and WB
  Music Corp, USA
Warner/Chappell Music Ltd,
  London W1Y 3FA

Bride and Groom
Music and lyrics by George and Ira
  Gershwin
© 1926 Chappell & Co, New
  World Music Co Ltd and WB
  Music Corp, USA
Warner/Chappell Music Ltd,
  London W1Y 3FA

My One and Only
Music and lyrics by George and Ira
  Gershwin
© 1927 Chappell & Co, New
  World Music Co Ltd and WB
  Music Corp, USA
Warner/Chappell Music Ltd,
  London W1Y 3FA

But Not for Me
Music and lyrics by George and Ira
  Gershwin
© 1930 Chappell & Co, New
  World Music Co Ltd and WB
  Music Corp, USA
Warner/Chappell Music Ltd,
  London W1Y 3FA

It Ain't Necessarily So
From *Porgy and Bess* (R)
Music and lyrics by George and Ira
  Gershwin, Dorothy and
  DuBose Heyward
© 1935 Chappell & Co USA
Warner/Chappell Music Ltd,
  London W1Y 3FA

Who Cares?
Music and lyrics by George and Ira
  Gershwin
© 1931 Chappell & Co, New
  World Music Co Ltd and WB
  Music Corp, USA
Warner/Chappell Music Ltd,
  London W1Y 3FA

Jubilee
by Cole Porter
© Warner/Chappell Music Ltd,
  London W1Y 3FA

Gershwin (R), George Gershwin
(R) and Ira Gershwin TM are
trademarks of Gershwin Enterprises.
Porgy and Bess (R) is a registered
trademark of Porgy and Bess
Enterprises.
All Rights Reserved